# I Still Want Fireworks

A Single-at-60's Odyssey Through

Life, Love & Online Dating

Judith Hill

# Table of Contents

## Chapter One
## Signing Up—The Penis Does the Picking

I still don't know why I did it.

Yes, my son told me to. He said everyone was doing it. *But if someone told you to jump off a bridge because everyone else was doing it, would you?* Wait! That's my line. To him. When he was nine years old, succumbing to peer pressure and getting caught smoking behind the school. But he's not nine anymore. He's 31 and wanting desperately for his mother to be happy. My being alone worries him.

"Come on, mom. You're hot for an older woman. I can't believe you can't find someone."

"They're not exactly falling out of the sky, Jason, men that want to date a 60-year-old."

"Well, you don't look 60."

"That doesn't help."

"Well, do something that will help."

"Such as?"

"Sign up for one of those dating sites. It worked for Daniel."

"Daniel was 27. And besides, your brother was looking to get married. I'm not."

"Doesn't matter. There's still men out there. You just need to find a way to meet them. Come on. Promise me. What do you have to lose?"

"My self-respect?"

"Really, mom, *really*?"

Near as I can recall that was just about how the conversation went that April day. A Pennsylvania resident these days, I had flown back to Phoenix to see my two oldest sons and my two grandsons. (My youngest son was deployed in Iraq—a whole other preoccupation, worry and fear.)

The morning following this dialogue with my middle child (ever the peacemaker and the problem-solver), I found myself back sitting on the back patio of my AZ home. Coffee cup in one hand, cell phone in the other, I was wasting time with Facebook—and trying to forget the date. It was the one year anniversary of my divorce. But because he had died nine weeks later, I had spent the next ten months looking for the comfort of a label. Married for 429 months and divorced for only two . . . seriously, what the eff was I? Divorcee, widow . . . didow? Did it matter anyway? Whatever I was, I was alone. And I didn't want to be.

Suddenly, an ad for the largest and most well-known of the online dating sites popped up.

Fortuitous? Precipitous? Or maybe just plain ironic? Who knows? I do know I had seen the ads for over a year. And ignored them.

This time I didn't.

Did I get suckered in by the pictures of good-looking men supposedly just waiting to find their soulmates? Probably. And probably, too, I was trying to prove a point. Falling in love was not in the cosmic cards for a cynical, soured on love, soon to be sixty-year-old didow. But maybe I was also daring the Universe to prove me wrong? Truth be told, I really *am* a romantic at heart. Hell! Once upon a time, I wrote romance novels for a living! So where was the harm, I asked myself. Either way it was a win-win situation. I was right—and found no one. Or I was wrong—because I actually did.

I set aside my coffee cup, my reservations—and my self-respect—and proceeded to follow the prompts:

Step #1. *Creating a **Profile***—a multi-step process that takes waaay more time than you'd think. First, you are first asked to describe in a paragraph (or more) yourself and the person you are looking for. If I'm being honest, I didn't put much time or effort into this. I didn't see the point. My experience with men is that most don't read. (A retired cop on this site actually wrote that reading makes his brain hurt! But I'm getting ahead of myself . . .) I dashed off what I realize now was a fairly flippant four or five line dare:

> *Intelligent, well-read, well-traveled. Stubborn at times, strong-willed, resilient. Classy and attractive on the outside, feisty ex-military brat on the inside—ergo the aforementioned traits. Looking for a man not intimidated by strength, someone willing to look beyond the layers...*

After composing this paragraph(s) most won't bother to read (see upcoming Step #3 for a further explanation), you'll be asked to answer specific questions in several main categories. Each particular question has a drop-down menu of answer choices. Just click on your correct (or should I say, *desired*) response—who's to know if you're answering truthfully? If you prefer not to answer a specific question, take the fifth. Choosing the "no answer" option will show up in your profile as a default "I'll tell you later" answer.

The first category and questions entail marital status; gender *(woman seeking man, man seeking woman,*

*man seeking man, or woman seeking woman*); the age you are looking for in a prospective match (with a drop-down choice of 18 to 99); and finally your horoscope sign. (Seriously? I thought that went out with the Age of Aquarius and the moon in the seventh house.) I've been told other online dating sites actually provide a link here which will inform you as to the sign you are most compatible with. (They'll also read your tea leaves if you download a screen shot of the last cup you drank. Just kidding.)

"Appearance" asks your height, eye and hair color. From salt and pepper to bald, every hair color choice is available. (I personally think they should include dyed-and-fried peroxide blonde, but that's just me.) The *"Which best describes your body type?"* question offers an interesting array of euphemisms at the weightier end of the spectrum, with *slender, about average, athletic and toned* progressing to *heavyset, a few extra pounds, stocky, big and beautiful, curvy, full-figured*, and of course no answer. ("Surgically enhanced" is not a choice. For the sake of truth in advertising perhaps it should be? But then again, the men seduced by cleavage probably don't care. Big boobs are big boobs.)

"Background/Values" asks which ethnicities best describe you. After you check the standard race-that-apply choices, you proceed to religion, level of education and what languages you speak.

In "Lifestyle" the first question wants to know how often you exercise. The *"Do you smoke?"* question offers an annoying—at least to me—option for the non-smoker: *no way*. (What's wrong with a simple "no"?) Other choices are *occasionally, daily, cigar aficionado* (Am I the only one who immediately thinks Monica Lewinsky?), *yes but trying to quit*, and no answer. How often you drink, your political stance and choice for pets are followed by *"Do you have/want kids?"* Occupation and yearly income are next,

8

with standard credit card application selections. The very last question inquires about your interests: coffee and conversation, dining out, museums, music, sporting events, etc..

Once you have completed the multiple choice portion of the test, you get to proceed to the short answer section. "In your own words" you are asked your idea of the perfect date, the last thing you read, what you do for fun, and what your favorite hot spots are. Coming up with a dating headline is the final step in Step #1. Mine was actually created later, a week down into the abyss, when I began to get an inkling as to what most men appeared to be truly wanting (more on this in Chapter 6).

> *Sass with class. I'm not interested in a text pal. Eyes-on is the only way to know a spark will flame.*

By the way and FYI, everything is submitted for approval: photo caption, written description, the photos themselves—although I'm not too sure how good a job they really do, since one of my photos presents sideways and another upside down. Once your submission has been approved, you receive an email to that effect.

Step #2. *Listing **Preferences**—*a repetition of Step #1. Only this time you do it about the person you are seeking. They call it "preferences." I call it your wish list. The same categories appear with the same drop-down menus. Simply check off the items on your shopping list or all that might apply. On my site, when your completed profile is viewed online, this wish list appears side-by-side with the traits that describe you. This no doubt copyrighted and proprietary secret soulmate-locator layout allows my site to highlight (yes, highlight—in bright yellow) the traits which supposedly prove compatibility—either common ground to show how much you and someone else match or desired qualities which demonstrate how well they meet your criterion.

Step #3. *Uploading the **default** Photo*—my personal favorite. After all, a picture is worth a thousand words and a face launched a thousand ships, right? This photo will pop up every time your profile or username does. Remember, one never gets a second chance to make a first impression! My site says you will *get 15x more response with a photo*. I'm pretty sure the statistic is higher. (Me personally, if there's no photo, I move on). In a user-friendly format for morons, a big square with a cartoon silhouette presents, indicating to where you are encouraged to upload at least one photo of yourself. While it is not mandatory, it is EXTREMELY IMPORTANT. Call me skeptical, but I know men. I was reared on military bases with thousands of them. I married one and birthed and raised three. Over the course of my nearly 60 years I have been intimate with dozens. Indeed, for ten years I was the only woman permitted to sit at a faculty lunch table occupied by six men who deliberately, with their crude humor and dirty jokes, grossed out and scared off every other female teacher in the school. So when I say I know . . . I KNOW. (At the very least, I fake it well. Ask the readers of *Affaire de Coeur* magazine who voted my male protagonist in *Fires in the Night* their "Outstanding Hero of 1991." Like the adage says: Write what you know . . .)

So, back to the photo . . . Granted, on the profile paragraph I didn't try too hard. But the photo was a different story. It needed to be good. There is not a man on the planet who is going to look past a photo of an unattractive woman and read a long paragraph, because he *still* wants to know if she might be "the one." It doesn't matter one damn bit whether or not they share common interests, values, and goals. If he doesn't find her attractive, he's moving on. Let's be real here. Men think with their cocks. And cocks are visual. (*Playboy©* for the articles, my ass!)

My daughter-in-law may have said it best. Three years ago, when they were online dating, she was my son's second choice because she lived three hours away and #1 lived only an hour and 15 minutes. To this day, she contends, however, that the real reason was because he thought the other one was "hotter." I tell her she is mistaken. He would have told me the truth back then. Besides, she is absolutely stunning! But she will not be dissuaded. In her own words she thusly –and quite succinctly –explains the male decision process as it pertains to online dating: The penis does the picking.

Which leads us back to the default photo. You are actually encouraged to download lots of pictures. "It helps tell your story" or some other b. s.. Regardless, the default photo is the one first seen. It has to be the best you can come up with. It may be all that is viewed. (See preceding paragraphs.) Ladies, we women have the definite advantage here. Hair, make-up and lighting can perform miracles. Think about those tabloid paparazzi photos of celebrities caught without!

And gentlemen, please, a word: Smile! I've seen more mug shot-esque photos than I can count. And while we are on the subject of profile pictures in general . . . would it kill you to shave or dress up a bit? The backwards ball cap on a fifty-plus-year-old looks ridiculous, and you're not fooling me. I know it's hiding a receding hair line. Worse than the ball caps are the bandanas. But then again, maybe some women *are* into the biker look. On second thought, I'll give you a pass on that one. What I won't give a pass to are the twenty-year-old photos. Seriously? I don't care that you once had hair and a waistline. Now you don't. And now is what counts.

Also, if I see another dumb-ass selfie in front of a bathroom mirror, a shower curtain, a closet or your bed,

I'm going to scream! And please, speaking of beds, I don't want to see you lying in yours. And what, pray tell, is up with the front seat in the car/seatbelt over the shoulder selfies? These are as ubiquitous to the women as to the men, and I don't get it. (To both genders, get a friend to take a decent picture.) Gentlemen, sit in a chair, lean against your car, kneel next to your dog. And speaking of dogs, hell yes! I have stopped on every man's photo that had a dog in it. Cropping out ex-wives or girlfriends doesn't work for me either. I can still see her hair, her shoulder, a hand on yours. I know she was there. Again, get a friend to take a real picture—a recent picture.

Ladies, I haven't bothered to check out your photos so I don't know what to critique. Although I did read a profile from a man who said he would not respond to any profile that featured cleavage and/or underwear shots. Really? Maybe it's a religious belief thing. I didn't bother to read his profile far enough through to learn his faith orientation.

As far as my own profile pic, I chose a photo taken a week earlier on a river cruise excursion for flight attendants. I have no idea why it looks like I was having such a good time, but it shows a genuine smile and a really, really good hair day. (I should probably mention that for the past twelve years I have been an inflight pretzel pusher and exit door point-it-outer, first for America West, then US Airways, and now for American Airlines. Gotta love those airline mergers!)

Step #4. *Selecting a **Username***—not as easy as you might think. Personally, some cutesy *phillyflygirl*-type crap was not me, nor was I about to hide my name and phone number in it (more on this later) or try to come up with a clever double entendre. I decided on the first email address I had when the World Wide Web and internet were first invented by Al Gore (kidding): *jamada*—the first two letters of my sons' first names.

Step #5. *Paying for* **Membership**—requires you to click on and agree to the site's terms and conditions before entering your credit card info. Caution: Step # 5 CANNOT be revoked. I know. I tried. Twenty minutes after signing up, I was on the phone trying to *un*sign up. No dice. (And no refund.) Once you hit that submit-to-pay button you have bought yourself a ticket down the rabbit-hole. A prompt email then arrives, congratulating you on joining the "leading online dating site . . . responsible for more dates, relationships, marriages . . ." blah blah blah. You'll also get a subscription confirmation with helpful hints and tips for success. Ta-da and *Voila!* Your "new beginning" is about to begin.

Welcome to Wonderland, Alice.


Note to reader: The preceding process is how it worked *for me.* All dating sites differ. Your experience can—and likely will—vary.

## Chapter Two
## Week 1—The Time-suck Begins

The first few days are (or at least for me they were) a blitzkrieg of overload. Not only do I not know what the hell I'm doing as far as negotiating the site, the emails seem unrelenting. Emails telling me I have received winks, notices of photo likes, "you're his fav" and "he's interested" memos, as well as daily matches. I realize this is a simple computer algorithm process. They are taking my wish list and finding compatible profiles. (Duh!) But never fear, if I don't like their suggestions, I soon discover there are also links to similar matches. (Oh goody. I reject 11 out of 12, but then they provide me with another dozen to discard??) Then there are matches wherein the men are actually given a numerical quantifier as to how well they match my preferences. My matches in this category of prospective relationships range from 83% to 99%. "Look what you share!" states the gushing email. (Wow. Me and *Niceguy4u* share a like for coffee and conversation and both have children that live away from home. Amazing! What are the odds? Oops. I forgot. They provide them— 83%, apparently.)

To be fair—and in the interest of full disclosure—I am not citing actual user IDs nor specific profiles. In the following sampling compilation of actual matches (which very much mirror the tone and tenor of what I received), I have merely changed the names and the most specific details to protect the innocent and cover my ass. (The very last thing I need is *Dogman46* coming after me in a slander suit!)

So back to the gallery of gags for week 1 . . . Again, a disclaimer: The usernames are merely representative! They are *not* the exact names of the matches provided by the online website from which I purchased a six month membership "guaranteed" to find me my someone special "or the next six months are free."

- One gentleman, who touts the fact he is a gentleman first and foremost, claims to be a member of my "toned and athletic" preference club. (His photo begs to differ.)
- A 6'4", PhD educated, 6 figure earner does indeed meet my height, education and income wants. But he is admitting to "an extra few pounds" and requesting his mate be the same.
- *Photoman*, 63, touts his career as a professional photographer—and dutifully as proof provides 20+ out-of-date pictures of himself with camera in hand. All feature an exotic background—and a guy with a 1970s head of hair. (I recognize the look—my high school boyfriend, circa 1974, Ft Collins, CO, had the same blond semi-fro.)
- A 67-year-old with a bald top and gray sides gives his hair color as black. (Yep, once upon a time, based on his eyebrows.)
- A B&W photo of Frankenstein from a 1930s horror movie. (This elicits a laugh, but no interest.)
- *Easylistener*, 39, prefers 40-55, but would be willing to expand

his pool even older "if that special spark ignites."

- *Damien*, 65, seeking more age-appropriate companionship in women 59-65, is a widower looking for someone to help him get over the loss of his wife. (The sad desperation in his profile is practically palpable—and far from enticing.)
- *Lonelyheart*, 48, is another widower. His profile reads less desperate and more interesting. His picture, in a suit—hallelujah!— ticks off a subconscious box. Height, body type, education and income? Check, check, check and check. At last! A feasible prospect. (And a definite "yes.")
- Another possible winner is *Lawyerlooking*, 52. He has actually already contacted me via the site, tagging one of my photos with a "Classic style" comment. (Flattery will get you everywhere, Ll.) He moves to my #1 slot, with *Lonelyheart* a close second.

The list of likely losers (sorry, pessimism showing), all of whom I will eventually contact, continues and concludes with:

- *Easywithanedge*, a retired detective
- *Jerseymike*, posing with his Black Labs
- *Delidude* (great smile)

- *Dancewithme* (great profile)
- *Builtbill* (yes, he was!)
- *Ready2go*, who includes a truly lovely and endearing photo of himself with his infant granddaughter at her baptism.

All in all, I estimated I had looked at more than 200 photos and profiles. In only seven or eight was I interested enough to take the next step. (What is that? 4%?) Still, despite the lousy odds given my truly depressing like-to-loser ratio, I resolved to soldier on. ONLINE DATING IS A NUMBERS GAME! Moreover, hope springs eternal. No one gets on a ship they know will sink. I had to believe this could work.

Because of *Lawyerlooking*'s witty and well-written profile, I emailed him first. When we exchanged probably four or five emails via the site that first day, I began to think I might have been totally wrong about this online dating thing. *Ll* had a great sense of humor and a self-deprecating wit I enjoyed. He also looked good in a suit, had a full head of dark hair, was obviously intelligent and made a good income. The next morning he wrote bright and early: "Good morning, lovely lady." I responded with smile and similar greeting and asked what type of law he practiced. That was it. I never received an answer to the question nor another email from him.

As confused I was, I was not discouraged. On to number two—not second on my personal list of choices, but rather next in my email box. I hadn't contacted *Easylistener*, but he had me. Of a generation that was taught manners (If someone writes to you, you write back!), I responded before I did much more than note his profile picture. A head and shoulders shot, sunglasses and watch cap, in front of an old castle. European obviously.

*That would work*, had been my initial thought—then I actually read his entire profile and looked at all his pictures. Oh, no, no, no. *Easy* was short, pot-bellied and very thin on top. (No wonder he was wearing a hat!) I politely and literally wrote him off.

On to *Lonelyheart*. Having learned a valuable lesson from *Easylistene*r, I went through *Lonelyheart's entire* profile first. Doing so, I ran a mental check list that had evolved rather naturally after the first 100 or so pics and profiles:

1. He didn't include a lot of pictures. A plus in his favor. There were only two. And no stupid selfies.
2. I liked his smile. It was more of a smirk, as if he thought this whole thing was stupid, but someone talked him into it. (I can relate.)
3. His username was not icky. No hidden—or not so hidden—innuendos. (Note: I will *not* respond to anyone who includes the number 69 anywhere in their profile!)

As fate would seem to have it, *Lonelyheart* and I were seemingly meant for each other. As he had been matched to me, I had been matched with him. Moreover, in the very moment I was writing him, he was actually writing me! (Whoa. Pause for karmic applause.) We began to email via the site. Then we exchanged numbers and began to text. I learned quite a bit about him. None of it bad. He was Italian, raised on a Third World continent to missionary parents. He worked out of town, was self-employed, a civil engineer. The texts were good. He was literate. More boxes were checked in my mental list:

4. He spoke of his relationship with his daughter, which told me family was very important to him.
5. He was—or seemed—very kind, empathetic. He wrote the right things. Not too personal, but interested.
6. He followed through, referencing what I might have previously written. (For example, when I told him I was taking my grandson to see a movie, his text the next morning asked which one we had decided to see.)

I was definitely feeling optimistic. *Lonely* and I texted for three more days until we simultaneously agreed we were both ready to speak by phone. At the end of the third day he called.

Ahhh . . . that long-awaited and all-important first phone conversation!

Crap! What a downer! His voice was weirdly high, not effeminate-high, but not a deep baritone by any stretch of the imagination. Plus, he had a sing-song intonation pattern that literally was as nails on a chalkboard, a product (I think) of his foreign upbringing. I actually texted him on purpose later that evening to avoid having to listen to him. I fervently hoped in person it would be better. The next morning, as I was waiting to board a flight, we spoke briefly. He had called, saying he had wanted to wish me a safe trip, but also to hear my voice. (Would that I could have said the same!)

During the flight I came up with a list of questions. (Lists . . . it's what I do.) My reasoning was fairly valid, I thought. If this really was the 21st century mode of dating, replacing awkward face-to-face meetings with incognito phone calls, this was the point where you get to learn about someone, right? I figured I'd start easy and build. Simple fluff to start: Favorite food, movie, book, type of music. Then more personal: Boxer or briefs? When was his birthday? What kind of car did he drive? How long he had lived in his house? Some philosophical stuff next: His biggest fault, fear, failure. Did he have a temper? If he could freeze time, when? If he had $20,000 to spend, on what would he spend it? If he didn't have his current job/career, what would he have been? Finally the *really* personal: His favorite part of a woman's body, biggest turn on and off. What would be a deal-breaker? When was his last relationship? The last time he got laid?

I figured the questions would spark conversation and give me a sense of the man. Boy, did they! That evening we spoke again. My first red flag rose with my first question. His favorite food was fast food. (Seriously?) He didn't cook, he told me. He was handy with the outdoors stuff, but figured his partner could take care of the inside. He liked to come home and relax, watch Netflix or TV, just tune out. Uh-oh. My inner voice started to warn me: Danger, Will Robinson, danger! (Only someone my age will recognize the reference.) I had spent my married life tied to a TV-addicted couch potato who did nothing inside the house. I wasn't looking for a repeat in my dating life.

Somehow *Lonely* and I ended up skipping the next two portions of my question and answer inquest. To this day, I don't know how, but we jumped straight to the *really* personal. His last relationship was with his wife, he told me, his last physical experience as well. He had been celibate for three years, but took care of his needs himself.

*Wtf! Did he just say what I think he said?* Before I could say "pull back," he plunged in.

"How about you?" he asked.

"A year long relationship that had ended a year ago," I answered, pretending I didn't know where he was going.

"But you do take care of yourself?" he pushed.

"Yes."

At this point you should probably be told a lil sum'em-sum'em about me. I don't know why, but I have *always* met a test that is supposed to shock or fluster me with a head-on approach. The more intimate and inappropriate the question, the more direct and nonplussed I have a tendency to be. It was why and how I won acceptance to that all-male-bunch lunch table I mentioned earlier. (If you are curious . . . my respond-correctly-and-gain-admittance question: "Are you loose or tight?" My answer? A Mona Lisa smile and a "It's relative" rejoinder. Yep. Sass with class—sometimes absent the class.)

*Lonelyheart* kept thrusting. "When was the last time you had an orgasm?" "Do you travel with a toy?" Believe it or not, these questions were not the kiss of death for this budding online romance. The *coup fatal* came when he mentioned how he had driven away his social friends after his wife died. He now only had friends from church. Curious, I asked the denomination. He said it was non-denominational.

"Born again?" I asked.

"Yes," he said.

And time stood still.

I live down the street from the township fire department. At least once a day their big red truck speeds by—siren blaring, lights flashing, huge American flag streaming behind. That's what it felt like then. At that moment the sirens went off, the strobes flashed, the red flag of warning snapped in the wind. One thought raced through my mind: *Oh, no. Oh, Hell no!*

We need to pause now for a necessary flashback. During the one year separation that had preceded my divorce, I'd been involved with a man I'd met in Zurich. He spent the entire length of our ten month relationship in a constant struggle with his guilt and desires. The seductress and the sinner. Forces combined, they won every battle. But in the end, the saint won the war. It took me a year to get over him. He was/is born again.)

I wasn't going down that road again—ever. *Lonelyheart* was going to remain lonely. The next morning I broke it off with him in a text. I told him I thought he was not ready to move on, he was looking for a safe and cheap and easy form of entertainment and sexual thrill with little to no effort or betrayal to his wife's memory. He was shocked I would draw such a conclusion when he had been just "having a conversation." Whatever he wanted to call it, it was over. In total, start to finish, it had been a 5-day relationship—8 emails via the site, 119 private texts of varying lengths, and 3 phone calls.

Thankfully, I had a flight to Frankfurt the next day. I needed the distance. My first week of online dating had been an unmitigated disaster, as far as I was concerned. Most fittingly, however, was the manner in which Rabbit-hole Week #1 officially ended.

The following night, at 3:40 am local in a German hotel room, my text message alert went off. "How are you?" read an anonymous text.

"Who is this?" I wrote back, awakened from a sound sleep and annoyed as f**k.

"Bob from XXXXX (my site)."

It took a moment for me to connect the dots . . .Bob aka *Ready2go* . . .the guy with the baby baptism photo . . . after a couple of exchanged emails and tired of the difficulty in going through the site, I had send him my number . . .

"Well, Bob from XXXXX," I typed back, "I am in Europe. It is 3:40 my time. I have a wake-up call in two hours. Can we continue this when I return to Philly tomorrow?"

"What are you wearing?"

Jesus, Mary and Joseph! Seriously, Dude? *Were you not the one in a church—holding a baby?* My Catholic upbringing/indoctrination reeled. I could not hit the "delete all" button on my phone fast enough.

The next day an email update arrived from my site summarizing my Week 1 progress: *25 Guys showed interest in you! You received 10 winks, 9 likes, 8 emails, 7 yes ratings. 3 Favs. Compared to successful members, you're off to an amazing start. Stay on the path to success by meeting more new people.* (A big pink and purple button labeled SEARCH NOW was helpfully provided.)

An amazing start? Really? Out of 24 site-provided matches, only one (1!) had evolved into anything. (And we all know how *Lonelyheart* went!)

But, no experience is without its lessons learned. In my first week of online dating I had learned three. I urge you to commit them to memory.

1. Read the **entire** profile before responding.
2. Voice **matters—nearly** as much as looks.
3. Regardless of lag time and difficulty maneuvering through the site, **do not immediately** give out your number.

Had I known *then* what I do *now*, Bob the Pervert might have revealed himself sooner.

## Chapter Three
## Week 2—Texting Toads

My military son has a favorite expression: "You will miss every shot you don't take." (You will probably miss it, too, if you don't try your hardest. Half-ass effort gets you half-ass results.)

At the beginning of Week 2 I decided I needed to take this entire thing more seriously. How could I legitimately expect a good result from a thrown-together profile? If I wanted to attract the right man, I needed to write the right profile. After all, if one asks for chocolate ice cream, one will get chocolate. Only a mind reader will know you really wanted Swiss mocha marshmallow crunch with almonds.

To that end, I rewrote my profile paragraph, presenting myself (I hoped) in a less sarcastic and (maybe) more vulnerable light.

*Independent, intelligent, well-traveled. Strong, resilient, stubborn. Attractive, cultured and classy on the outside, but feisty ex-military brat on the inside—ergo the aforementioned qualities. Honest. Looking for someone not intimidated by strength, who sees beyond the surface and the shell, who undermines my walls to reach my soul. I am the strongest, most independent woman you are likely to meet. But I'm also a sucker for dogs and babies and sappy Budweiser Clydesdale commercials. I've lived enough life to know who I am, what I am, and what I want. I want a gentleman who will drape his coat across my shoulders when the air turns chilly; a man who will take the lead and decide the way, whether it is the restaurant to choose or street to take, the wine or entree to order; a mate who will spark my intellect, challenge my boundaries and fill my empty spaces.*

It was still reserved, even standoffish, but that's me. Nor was I sugar-coating anything. I didn't want to cuddle on the couch and take long walks on the beach. I wanted the triumvirate: intellectual, emotional *and* physical appeal.

I also added three pictures and captions to all six. The profile picture I dated for the express purpose of making it known it was a recent picture. I identified my oldest grandson as such and stated "Yes, I am a grandmother." The picture with my youngest son at his wedding I explained was taken nine days before he left for Afghanistan. The full length shot taken at a local Veteran's Day parade gave a good likeness of my size and shape. Beneath it I identified myself as the proud mother of a currently deployed soldier. I added a photo with my middle son, all 75 cross-fit inches of him, with the corresponding caption: "I grow them big—the intimidated need not apply." A selfie that made me look svelte and extremely sexy was also included, its caption reading: "Since a dumbass mirror selfie is apparently *de rigueur*, here's mine." Lastly, a picture of me in full flight attendant regalia working a First Class flight to Paris.

Yes, I realized my sharp personality and innate sarcasm were doing more than peek out. And yes, the thought occurred I was probably going to scare them off with my attitude and vocabulary. But I didn't care. The man I wanted then (and still do!) would recognize the wit. And he sure as hell would know what *de rigueur* means! (Or at least have the wherewithal to look it up.) I can't do dumb. Blue collar is one thing. But illiterate is another. The guy who wrote the last thing he read was his water bill had better be trying to be funny. I had just finished a 640 page book on how and why France lost to Nazi Germany in 1940. An intellectual challenge wasn't coming from a man who doesn't read or one who can't spell. ("dose" for "does," really??)

In my defense, some self-proclaimed experts (who actually get paid to give advice on online dating) contend that making yourself appear as a challenge that has daunted others may have its upside. Women love the thought of snagging the guy other women just couldn't catch. (It's a staple of every romance novel ever written!) Men, on the other hand, just love the hunt. The more difficult the prey, the greater the thrill. Unfortunately (in my experience, at least), the relationship hunt is—for most men—a "catch and immediately release" sport.

*Lonelyheart* had told me there were a lot of crazies out there. (Damn, he had started out so promising! Oh well . . . *c'est le vie*.) Truth be told, I *was* afraid of falling into that crazy column. But if I scared them off at the get-go, where was the loss? Wasn't I looking for the one *not* frightened away by intellect and strength?

On the cusp of Weeks 1 and 2, I came across the profile of an ex-lawyer, 42, foreign-born, who was not a match to me per se, but rather someone similar to someone I had "liked." (Yes. You get those messages too: "Hello, *jamada*. If you liked X, you may like Z.") I definitely *did* like Z. The problem was I was a couple years past his age preference. And speaking of preference, he was most specific in his—graduate degree and/or PhD. I was also not his religious choice. Undeterred, I wrote. I explained my familial connection to his faith and included the fact I had written a novel about a specific group in his people's history. He actually responded the next day. He said I sounded "special" and provided his name and number. We started to text. Pretty hot and heavily, in fact. We met in the flesh the next night. (As of this chapter's final edit, it has been nearly three weeks now. Z and I still text and play some mutually entertaining phone sex game.)

The irony is I really don't want an email buddy or even a phone sex pal, as fun as it sometimes is. Neither am I interested in "online" dating as it apparently exists. If, after a few emails and texts and a couple phone calls, a man is not interested enough to want to meet and lay eyes on, then please. Have him do me the favor of moving on. This is not my inner bitch talking, merely my innate good sense speaking. I already have a man, an extremely good-looking—albeit too young—one, who enjoys online dating's siren song to single men everywhere:   safe excitement and vicarious thrills with no expense of effort or money and damn little time. I don't need another.

The problem for me lies in my insistence upon physical attraction. If it doesn't present itself in the photo, there is no way for me to proceed, to judge, gauge or discover whether or not the intellectual and emotional aspects of my triumvirate are present. I know attraction isn't always sparked solely by physical appeal, but I can't look past some really unappealing men.

And still my site's algorithm does its thing . . . *You caught his attention! He's interested in you! See who saw your profile and is interested!* shout the email alerts. Invariably, when I open up the site to view the actual profiles, I want to cry, scream or laugh. A few cases in point:

- *Swivelhips* looks like he's 70 and more capable of breaking them than twisting them
- *Itstime* (no, it's not!) is lying in bed with his head on a pillow
- *Mike228163* looks homeless and kind of scary
- *Lastchance*, 57, is worse. He looks like a serial killer. Never married, the rest of his profile is blank, every question reads "I'll tell you later" (no, you won't)

Eventually—mercifully—Week 2 draws to a close with yet another list of potential matches, rated to match me and my preferences within a 83-86% range. Really? Of the 24 possibles, half are at the very highest end of my age preference. Two are not my race and three are separated—a no-go item for me. Only one sparks my interest with a comment about Sartre and Vonnegut, both of whom I have read and enjoyed. I write to him, and he never replies.

Any way I look at it, this is depressing. Not only the lack of viable candidates, but the rejection. You can see who has viewed you. If no contact is forthcoming, you can pretty much surmise you have been rejected out of hand. (Of course you are doing the same to them.) Then there are the ones you actually reach out to who don't email back. More rejection. And more frustration because apparently some aren't even able to view or return your email since they are not paying members, but merely freebie looky-loos. It's also possible they were once legit. But since they haven't renewed their memberships, they are now unattainable. Or maybe they were actually never on the site at all? (Several lawsuits have been filed over this practice. Seeding the pool, as it were.)

The amount of time this requires is ridiculous. And it is a constant roller coaster of emotion. With each and every email, wink, like or outreach received, hope goes uuup (until you see the picture) and reality crashes dooown.

I also cannot shut off my inner skeptic. The same question pops into my head every single time: Why is this guy even online anyway? There has to be something wrong with him—otherwise he wouldn't be alone and looking. (Of course, the widowers do have a get out of jail free card on this one.) Even the fact my handsome, accomplished, Air Force Academy-educated son resorted to Match.com does not assuage my leeriness. I am certain most are simply surfing, drawn by curiosity, voyeurism and the ease of anonymity. Online "dating" is cheap entertainment and a perfect form of porn—virtual *and* interactive! The "I'm looking to meet interesting people" line is a load of crap. Based upon my experience thus far, no one wants to "meet" anyone or "date" in the conventional sense. They want to text until they want to "see" you. (Think phone sex with visual aids.)

Of course, I realize I am online, too. (So I am a hypocrite as well as a judgmental bitch.) But my opinion is far from solely held. A woman who had been spammed from my hacked profile (see Chapter 12) wrote me that this was her first site ever and she was feeling "quite overwhelmed with the weird looking people out there emailing [her] and they mostly look like pedophiles." I couldn't agree more. Though I've never had the word "pedophile" pop into my head, I sure as hell have thought "felon" more times than I can count. And women are not alone in this sense of being over—and under—whelmed. I actually emailed a guy, who in his profile wrote "save me from this site." BTW, I never heard back from him either. So there it is. My conclusion at the conclusion of my second week: They (and me, I guess) are all lonely, horny losers grasping at a last straw and the possibility of free phone fun.

And yet my cheery week's end Dear Dater email tells me I'm doing "great." My status update features that same damn big pink/purple button for me to conveniently click and respond to my winkers, emailers, favers, likers and yesers. My progress report also informs that I have sent eight more emails than their "average successful dater."

I'm torn by the temptation to send a response:

> *Dear Dating Site,*
> *How about measuring the success of my online **dating** by the number of actual **dates**? Oh, wait, no. Never mind. That wouldn't work. Because that number is **ZERO!***

## Chapter Four
## Week Three—Turnoffs and Red Flags

After a couple of weeks or so, I began to notice things. You know the adage, if it walks like a duck and quacks like a duck . . .

Of all the things about online dating profiles that bother me in general, the number one turnoff: no photo. I have seen some truly unattractive and even scary looking men who had no problem posting their mug shot. If a man hasn't uploaded at least one picture of himself, I have to wonder: Jeeze! How bad *can* he be? Big Big Bill, Toothless Biker Dan and Inmate Steve the Living Tattoo had no qualms.

Speaking of pictures . . . What's with the sunsets, beach views and mountain vistas? I truly don't care about your vacation, so neither do I want to see its montage. And if it's some kind of subliminal hint, as in "If you date me, I'll take you here." No thanks. I fly for free. I'll take myself.

And whether it's just this part of the country or the male mid-life crisis incarnate . . . what's with the motorcycle and boat pictures? I swear every other man posts them. And as long as we are on an aquatic note . . . I am not into the proudly displayed dead fish pics either. Dead deer do it for me even less. Yes, my brain tells me it is a legitimate and necessary-for-the-balance-of-nature sport—but regardless of how many points the poor thing has (had), my heart cries, "He murdered Bambi's mom!" Not really a fan of the pictures trying to demonstrate how physically active you are either. Gym pictures flexing in the mirror, bike helmets and spandex shorts, hiking with a huge-ass backpack or shirtless jogging . . . not impressing me. Sorry. Most men my age look exactly what they are: Trying too hard.

My second turnoff (it's actually my first, but without a photo I usually don't get far enough to discover it): *separated* as a marital status. Nope. Not interested. You can't have your cake and eat it too. Get the decree finalized, then go looking. I'm not actually crazy about *never married* either. It begs the question: Why the hell not? Only in romance novels (I know. I wrote 'em.) is a fantastic, gorgeous, perfectly perfect in every way man still single at 50. I gotta think something's wrong with him. Of course *widowed* carries its own baggage. If his was a bad marriage, he is now free. Like a kid loose in a candy store, he's gonna want it all. Settling down and being monogamous after years of the ball and chain scenario are not likely items on his immediate to-do list. And if his marriage was good, that's worse. He's looking for a substitute. He can say "fresh start," but it's probably not the reason he's on an online dating site. He's lonely and looking for safe fun. A way to get his rocks off without actually cheating on his dead missus.

Which takes us now to *divorced*. Ladies, beware the "no drama" line in his profile! He wants a clean slate from you, but chances are good he's requesting such because his own chalkboard is covered with crazy ex-wife bullshit. And if she cheated on him, he's going to view you through the same myopic lens. It's hard to trust anyone when someone has broken your trust. Just my opinion. But an opinion I can back up with a hundred profiles that mention the words *honest, loyal*, and *no games* as traits the men on my site are looking for in their next relationship. Regardless, watch where you step, Alice. 'Cause in Dot Com Rabbit-hole Wonderland, none of the above choices are without their pitfalls.

A man's listed age preference for his ideal date is another potential turnoff, since it presents, as pretty tangible proof, both his mindset and his motivation. Beyond the gross and totally obvious 49-year-old man seeking women 18-29, there is the equally offensive 45-year-old targeting *both* extremes: 20-80 is your preference? Really? (Apparently "breathing" was not a listed option.) I have to wonder no less about the 29-year-old who is seeking women 45-70. (Can you say Sugar Momma?) I'm not one to talk. My preference is 42-60. And while I have gone even younger, I do draw the line at anyone younger than my own offspring. I expect the same restraint and good sense from the opposite gender.

Extremely narrow preferences such as 31-35 earn their own brand of turn off veering into Red Flag Territory. Either a man is looking for a precise replacement, or his specificity results from a fantasy ideal he has conjured in his mind. Neither scenario bodes well for the lucky woman unlucky enough to match his want. (Side note: One man who had "winked" at me had listed blue eyes, white or gray hair as a preference, a Master's Degree and a retired status. Either he was shopping with a *really* detailed grocery list— or he had screwed up and listed his own particulars as desires for his mate. An honest mistake. But shouldn't an individual, who claims to make 200,000+, have a better eye for detail and know to double-check his work before submitting it?)

On the other hand, a yellow flag goes to those men who don't bother with any preferences at all. Age 18-73? Height 3' to 7'? Any and all options for race, hair color, education, income, body type, etc. and/or no preference for any and all lifestyle questions? This tells me one of two things about you. #1: You are desperate and your only preference is a pulse. Or #2: You are too lazy to fill out the damn questions! Either way you are a no-go for me.

The next object of my derision is usernames . . . three words: yuck, ick, eww. First and foremost, to the online daters of the male persuasion, PLEASE STOP INCLUDING THE NUMBER 69 IN YOUR USERNAME! Someone else may feel very differently, but personally, it elicits nothing but a groan. It is neither amusing nor clever. And it certainly is not original or enticing. It is, in fact, an unmitigated turnoff and an absolute red flag. Yellow flags fly immediately with those men who include their phones numbers in their usernames. Other men are slightly less overt. Asking obvious questions in their written profiles, they challenge their reader to solve the puzzle. Oh goody! A treasure map/scavenger hunt/trivial pursuit game. Answer correctly and you'll be able to text or chat directly. These "hidden in plain sight" questions, whose answers (i.e. the number of legs on an octopus) ultimately supply the digits of his contact number, might earn a point or two for clever, but they are no less irritating or off-putting. The purpose of such subterfuge is to circumvent the site— which I have learned the hard way is there for a good reason besides making money for its shareholders. (FYI and BTW . . . my site's shares rose 7% last week after beating Q 1 estimates.)

Ladies, think before you act. In this day and age of caller ID, if you contact him, he'll have your number. If you don't mind an absolute stranger having it, then go for it. There is a reason why the site doesn't just include it from the get-go. Yes, going through the site and emailing is a pain. But so are middle of the night phone calls and texts from perverts you gave your number to. Trust me on this one!

I am also not a fan of the cutesy/subliminal message username, for example *ineedu*, *kravnluv* and *go4it*. (One day I counted 14 men using "*go4it*"s—and that didn't include its innumerable variants, i.e. *letsgo4it, Ltsgo4it, ynotgo4it*.) It's like vanity license plates, trying to figure them out sometimes. It just doesn't seem *2b* worth the *frt*. Any username with "God" in it isn't really a winner for me either. A lot of men include some reference to a sports team as well. As big a part as sports can play in some men's lives, I'm not surprised. I just wonder though how many men would be chomping at the bit to date *iluvshooz* or *ibr8k4dsw*? On second thought, never mind. If she is hot enough, most men wouldn't care what she called herself.

The written paragraph portion of the profile is a veritable minefield. Ladies, negotiate this section very carefully! The ground may look smooth, but you need to watch out for what lies beneath the surface. Keep your eyes open for signs of incongruity and always trust your instincts. *What, how* and *why* are the watchwords here. Indeed, *how* he expresses himself may be even more important than *what* he says. Language, vocabulary and grammar are important clues not to be overlooked or dismissed. I am talking now about more than the annoying misspelled word. (Seriously, though! Spellcheck!) If he claims to be college-educated and earning six figures, should he not be capable of complete sentences and proper capitalization? (For example, i hate i for I—my own damn computer even auto corrects it.) Frauds and scams are rampant in our computer age in general, and in online dating in particular. Many of these originate overseas. The FBI lists slightly "off" language as one of the first clues the person you are corresponding with is in another country. (See Chapters 8 and 22 for more information on frauds and scams.) Z did this in his texts. However, "I just going to have" or "sorry I am a bad company today," lent credence to his foreign-born and educated claim.

Speaking of claims . . . double-check his photos after you read his paragraph. Car, house, yard, clothes, furniture should all appear to go with the person he is purporting to be. If Mr. Self-employed Entrepreneur making 100,000+ a year is a casual drinker, why are there liquor bottles galore on the Formica counter of his tract-house looking kitchen? Nor do lawyers live in double wide trailers or drive old pick-up trucks, as a rule. Seriously, 70s paneling and American Colonial furniture or 80s Southwest from a guy who claims to be a real estate developer/house flipper earning 150,000+ k? Maybe he should concentrate his efforts a little closer to home? Then again, they say the shoemaker's kid has the worst shoes . . .

Even small details can provide information as to his personality. Look closely. Is his house neat or messy? Is his yard well-maintained or a weed patch? Female clothing scattered about in a bedroom should definitely merit a second thought. Equally problematic is a photo that looks too good, too professional, too posed. A fellow flight attendant found herself very attracted to a man who had contacted her via a dating site. They exchanged multiple emails, and things looked promising indeed. Then she showed his picture to her twenty-something-year-old daughter—who immediately pulled up the same image on google image. Mom's dream match was Halle Barrie's boyfriend.

An excellent indication of who this person is may be gleaned from what he writes about himself. But sometimes what he writes about the woman he is seeking speaks even louder. Either way, ask yourself why he would write what he has written and try to read between the lines. It may save you from making a serious mistake—or it could eliminate a great guy. Roll of the dice, I guess. Some of my favorite red flag statements and my interpretations and reactions follow. Note, I have not changed or altered these in any way. The grammar mistakes within are theirs.

- *I love spooning in bed. Another turn on is holding hands in public displays of affection from my significant other.* (In other words . . . it no longer works? Never have I known a virile man to choose cuddling and hand holding over the real deal.)
- *It is important that we each have the space to pursue our own interests and time spend*

*with our own friends.* (So you want a long leash and a relationship on your terms?)

- *Thanks for looking anyways* (He already knows he's a loser?)
- *My search has not been without prayer and consideration.* (Ouch. Part sad, part guilt and all bad.)
- *I look better in person* (I doubt it.)
- *I might be a closet Chippendale, but only do private shows, 1 on 1.* (A lap dance from a 60-year-old? No, thanks. I didn't much care for it when I was 30 and the men were in their 20s.)
- *I've counseled nutrition for decades and use the best supplements, and it's kept me looking younger than biologic age...usually take for mid 40s or mid 50s at most, I'm actually 65, not 55...try to keep up with me...* (Honey, your hair dye has given you a false sense of reality. Trust me, you look 65.)
- *She must be social, happy and without grudges. Her past must be her past.* (Wow. Let me guess about your ex.)
- *Retired from dentistry for photography ... have an amazing career/studio—looking for a woman who is photogenic and receptive to being adored and captured with my artistry, all over the world* (No way, no how. I hate having my picture taken and I'm pretty sure your ego would fill the frame anyways.)
- *. . . all I can say here now is that these dating sites are frustrating, I've been abused, spent lots of $$ to find out the other person was never interested or was hungry and thirsty.* (Another ouch. But either she

was a *really* good actress, you can't read a woman for shit—or you saw what you wanted to.)

- *I have so many tremendous great qualities!* (Dude, I'm pretty sure when they tell you to talk about your qualities they mean to *list* them.)
- *Not a couch potato except for cuddling and romance* (Wanna bet?)
- *Retired homebody funlovein cookout NASCAR football fishing shooting cars outing fixing up old houses* (I'm sure there's a red neck woman out there for you, good buddy. But she ain't me.)
- *I have so much that I could say here (a ton of characters are left), but I'll save that for later.* (Maybe you shouldn't. Lazy isn't an attractive quality, and the strong silent type only works in person—not on paper.)
- *. . . maybe she would like me to train her in the gym.* (Hmmm . . . I don't know a woman anywhere—even the ones in good shape—who would take this statement well. Regardless of your intent, Muscle Man, you have in essence told her she isn't good enough the way she is now.)

So back to the paragraph profiles . . . Gentlemen, too short is a problem, but so is too long. At some point after four or five paragraphs, I don't want to know any more. You've crossed the line between interesting and detailed to self-indulgent bore. You are either preaching or ranting. Neither is an alluring draw. Hold something back. Then there is the opposite extreme—the profiles that are essentially blank save a single sentence claiming you are "working" on your profile or considering what to write. Contact me when it's done and you have posted a picture. Ladies, if you are good-looking, you  need not worry. You could spit on paper, and men would flock. If you are average-looking, though, you'll have to try harder.

My best advice to both genders is to be honest— about yourself *and* what you are seeking. But moderation is key. Too much is too much. Be interesting and refrain from mentioning the past. If your status is widowed, enough said. Your profile need not go into detail about the length of the illness and how after your months/years of mourning you are finally ready to find love again. Avoid negative statements such as "I'm lonely" or "I'm giving this one last shot." If in doubt, have a friend (preferably of the opposite gender) look at your profile.  According to a 2015 Pew Research Center online post, 1 in 5  online daters has turned to someone else for help with their profile, either to help create it or to view it.  Unsurprisingly, women are nearly twice as likely as men to ask a friend for input or feedback.

I am honestly torn on this subject. On one hand I'd like to think it's possible to describe yourself in such a way as to spark another person's genuine interest. But on the other, I don't believe a lack of physical attraction can be compensated for by even the best profile ever written. Conversely, if that physical spark ignites, there probably isn't a profile awful enough that will douse it.  At least not until you have been burned badly enough . . .  Or one time too many.

# Chapter Five
## Week 4 –To Settle or Not to Settle?

With apologies to Shakespeare, the above title question is a good one. It is a question I firmly believe every woman going down the dot com dating hole is going to have to answer fairly early on. If you can't be with the one you love, honey—do you just love the one you're with?

I am no expert. My Master's is in Mothering and my PhD in Life. I have absolutely no education or formal training to back up my thoughts. I have only opinion, personal experience, gut instinct and a pretty decent (most of the time) moral compass. They have not always served me well, but neither have I ever gotten myself into a situation I couldn't get out of—if I wanted to badly enough. Remember my profile? Strong, resilient, firm-willed, and opinionated.

Choice has consequence. Make a mistake once, and it's a mistake. Make the same mistake again, and it's now a decision. Those who fail to learn from history are doomed to repeat it. Old ways won't open new doors. Stupid is doing the same thing over and over and expecting a different outcome. Clichés and proverbs all. They are as numerous as ticks on a mangy dog. But the problem with clichés and proverbs is that they are inspired by—and grounded in—*truth*. A cliché is born when something occurs so frequently as to be utterly unsurprising. A proverb, on the other hand, is a pearl of wisdom, begotten by the grit of experience to develop into a seed of knowledge and a gem of moral advice. A lesson to be learned. For the simple reason they are proverbs and clichés, they are often discounted and even dismissed as banal or untrue. Life has taught me the very opposite.

Each of the aforementioned clichés and proverbs addresses the same behavior—that of knowingly repeating an action or a pattern that has led to disaster in the past. This lack of learning from one's mistakes has major relevance in the dating process—whether it be traditional dating or online. I am the most guilty of anyone in this regard, and I absolutely and freely admit it. I just don't know if I can—or am at this point ready—to change my pattern. More specifically my preference pattern.

I have a "type." Always have. Dark-haired (preferably long), somewhat ethnic/exotic, arrogant. If one were to line up the photos of every guy I have been with since I started dating some 45 years ago, I have no doubt 90% would be eerily similar in looks. In my high school, college and pre-marriage years they were Italian, Mexican, Greek—hell, there was even a Sikh in there! Now returned to dating, I have not changed much. The only difference is that with age (or international flying?) I seem to be more enamored of foreign men and less impressed by American. But I digress . . .

Returning to the subject of preferences as they relate to online dating. They matter. A lot. Or at least as they pertain to describing your perfect date match. Think back to the signing-up process wherein you were flat-out asked to list and/or select your desired body type, hair and eye color, race, education, etc.. Choice has consequence, Alice! In other words, in this grown-up version of *Build a Bear Workshop©,* if you indicated that income and education didn't matter, you can't be surprised if your rabbit-hole Romeo is a high school-educated low income wage earner. Ergo, if you really do have a sense of what or who you want, go for it. With literally millions in the online pool, you might just catch him. Nothing ventured, nothing gained. Be specific and be honest. If short men really do turn you off, don't drop the drop-down box to 5'7". Want a tough teddy bear with callouses on his hands? Then say so. Dream large. At least to start. You can always go back and make changes when reality rains on your parade.

I had to.

Upon signing up, the question of my age preference was not an easy one. I don't feel nearly sixty. I don't act nearly sixty. And I am repeatedly told I do not look sixty. So screw it! I wasn't looking to screw sixty! Not while— and if—I could get or attract younger. Besides, I'd actually tried dating my age and didn't like it. (Right after moving to Philly, I started to see a very nice man, my age thereabouts [62]. He bored me to tears.) Hence, when I'd first looked at the age drop-down menu, I knew I needed to list my age preference truthfully. However, in concession to "we really need to be real here," I *had* dialed up the dial from Zurich (38) and dropped down the drop-down to 42-60.

By Week 4 I was confronting the consequences of my choice.

AARP might publish an article in their magazine touting the frequency of younger men dating older women, but my online experiences thus far have proven far different. Clearly, the 37-year-old long-haired Tunisian concierge who picked me up in a Munich hotel lobby does *not* have a slightly older brother or cousin online dating in the greater Philadelphia area! F**K! (Not bloody likely at this rate!) I am so tired of looking at photos of men whom I literally would not touch if we were the last two human beings on the planet and the future of mankind depended upon it. (Ok, bad analogy. I'm a dozen years past child-bearing—but the sentiment remains.)

In a word: NO. No, to the Duck Dynasty reject with his straggly-ass gray beard all the way down to his ginormous beer belly. (Hello? Did I not list athletic and toned as my body type preference?). No, to Mr. 4 Chins Charlie. (Making up perhaps for the 2 hairs on top of his head?) And no—regrettably at times—to every African-

41

American. Right, wrong or indifferent, I prefer to not date out of my race.

And by the way, I prefer tall. And I listed my preference accordingly. I don't care that I'm 5'3" and can wear 3 inch heels and still not be taller than a 5'7" guy. I want tall. So why, considering my generous 5'9" parameters, am I getting 5'6" candidates? (I can only assume the same yahoo who approved my upside photo is also coming up with my matches—and totally ignoring my stated preferences in the process.)

"No" as well, to every man older than 60. No, to the 42-year-old baseball coach making 35k a year, and no, to the tattooed biker-looking artist claiming less than that. These last were men whose profiles I actually perused past the photo. The vast majority though I honestly rejected on looks alone.

I know I'm being cruel and unfair. Certainly plenty of nasty, hurtful, critical (albeit true) comments can be thrown at my picture. (Trust me. I'm a better self-critic than any stranger could ever be.) But fact is fact. Not only do our first impressions have a tendency to stick, they happen quick! Research has proven that it takes *less than one second* for a person to form a first impression of another. In fact, within one-tenth second of seeing someone's face, we have made up our mind not only about their attractiveness, but their likeability, trustworthiness, competence and aggressiveness as well! It's an intuitive, innate capability evolved into Homo sapiens' primordial hard-wiring out of pure Darwinian necessity. In those earliest "fight or flight" days, the ability to discern friend from foe in a literal split second meant literal life or death. Talk about your life skill!

So this is primitive man's (and woman's) gift to us today—the talent of nano-second "no" ing a photo array of wannabe mates and dates on a dot com site? Ain't progress great? Because (again according to bona fide research) within 30 seconds we have also made up our mind if we would sleep with that person or not. Heady stuff . . . a first impression.  Much of what inspires that first impression is physical appearance.  Confidence, voice, passion and personality are factors as well, but the lion's share rests on looks. Physical appeal is 90% the thing (my number now and not the researchers') that strikes the spark that lights the attraction that fires the mating urge. Again, we are talking about primordial programming. This instinct to seek the most attractive with which to mate not only transcends species, but is actually ironically reversed in most of the animal kingdom wherein the male is much better looking than the female. Hello, peacock? Hello, pen hen? Why do you think Lassie on TV and in the movies was always a male dog? And speaking earlier about lions—what about that mane?

But back to people and physical attraction and attractiveness and online dating site profile photos . . . Yes, I know a photo does not always accurately portray its subject.  Some people don't photograph well. I have a beautiful girlfriend in Germany whose every picture fails to do her justice. Then there is the obvious as previously mentioned—most of the photos on this site suck! Amateur hour meets closet selfie meets Facebook vacay pics meets family photo album! Truly, I get it. A wonderful man may be eliminated from my consideration for no better a reason than his photo was bad.

Paradoxically, the opposite holds true as well. Some people *do* photograph well. I am sure more than one man on an online dating site has fallen for a woman who in real life looks NOTHING like her photo. Forty pounds ago, a different hair color or the absence of salon extensions are false advertising at its worst (best?). Then there is the artful quasi-deception. My oldest son tells the story of a girl he met online dating several years ago. Every photo she posted was a headshot. In each and every one, regardless of hairstyle or degree of makeup, she was really pretty. They agreed to meet face-to-face at a local bar. She was already seated when he arrived. Everything was going well and according to plan—until she stood up to use the ladies' room. In my son's words, "Mom, she was built like a lake buoy! Small on top and huge on the bottom. It wasn't what I expected at all." It's a story as nearly old as time. A case in point: Henry VIII, who fell in love with Anne of Cleves based solely upon an incredibly flattering painting. When the German princess showed up in the flesh, England's serial marrying king couldn't divorce her fat Teutonic ass fast enough. A blessing in disguise for the poor girl— considering the fate of all his other wives save the last.

In fact, my son claims the girls he met online so often misrepresented their looks that he began to utilize an escape plan he had heard about on a syndicated radio show. I should first explain. According to my son's thinking, once eyes have met and words are exchanged, a decent guy is pretty much committed to see the date through to at least one round of drinks. And even an SOS text from a buddy isn't going to get him off the paying hook. The man pays. Period. My son's solution therefore was to avoid from the get-go the initial contact if the girl was not as advertised. A no-show was better than a kiss-off, was his contention. He would ask the girl what she would be wearing and tell her he was wearing a blue shirt, for example. A time to meet would be set. He would then purposely arrive late, wearing a different color shirt than he had told her. This allowed him to scope her out in anonymity. If she failed the eye test, he was out the door—gone with her nary the wiser that she had been scrutinized and found lacking. Ingenious, I have to admit. (I may use it myself—if I ever actually get asked out.)

According to my son's radio host mentor (who obviously has read the same research I have) if the chemistry is there, it happens fast. If it isn't there, no expensive dinners and nice-guy behavior are going to change her mind. She might say she doesn't put out on the first date, but shock jock Tom Leykis guarantees his target-audience male listener, "She has for somebody—just not *for you.*" Clearly this guy knows there is ratings' gold in controversy. This self-proclaimed expert bills himself as a teacher and instructor, dedicated to the cause of teaching men "how to get more tail for less money." "Dating equals porking," he crows, so men need to "stop their nice-guy instincts." After all, (I am paraphrasing his *spiel* now) 60% of her is a deliberate scam—dyed hair, fake nails, boobs—so men need to wake up and not waste weeks or months. This dating dali's avowed formula for success is based upon a singular, inviolate truth (verified by research!): A woman decides in 30 seconds "yes" or "no" she will sleep with a guy. Therefore, if after three dates and $100, the relationship is not moving in that direction, the guy needs to move on "because he is in the friend zone." An outlay of money does not or will not equate to more sex—or any.

As distasteful as I may find this guy's language and delivery, I can't honestly argue with the truth of his premise—except perhaps to dispute his—and research's—timeframe. I personally pretty much know in a nano-second. (3 tops!) And while I have succumbed after a few months of "nice-guy behavior and expensive dinners," I attribute that to wine and a long dry spell.

But let's leave my son's online dating practices in the past where they belong, and return to the present and my question of settling or not. After nearly three weeks of online dating—more accurately—of being on line on an online dating site, I realized a second painful truth: Not only were the vast majority of my matches, likes, favs and winks still failing the nano-second test, the number of men responding to my profile seemed to be diminishing. Going back and actually counting (yes, the site allows for all kinds of tracking), my suspicion was confirmed. In my first week online, 22 men had "liked" my photo. My second week netted 10 men. But by week 3 only three men were interested enough to hit that "like" button. Talk about depressing and demoralizing!

FYI: you can also select a link to look and see every person who has ever viewed you. Seeing the sheer number of men who passed and the *losers* who deemed *me* unworthy of their attention is a blow to ego and self-esteem I don't know many women could shake off. A second punch in the gut landed when I followed yet another link— and saw in black and white the truly small number of men I had contacted (a tiny fraction of the 200+ a week matches I've been sent), and then compared the even smaller number of favorable outcomes via return emails.

I know by now this is getting redundant—and even boring. But that's the online dating experience. The same old same old until you think you can't click another click. It's all part and parcel of dot com dating rabbit-hole hell: Out-reaches on your part that get no response. (And no, don't go thinking it could be a computer glitch. They got it—they just don't respond because they don't want to respond.) Emails that get a polite response. (Period) And emails that turn into a pleasant back and forth exchange— and then die. No explanation given. But in case you don't believe me (yet) here's a perfect example: A widowed father, with whom I exchanged 10 very cordial and seemingly promising emails, was leaving town for his college daughter's graduation. He wrote he would be in touch when he returned. He lied.

In fact, into week 4, I wonder if they all don't—lie, that is. There is absolutely no way some of the ages given can match the photo provided. Studies bear me out. While women online will most typically lie about their weight, shaving off pounds, men shave off years. After all, it's not as if proof of age is required when signing up on a dating site.

But let's leave the subject of my matches' disappointing looks and move on to their written profile paragraphs. After three weeks my impression is mixed. Quite honestly, I have read several very interesting profiles and a couple truly intriguing ones. Well written, thoughtful, humorous, they paint an infinitely more attractive picture of the man than does his photo. Based on their written profile alone, I contacted several I would have rejected for appearance. The fact they did not respond in kind is beside the point here. The point I am making is that the vast majority of written profiles fall far short of intriguing or even interesting.

Many are simply awful, while others are incongruous to the person who supposedly wrote it. Grammar mistake-ridden, they reflect a high school education at best. (Tell me, how does a graduate degree level of education fail to engender basic subject verb agreement?) The remainder are ridiculously generic—fun loving guy, nice guy, romantic guy looking for his queen (God, I hate that term!). They all want the same: someone to cuddle on the couch with, a companion to travel with, a woman to share their lives with. Just a comment: I really am annoyed by a sixty-plus-year-old man stating he is looking for a "girl." Of course, often their preferences do indeed bear that out. A charter member of my cringe club: a 63-year-old seeking a woman 18-35. I'm pretty sure I know what he's really looking for—and it ain't long walks and good conversation.

Along those lines, many written profiles are forthright enough to list libido, spark, passion or romance as a definitive definite want. No judgment here. It's what I want as well—ergo my younger age preference. This is one *girl* who has seen one too many ED commercials on TV. (How many men is it again, who "suffer from some form of erectile dysfunction?") Ladies, it's one thing if the man whom you have loved and been married to for decades begins to have a little trouble in the get it up and keep it up department. It is a whole other matter entirely to wander willingly into Limp Dick Land.

So back to all these nice, fun-loving and romantic gentlemen who know how to treat their women . . . a question: If you are such a great catch, why are you still uncaught? I'll give the widowers a pass on this one. But seriously. If these men are indeed as their profiles describe, why are they divorced—or worse never married at all? And the ones who list themselves as separated? Ahhhh . . . no. It's one thing to meet someone, and the unanticipated happens. It's another to deliberately go looking before the judge signs the decree. But that's just me. Speaking of divorce, I know I have made the point previously, but there must *really* be a lot of cheating, lying, game-playing ex-wives out there given the frequency of men specifically listing honesty and fidelity and no baggage and drama as must-haves. But I could be wrong.

I could be wrong in all of this. Most wrong perhaps in my Week 4 attitude. My apathy has reached a new high (or is it low?). Part of the problem—ok, ALL of the problem—is that I have lost real interest in finding Mr. Right. Mainly because at the end of Week 1, I found Mr. Wrong, aka Z. Remember that paragraph a while back about patterns and disasters? Well, I am no doubt in the midst of one in the making right now. That is the problem of falling for fireworks, one inevitably gets burned. But life is for living. And for the moment, I am living. Yes, Z is my "type", and yes, he is too young for any long-term duration. And yes, I went too far too fast and broke every rule of online dating. Or did I?

Online dating is not the dating I knew 40+ years ago. If it isn't an entirely different animal altogether, then it has certainly changed in the course of four decades! The one thing that has not changed, however, is me. After three weeks of failures, I am still not ready to settle. High school me couldn't just accept an invitation to go out without that spark any more than nearly sixty-year old me can hit like, wink, or fav. No spark, no point.


Postscript: My weekly progress report dutifully reflects my decrease in activity and interest and offers a not-so-subtle secret hint/remedy, essentially a "Dear Dater, try harder and send an email a day this coming week." Helpfully, another big damn pinkish-purple button is displayed through which I can search and "start a conversation with a few of the newest members that have just joined in [my] area." Such would increase my chances of meeting someone 42%, they tell me. Great. I'll get right on that. (Not.)

*Dear Dating Site: Here's a little secret backatcha:* ***More*** *does not mean* ***better****!*

## Chapter Six
## Week 5 – Talk Dirty to Me

I haven't figured it all out yet exactly. But going into Week 5 I am fairly convinced online dating is designed to achieve in a week what traditional, old-school dating took a month to accomplish. Moreover, with a substantial savings of *time, effort*, and m*oney*, online dating had to have been created by a man. (It was. I checked.) Please consider if you will the following:

The profile picture saves the time, effort and money of a blind date. No longer must a guy be set up by his friends. No more being blindsided by Joey's girlfriend's girlfriend who was supposed to be really cute, but who in the flesh has the worst case of acne and buck teeth you've ever seen. (Yes. A cruel and unkind and grossly exaggerated example. But you get my point.) In the comfort of his own living room, a guy can sit in his boxers and slide and swipe and window shop to his heart's content the catalog of cuties at his literal figure tip. Click a button and send a wink, a like, a "she's your fav" message. Maybe send an email. Chances are good she will type 4x as much as you do, so you are saved the effort of keeping the "conversation" going. Then, when you get tired of the lag time and weary of having to not only read but *spell*, you can suggest an exchange of phone numbers.

Now it gets infinitely better. Here comes the truly fun part! Between the photo and a phone call, you are now set for both visual and aural stimulation. You let her go on and yap about crap you really don't care two shits about. After all, this is the phase of online dating wherein a sense of acquaintance builds. Even though you've never laid eyes on each other, you are getting the sense of knowing one another—to the point where a few lines may be crossed. Think first base in high school. (Only coping a feel online probably has more to do with asking her when her last relationship and/or orgasm was.) If she doesn't shy away and hang up, you proceed to more intimately feel her out. Do you like kissing? Do you use tongue? You tell her you are a boob man, or an ass man, and you wait to hear her reaction. You tell her the best thing about sex is the spooning after, holding a woman close (bullshit). Then you tell her you would like to do that with her. Would she like it as well? You tell her how sexy her voice is and how hard you have gotten just hearing it. You can't help yourself. She is special. This has never happened before. You ask what she's wearing. Is she becoming aroused as well? The two of you may well get caught up in the moment, and a mutually satisfying experience might occur. And even if she doesn't get into it, you can run the conversation through your head later and achieve the desired result solo.

How perfect is this? Without having to shave, dress, leave the house, or shell out even the cost of a Starbucks coffee, you have enjoyed the safest form of sex there is. If she's really good, you can repeat the experience God knows how many times before you actually meet her. (If you ever do. Because let's be real. If she had knocked your socks off, you couldn't have waited to ask her out!) If she is only so-so, you can move on to the next match on your weekly list. And there's the true beauty of the system: There's a nearly never-ending supply! Moreover, it's a numbers game. They tell you so. They even try to upsell you to get even more matches a day. You literally can go through dozens a day and never leave your house or spend a cent.

I actually have a mental picture of a guy sitting at home on his lap top and cell. He's texting and emailing several women at once. Such a scenario certainly explains the generic questions, the fact he doesn't ever use your name—just "sweetie" or "beautiful" or some such sickening sobriquet—and he certainly doesn't seem to remember what you told him yesterday or what he told you. He repeats himself, telling you shit you already know. Plus, it's the only thing that really explains the insane lag time it sometimes takes for him to reply. (Jaded? Suspicious? You bet!) But how perfect is this? Convenient excuses about work and having your kids for the weekend can put her off for weeks. There really is no need to meet face to face. Because if you did, she would know you've been using your buddy's cousin's picture. Or worse—your phone *femme fatale* might turn out to be Joey's girlfriend's girlfriend.

Ladies, I'm not telling you not to. I'm just warning you to be aware of what's happening. *Loverboyonline* has to expend no money and next to little time and effort to get his rocks off! If he plays his cards right (and I have good cause to believe this is a pretty prevalent occurrence), aural sex can be achieved pretty easily. I'm not knocking it. Hell, I've done it. But know what is going on.

The entire concept, process and system is naturally rigged to favor the male. (Suspecting there are more men online dating than women, I checked. There are. In fact, the inventers of the original site actually hired a woman to help make it more appealing to women!) The anonymity appeals to them, especially the ones who don't bother to even post a photo. I look at the 25 men who have, to date, (no pun intended) provided tangible proof of their interest in me via winks, likes, favs, and outreach emails. Not one has made mention of an actual date. I can only surmise they are quite happy with the status quo. But texting, emails and phone calls are not what women—or at least what I—want. It's what the men want. A conservation of time, effort and cost while achieving the maximum result. Women, on the other hand, crave the waste. They want to dress up and go out.

Please know I am exaggerating for the purpose of making a point. Additionally, I may well be the only woman online dating to experience these things—but I highly doubt it. Yet it doesn't mean I can't be wrong—or at least off base. Certainly my attitude could use improvement. After 4 1/2 weeks of online dating my apathy has reached new heights (or should it be depths?) Part of the problem—okay ALL of the problem—is that I'm still "dating" Z. (Pause here for another disclaimer: Ladies, don't do as I do. Do as I say and learn from my mistakes.) Very, very early on (too early!) he and I went through many of the aforementioned steps. But we *did* meet face to face the second night. I needed to know he matched his picture. (He did.) Now I'm having a terrible time looking further. Though I know damn well he isn't the right one, I am hooked on the wrong one. For now.

But one positive about growing old(er) (supposedly) is growing wise(r). I know Z won't last. Heading in Week 5, I know I need to keep looking. Besides, I still have five months left on my six month "guaranteed to find you someone special" membership.

According to a July 2015 *Consumer Rankings* report, monthly visitors to my online site number in the millions! A May 13, 2016 article in The *New York Post* by Stephanie Faris states, "Men drastically outnumber women on many dating apps." So shouldn't I be able to find just *one*?

Statistics say online dating works. Consider the following statements culled from Match.com (the #2 online dating site in 2016, again according to *Consumer Rankings):*

> ➢ . . . *1 in 6 of the couples married in the last 3 years met each other on an online dating site . . .*

> ➢ . . . *1 out of 5 single people have dated*

*someone they met on a
dating website . . .*

> ➢ *In the last year more than
twice as many marriages
occurred between people
who met on an online site
than met in bars, at clubs
and other social events
combined . . .*

With the start of Week 5, I considered the
possibility that the problem was neither the concept nor the
practice of online dating. It was the participant—me. I
decided that perhaps an attitude adjustment was in order.
Whether the stigma of online dating had colored my view
from day one, or a lack of immediate result had jaded me
into believing this was not going to work, the point
remained: Believing in failure begets failure. Maybe I had
just set my sites too high? Maybe I should settle—a little.
Instead of rejecting every man who did not meet my ideal
mate expectations, perhaps I should judge each upon his
own merit? After all, I have friends (good friends whom I
love without measure) who are not the perfect friends and
sons who sometimes fall so short of that mark I would have
disavowed them long ago did I adhere to the same rigid
standard I was using with the profiles filling my inbox.
Plus, I had been haunted of late by my mother's voice. She
died a couple years ago, but sometimes I swear I hear her in
my head as clearly as if she were standing beside me. She
used to admonish me (ok, she used to yell at me) when I
was dating in high school and not particularly taken with a
boy who had asked out: "For Christ's sake! You don't
have to marry him! Just go out with him. You might find
that you actually like him."

I decided to listen to my mom. I would try to shelve my cynicism. A new week a new tact—in both senses of the word. I would be a kinder, gentler online dater. Less critical and judgmental, less shallow, more open to men outside my "type" box. And I would employ a new method for judging the men who expressed interest in me, as well as those the site selected. Ala the reality show *The Voice*, wherein the judges do not initially see the singers (and so are making their selections upon the talent alone and not the contestant's physical appearance), I would conduct my own blind auditions. If possible I would not hit the "show image" button on my cell. If the photo came up regardless, I would try to put my thumb over it immediately. I would read the written profile first and reserve judgement until I had seen what he had to say. As far as an online dating situation would permit, this was as close as I could come to just going out with them and maybe finding out I actually liked them. (Ok, Mom?)

Easier said than done. We all know what a certain road is paved with. Try as I might, if there was a photo, I looked at it. I couldn't help it. But focusing on appearance had gotten me literally nowhere and no one, save a phone sex friend. I strove to silence the visual critic and let logic speak. The act of picking potential partners purely by looks, culling by cuteness, or selecting by sexiness is shallow at its lowest. I get it. By doing so, I could well be missing out.

I need look no further than to one of my dearest friends in Philly for a perfect example. Tall, blond, gorgeous, she is also a flight attendant. Smart as hell (her graduate degree is in Bio-chemistry!) and gifted with a wicked sense of humor that has me often in tears, she fell in love with a short bald guy. She would never have gone out with him in the first place based upon his looks. And in fact, she didn't. Their first few interactions were in a group setting. They shared a large pool of common friends, and those friends urged her to go out with him. She refused. But eventually getting to know him better in group activities allowed her to discover how much fun he was. Despite his shortcomings, he possessed—for her—a seductive combination of goofy enthusiasm and daring adventure. Every lock has a key, you know. To her utter bewilderment, she entered into a passionate love affair with him that lasted a year. He was the one to break it off. She still misses him—and continues to measure each new man by "the short little bald shit."

But it's not just women who fall in love past the looks. In the mid-1990s my then husband invited a colleague from IBM to dinner. He was drop-dead gorgeous: long dark hair in a neat pony tail, a perfectly tailored gray suit, piercing green eyes—it was all I could do not to drool. And he was as kind and intelligent and gracious as he was good-looking. (To this day he is the only man who has ever had dinner at my house and sent a thank you card.) I don't even remember his name, but I've never forgotten him. He told me about the woman he was going to marry. He had met her at a company barbeque. She was the sister of a co-worker. Believe it or not (and I couldn't then and still don't now) that 6'2", 36-year-old, never married, hunk of male perfection had fallen for a 45-year-old divorcee with three kids! Online dating sites didn't really exist at the time of this love story's inception, but I can guarantee if it did: *Dropdeadgorgeous* would not have listed his preference as slightly overweight 45-year-old divorcee with children.

Another story I love about true love conquering all odds was told to me by another flight attendant. The woman was around 60 herself when she relayed to me her mother's story. Devotedly Catholic and the mother of seven (no surprise there), her mother had left her father when she was in her mid-forties. Wait, it gets better! She left him for her 22-year-old priest! Now nearly forty years later, that man (who left the priesthood) is still so madly in love with his wife—my colleague's mother—that every single day he brings her flowers. (Pause for collective ahhhhhhhhh.)

It is said what is meant to be will always find its way to be. The heart wants what the heart wants. Age is a number. Opposites attract. No accounting for taste. Love is blind. You'd never picture them together. We have all quoted those sayings. And to some degree we all believe in their truth. Because life has shown us proof and provided examples.

A closet romantic, I want to believe. I want to believe it could happen to me. Which then begs the uncomfortable question: Which am I? Am I the woman who falls in love beneath her standard? Or am I the woman beneath *his*?

Because Z was still a presence, I was still less than highly motivated to find Mr. Right. (Question: When did "seeing" become a euphemism for what Adele calls "doing what lovers do"?) Has online dating really provided an entirely different avenue for male/female interaction? What teenagers and young adults used to do in the 1970s in the back seat of a car at a drive-in movie on a "real" date has devolved from first base, second base, third base, home run into 2016's senior citizen sexting? If Z and Bob the Perv and *Lonelyheart* are any indication . . . yes. It's faster, cheaper, easier and safer, to be sure. A whole new world . . . and ergo my new focus. Instead of striving for Mr. Right, I aspired to Mr. Interesting. I was back to concentrating on the profiles—'cause now the photos didn't matter. (Genius!)

Unfortunately, reading only the profiles (or trying to) brought much of the same reaction as viewing their photos: Yuck! Yuck to the man who wrote, "If you are willing to spend your Saturday and Sunday spoiling that special someone in your life, let's text." (Wow. Dude, I think the website you're looking for is match.geisha/concubine.com.) Another red flag profile rose with the architect "ready to relocate for love and happiness." I passed as well on bluecollarbenny, who listed his high points as having a high school education and being retired.

A mental checklist for profiles subconsciously formed, just as had happened when I was only looking at photos. Lists . . . it's what I do.

- ✓ Generic or original?
- ✓ Actually articulate or simply stupid?
- ✓ Grammar, vocabulary, punctuation, spelling?
- ✓ Content?
- ✓ Compatibility?

(Regardless of how well-written his profile was, if he was into golf, camping, horror movies or 20k marathons, this would never work.)

Neither would it work if his age preference was closer to 30 or 40 than 60. (Don't ask how we were even matched in the first place with that gap. The same yahoo approving upside photos, I'm sure.) Inevitably, if I liked a profile and also the photo, he was looking for younger. I found myself drifting back to old habits. I was willing to overlook the photo if the profile was really great. But so-so profiles? They needed to also pass the photo test. Among those who did not:  A Mr. Rogers look-a-like in a brown button-up sweater cardigan, *Howie232* (who posted 3 photos—all bowling—and dated 2008) and *wandererwally* (another mid-life crisis on his motorcycle claiming to be 58 but looking 68).

And then I found it—the Holy Grail among stupid, boring, generic, grammar-challenged profiles. Claiming to be 66 with an accompanying photo that begged to differ, white-haired *SCScsponder* had a few extra pounds to be sure—but also a truly great profile. He had been a journalist who had covered the largest three wars in the last three decades. He was droll and witty and outright funny! What a fascinating life he had led, I thought. What an interesting person he must be, I thought. What the hell, I thought.

I wrote to *SCScsponder* and explained that while he was out of my preferred age range, he was someone I really would like to get to know. We exchanged numerous emails. His were always well-written and entertaining. Intrigued with his life and career, I actually googled him and discovered he was a multi-published author, having penned books on politics and world events. On the 16th email he invited me to lunch sometime. I was absolutely receptive to the idea. His emails made me laugh. Humor is an attracting quality, after all. Look at Anne Bancroft with Mel Brooks—and any woman who ever slept with Woody Allen. In fact, a sense of humor is often listed as the #1 quality women look for in a man. The celebrity ranks bear solid witness to such pairings. Consider the following not conventionally sexy by any means men: Cheech Marin (currently married to a gorgeous Russian pianist), Jerry Seinfeld, Sacha Cohen, Seth Rogan, Kevin Hart . . . they are all married to beautiful women. If you don't believe me, google "funny men and hot wives." (Of course, it might also just be rich men and hot wives . . .)

When *SCScsponder* suggested we might try a real phone call, I had no reservations against. (I should have had.) He was in the kindest word: boring. He wanted to talk about himself. Not really an issue per se, except he repeated himself and spoke so slowly I thought I would lose my mind. He also constantly asked me to repeat myself. I figured he was probably hard of hearing. There were lots of pauses wherein one of us looked for something to say. The one conversation that flowed concerning WWII history revealed an unpleasant aspect to his personality. He wanted to lecture and show off his knowledge. I know about Russian History. I have a minor in it. But he wasn't receptive to or even interested in my thoughts, glossing over them to return to his own. Like most his age with, I will grant you, huge accomplishments, he was stuck in the past. Then he actually cut me off in mid-sentence when I said the date he had proposed to meet for lunch would not work for me. He acted like my explanation was a lie to break it off kindly. It wasn't, but at that point I didn't care anymore anyway. I was not interested in a face to face snooze fest. After we signed off I did the math. An event he claimed to have witnessed took place in the early 70s. I very much doubt he was a 13-year-old reporter at the time, making him a liar about his age. Gee, color me surprised! So much for judging on profile.

Not that the photo offers any better, given my week's highlights:

- the selfie in the bathroom with a half empty roll of toilet paper on the counter, front and center!
- another bathroom selfie, this one half-naked with a huge beer gut being the only thing *not* covered in star tattoos
- yet another half-naked in front of the shower curtain selfie of a 49-year-old, seeking 19-35
- a 60-year-old widower lying bare-chested in bed, who says he's ready to start the next phase of his life
- and the winner of all time—so far—*Fisher58*: a naked selfie shot from below so it's (technically) decent, while standing in front of his fishing poles (subliminal?), surgery scars on display, maybe trying to flex with his free arm. (It was hard to tell with his flabby old man arms hanging down.)

I actually found one photo that elicited a tingle, however. Great eyes, dark hair, beard (yes, type), a widower, 50, good profile. I sent 2 emails and received no response. A so-so photo of a silver-haired 60-year-old widower, an architect by profession, in a sport coat, holding a flute of champagne (classier than the bikers on their motorcycles), featured a too long profile that went a bit preachy. If there is a romantic connection, he "would like it to be an exclusive thing," he wrote. The sentiment is fine, just a little early to state it, I think. I sent an email anyway. I also sent an email to a Russell Crowe look-a-like before I read his profile. He was 49, a lawyer, seeking 33-40. I never heard from either of them either.

Specific lines culled from the profiles I read this week include the following favorites:

- *Looking for someone willing to communicate what his needs are.* (his???)
- *Lost faith in love and marriage but hoping to change it.*
- *I dislike Gossips, Cheats, liars, Polygamous act and also a woman who takes advantages of her man.*
- *I will be there for her at all times, keep her warm and keep her heart beating at a smooth pace.* (??? Does he have an in-home defibrillator?)

Of course, no weekly recap would be complete without mentioning my site-selected matches. The winner for the week was a 65-year-old, retired lawyer, a widower who plays golf (I hate it), who looked much, much older (out of my age preference regardless). So what exactly did we have so much in common that my site's algorithm program would have put him into contention as a potential match? Are you ready? He was also a dog lover who likes dining out. Wow.

By the way, I received two Photo likes. One from another widower, 64, who wrote: *I know God and desire a stronger relationship with Him.* The other came from a bald, heavy set 56-year-old with a sheep dog. His profile states chemistry is important and he *needs a lady who's not afraid to try new things.*

Right on schedule, my weekly progress report arrives, informing that once again I'd sent three more emails than the average dater. This time though, my "atta, girl" also contains an upsell offer: "Congratulations! You're doing great! Now up your chances by getting even more matches!" Question: If I was doing worse, would they really say so with a "Don't despair you are getting there!" salutation? I can see it now: "Dear Dater, Yes, you've sent and received less emails than the average successful dater, but help in on the way! (And available for a small fee.) Get more matches, more alerts and more attention (for more $). Remember. Increase your numbers, increase your odds!"

*Dear Site, You **do** know a thousand times zero is still **zero**?*

## Chapter Seven
## Month 1 — No Exit

I have never participated in anything even remotely related to "speed dating." Such did not exist in the decade I was dating. I have of course seen the concept portrayed on TV: a *Law and Order Special Victims* episode, wherein Detective Olivia Benson went undercover to catch a rapist who was finding his victims through a speed dating service. Not the most positive of reference points to be sure, but neither a source of concern. What did disturb me was the fact the damn venue was changed twice. I had to wonder, how incompetent *were* the people running this thing? I did, however, appreciate the cosmic irony that the event would take place on my one month anniversary of joining the site.

Two days prior I received a confirmation/reminder email. Along with the particulars of place and time was a list of helpful suggestions:

1. Be on time. (Seriously! Do we have to say this? Has society so degraded? Or is my military-brat upbringing showing? Their watchword: "If you are on time, you are late.")
2. Pay attention to get attention. (Again, is this not common sense and courtesy?)
3. Keep an open mind. (Oops. Going to have trouble with that one!)
4. Relax, everyone's single (Or so they say)

5. Talk more, text less
(Again. Really???)

Along with this list of to-dos and to-don'ts was an itinerary of the evening's planned events: shared appetizers, ice breakers, the dating itself, and time to chat after with anyone who captured (my) interest. Oh, and the day following the event, a list would be provided with email addresses of all participants. (So I could keep the good times rolling?) Good lord! If I hadn't met someone I was interested enough in to give my number to right then and there, I sure as hell didn't want their email address so we could write. I am **not** looking for a pen pal! (Yep, that open mind thing was going to be a problem.)

The day before the event I did what most women will relate to. I decided what to wear. Venue, time of day and weather all have some bearing on a gal's wardrobe choice. But the number one determiner is what she feels good in. Whether that means comfort or confidence is up to the individual. Every woman has her go-tos—her favorite outfits. Regardless of the size of her closet—and unless she has something brand new or purchased specifically for that event—she is going to go to the tried and true. Ladies, you know what I am talking about: that little black dress that hides your stomach, the blouse everyone always compliments you on, the skirt that hits that perfect length, the jeans that hug your ass but somehow not your thighs . . . we all have them and we wear them to death. Why do you suppose that spring-cleaning tip is so effective? The one that says to hang everything in your closet with the hanger going the wrong way, turning it the right way when it is worn, then tossing or donating everything still hanging backward at the end of the season.

Most women favor a look, a style, a color palette. Peek in my closet and you will see black, gray, brown, navy, olive green and maroon. Remember color draping?

No way will you find "spring tones and pastels" hanging on my rod—hangers backwards or not. I also tend to overdress, mostly because I don't wear pants and always wear heels. I love them in all colors and had actually bought a pair of red high heels a few days earlier. (Side note: My airline is changing uniforms this fall. The new uniform will be dark gray and feature red accents, including shoes. ) When I saw these red heels at DWS, I figured it was fate. The fact they were comfortable as hell sealed the deal. Never one to buy something and let it sit in the closet, I knew I was going to wear those damn heels for my big night out. A gray pencil skirt and a ¾ length sleeve, scoop-necked shirt and a skinny red belt completed my choice. Not too much or too little. I know what looks good on me, and no woman over 55 should go sleeveless if she can help it! (I remember laughing 20 years ago at a 60ish friend of mine who hated her upper arms. Boy, do I know *now* where she was coming from then!)

With my outfit decided, the whole speed dating thing became somehow more real than a circled date on the calendar. I had signed up for the thing nearly a month ago when I was brand new to the site. I had forgotten (or didn't notice) the targeted age group for this little soiree was 50-69. Fast forward four weeks and my expectations reflected my experience. I'd easily seen 300 photos of that age group on my dating site and could count on one hand the number I found attractive. Either the Philly winters or lifestyle are harsher than I ever realized, or most are lying about their age. To say I was less than optimist was an understatement. My "open" mind needed a crow bar.

Truthfully, I didn't know exactly what to expect. I envisioned however an evening with mostly women and really desperate men (because no sane man would buy into this). I could only hope the people putting this on had had the good sense to assemble the participants equally by gender. So, assuming there were a comparable number of men to women, what else did I expect?

I expected the Black men to be dressed to the nines. Black men know how to dress—and dress *well*. The white guys, on the other hand, would fall into three categories: Those that pulled that old moth-eaten suit from the back of the closet. (You know the one: reserved for weddings and funerals, twenty years out of style and a J.C. Penny's $99 special that came with a second pair of pants!) The second group would be wearing slacks, an open neck short-sleeved dress shirt and a sports coat. Based on the profile pictures I had been seeing, I figured at least one would be rocking a Guido gold chain and/or big ass watch—east coast/Philly wise guy cool (maybe in the 1970s, which is probably when they last dated). The last group would opt for business casual. (God, I hate the term and the look!) Khakis, polo, Dockers. Comfort over style, always. (Besides, the shirt was free from that conference they attended seven years ago and it's hardly been worn.)

My presumptions about the women were in much greater detail. Women study other women infinitely more than they do men. Women dress for other women. Our whole lives we have compared ourselves to one another. And sometimes fate plays fair. The inequities of earlier life even out in later age. The popular cheerleader packs on pounds, the star quarterback goes bald and the nerd becomes a millionaire with a dot com site. I was chubby til twelve and geeky til twenty. My ex would tell anyone who listened that when he met me, I was "a dog." (Nice, huh?) Nowadays karma has paid me back. I have a better figure and sense of style than 80% of the women in this 50-69 year old age group. Remember, I work with thousands of them. I know what my contemporaries look like. I also have not chopped off my hair. (Please tell me *where* it is written that woman after a certain age should go short!) Few of them wear makeup either. But they do *all* have the gel nails! And sensible shoes. If they wear hose at all, it is probably knee-highs. When called upon to "dress up," most wear what I term "church-lady" dresses. Except for the Black women. Again, they know how to dress, and their shoes put mine to shame. Plus, they don't give a damn about body image. No, I take that back. They don't give a damn about *society's* preconceptions of body image. They will wear short and tight and bold and sassy. And good lord, do they have gorgeous jewelry—real and costume both!

In regard to this speed dating event, I should issue a disclaimer. My assumptions were/are based the assumption that the cross-section of women at this event would be a true cross-section of American women. If this thing only attracted the upper 20% end of the spectrum, I would fall somewhere in the middle. If they were widowed and blue collar, they would closely resemble the previous paragraph's description. The ones who would outclass me have money, plastic surgery and better genes on their side. What the hell *they* would be doing at this event was beyond me. But they would be divorcees with time and means. Hair, nails, boobs, designer purse, Swarovski crystal encrusted iPhone case . . . I know the ilk well: Queen bees. They'd be coming in pairs or even small groups because they hunt in packs. The middle group would look like they just got off work at the bank (pant suits and low pumps). I expected at least one in this gaggle to be way over-dressed (think sequins). The last group would be dressed for comfort and look more like they were shopping for groceries than a date (capris and sandals).

Between the genders, the smell of cologne and perfume would be overwhelming.


The day of I felt as if I was going to throw up. Nervous and scared didn't begin to describe. One can attempt to rationalize with one's self, but feelings are real no matter how irrational. I knew the worst thing that could happen was a couple hour long experience that would transport me back in time to standing on the sideline of an 8th grade dance, wishing against all probability to the contrary I would get asked to dance. It still didn't help. My nerves were unsettled as well by the fact I would be driving 40 minutes from my comfort zone. I'd had my car shipped from Phoenix and had had it in Philly only a few days. Driving and directions were very much still a challenge.

Just before I left my house, Z texted and took my mind off my fears. I told him where I was headed—unless he could make me a better offer. He laughed and said he was still at work. So off I went.

Thank God for GPS, which led me unerringly to the town of Conshohocken (yeah, couldn't make up that name if I tried!) and then, via a series of small side streets, to the restaurant hosting the event. Located pretty much in a residential area, it had an absurdly small parking lot, completely full. Because of the neighborhood nature of the street there was little to no street parking. I drove several blocks and parked in the unpaved parking lot of a strip club called The Heaven. (Seriously, I'm not making this up either!)

As I was walking up the street to the restaurant, Z texted again, wanting to know when it would be over. I gave my best estimate and begged him to save me. Again he sent a laughing emoticon. Knowing I had a fallback girded me against failure and in a way allowed me to erect a force field of sorts. How badly could the impending rejection of probable losers hurt knowing I have attracted him? was my reasoning.

The Mexican restaurant and its outdoor patio were packed with families and couples. It became very clear very quickly however who was there for the speed dating. An entire backroom had been reserved. Two women were in line ahead of me at the sign-in table. Slacks and tops, the came-from-work look, short hair, ugly shoes, mid 50s. *Did I nail it or what?* I laughed to myself. They asked if there were going to be any men attending this. They had a valid point. Looking around, I saw a handful of women and no men. The facilitator, a very personable Black girl assured them there would be, but then in the next breath she hurried to explain that though they try to make it even, they have no control over people canceling. Another woman approached the sign-in table. She was early 50s, attractive with long dark hair, bangs, heels (not my taste, but still points earned) and a colorful Pucci-like print dress. Another, hopeful she speed-dater already checked in, was a blond (more gray than blond), with shoulder-length hair. She was wearing a sleeveless knee-length sundress with wide black crisscross straps, a $19 Ross summer special. I spotted a Black woman in a floor length blue print sundress—very underdressed in comparison to my guesstimate at the beginning of this chapter. An Asian woman with glasses in a church lady dress crossed my range of sight next. The facilitator instructed us to take a blank name tag and write on it something we could teach well. Then, with a good twenty minutes yet to kill, she directed us to the cash bar.

The restaurant was woefully short-staffed. (The minimalist responsible for the parking lot does the shift schedule too?) Only two bartenders, trying to take care of the entire bar and fill drink orders for the wait staff. A bald on top he-dater wearing a name tag with "sailing" written on it ended up beside me. We started talking, having spotted one another's tag. I had written "German" on mine. (I taught it for a dozen years, I figured I was qualified.) He was from Boston, Jewish. He said he had been to another one of these and had been disappointed. I asked why. He said the attendees were not "a very dynamic group." When pressed to explain, he said no one seemed to make much effort with their appearance. I assumed he meant the women, because he certainly was winning no style contest: dark polo shirt, wrinkled slacks. We waited an incredibly long time to have our drink orders taken and filled. I learned the sailor had recently been to the Mojave and was an amateur photographer. He made no effort to buy my Malbec, yet gave me his card and told me to call him if I wanted to go out. (When the Mohave freezes over, Ansel.)

We moved back into the foyer where there were now four of us speed daters, all wearing the stupid name tags. A guy with a sports coat he wasn't wearing (I didn't blame him. It was hotter than hell in the restaurant.), the sailor, me and another guy—short, another Jewish guy who particularly glommed on to me. I am often mistaken for Jewish, so I wasn't surprised both had migrated to me. Based on polite small talk and the ages of their children, 28 -21, I figured all three were 5 to 10 years younger than me. At about this point in time, the facilitator instructed the women to find seats. I went to a table by the window. Each table had a number card, 1-15. Mine was 6.

Seated at the table beside me, but on the opposite side, was an older woman, mid 60s, a retired saleswoman dressed in a dark blouse and slacks with a wide colorful belt. She introduced herself, and we spoke briefly. Along the wall behind me, and visible in my peripheral vison if I turned in my chair, sat a blond with short hair wearing pants and a sleeveless top. Smart considering how hot it was in the room, but not a good look. At the table beside the saleswoman was the Asian church lady and beside her the attractive brunette. I also saw the blond in the sundress. I tried to scope out the room and count the attendees without looking too obvious. Then the fun started.

The men were supposed to select a table and sit and talk with the woman seated there for 5 minutes until the facilitator called time. When I had counted, I'd come up with 11 women and 8 men. For the first round I and apparently 2 others would be "dateless." I texted Z. He was still working.

Round 2 began, and a guy in a print short-sleeved shirt sat down and introduced himself.

"So tell me about Judith. Are you German?" He indicated my name tag.

"No. military brat."

He asked me to say something in German. To my profound surprise, he translated the gist of it correctly. Apparently his grandparents had been German, and he had studied it in high school. He kept the conversation about me. Most of his questions were those I had gotten for the last dozen years, ever since I started to fly. (To explain . . . with a workforce of thousands and hundreds of destination cities, the vast majority of flights I have worked have begun with a flight crew of virtual strangers. In close quarters together, for sometimes as long as four days, most flight attendants inevitably open up to one another on pretty personal levels. We call it "jumpseat therapy." My bio is therefore down pretty pat.) My German-understanding "date" said I had had an interesting life. *Not really*, was my thought.

The men pretty much resembled one another. Only one man in the entire room had an entire head of hair. It became obvious early on that most had done this before. Each "date" began the same. "Hi, I'm so-and-so." I would stick out my hand (European upbringing) and introduce myself. "It's nice to meet you," I would lie. I found myself in full flight attendant mode. Polite, friendly, smiling on the outside, bored and not giving a shit on the in. I was still uncomfortable, so my accent was more pronounced than usual. I have had it since junior high when my father was transferred back stateside from Germany. It comes out when I am nervous, an unintentional façade I hide behind, I think.

I don't remember the order of the next four or five men who sat down and talked with me. I do however remember things about each: One was completely bald. He had suffered a stroke and labored valiantly to converse. I gave him credit for even trying. He touched my arm repeatedly to convey what his speech could not. I felt really sorry for him. For my next "date" not so much.

By the time he reached my table he was drunk. He was also bitter, complaining about the venue and the evening, and the online site. He wasn't even a member any more, but still received the emails. His major complaint appeared to be about dating in general, specifically spending money on women who just wanted to date. "Harry on Friday, me on Saturday, Joe on Sunday," he said. He had no problem spending money if it would lead to something. His life was good. He had a lot of friends, just wanted a woman to share it. But women on these sites didn't want that, he repeatedly claimed. They were all divorced. Been there done that, was their attitudes. Now they just wanted to date. He informed me there were "as many A-hole women as A-hole men" on the sites. I was not surprised he had never been married.

Another was a truck driver, a big guy, Italian, tall, over 6' 4", Hawaiian shirt. He said I looked like a flight attendant. I asked him what that mean. Beautiful and smart was his answer. No girl on the planet doesn't like a compliment. But he didn't appeal. I was dateless the next round and went looking for the appetizers. The Black woman was parked alone over by the table that held a couple little plates of cheese quesadillas. She and I exchanged a few words that relayed mutual commiseration. I was not surprised to see her soon gone. I had earlier seen a second church lady dressed women with a bowl of guacamole, but there was none now to be had.

The sailing guy from the bar returned, and then I was "dateless" again. The facilitator came over and sat next to me. She greeted me with a huge smile and inquired how it was going.

"So where is my Prince Charming?" I asked.

"You know you got to kiss a lot of frogs," she answered, still smiling.

"So in the cosmic order of things it's written the exact number, say 625, before I find him?"

"Exactly," she answered. "So after tonight you get to cross off eight more."

"Wonderful. Only 617 to go."

She laughed.

I asked her how she got into doing this. She had some kind of marketing degree. Did she like it? She did. But admitted she had seen a lot of things. I said I could imagine. I waved my hand to encompass the room.

"I think I'm in Hell," I said.

"Girl, you got it going on!" she refuted. "Men don't want leave your table."

I laughed. "Seriously? I sure didn't get that."

She said I was classy and beautiful and I'd get asked out "for sure." I shook my head and told her after a month online I had not been asked out once (and that included Z who was getting all the fringe benefits with none of the cash outlay). I told her all I had had were a couple pervs who wanted phone sex buddies or those that wanted to just email or text. She said it happens a lot. She told me she was divorced and had been online herself. One guy had actually gone above and beyond the well-known "cock shot" photo. (Or maybe he was taking it literal?) In any case, he send her a video "with all the sound effects." (Well that was definitely going in the book! I thought.)

Finally the last gut sat at my table. He lamented that it was all too focused on appearance. He talked about looking at high school yearbooks. Lots were not that attractive, he said, but back in the day you got to know somebody and so went out. He asked me if I would be interested in a date. I felt bad for him. I lied and said, "Of course."

The evening was thankfully over at that point. The very first guy returned and sat down. Before we had said too much, my cell phone rang. I excused myself to answer the call. My girlfriend wanted to know how it was going. "Disaster" was my sum it up in one word answer. I went back to the table, and told my first "date" my roommate had locked herself out and I needed to go. Half a lie. I needed to go. I wanted out of there.

I talked to her all the way to my car and then sat there in The Heaven's parking lot for another 20 minutes. Z had never gotten back to me. A lousy evening ended lousy, I told her. She laughed and then came clean. "Now that it was over" she told me another friend had said the same thing about speed dating. Why the hell hadn't she told me that beforehand? She hadn't wanted to influence me. Besides, there was always the chance something good might happen. The only good thing about the night was that I got home easily over unfamiliar highways. I was home by 10. Except for this chapter, it had been a waste of $46 ($35 for the event and $11 for the wine plus tip).

Next day, as promised, I received the email with participants' contact info. "Reconnect with the people you met or missed," was the tagline. They asked for feedback as well. I complimented the facilitator and reamed the venue. The parking sucked, they needed another bartender and it had been hellaciously hot. I had used my table number card as a fan the whole time. And the appetizers had been a joke. $35 times the 30 attendees they expected should have produced more than the measly spread I saw. And I doubted they paid the facilitator much. Hell, she didn't even have a bell, as the drunk had pointed out.

I looked through the pictures and ages of the attendees. The women were 51-67 in age. I was shocked to learn I was the second oldest there. One woman listed as 51

I would have easily tagged to be a decade older. And while their ages may have surprised, my fellow female speed daters had not surprised much in regard to appearance and dress. I had been wrong about the sequins though. No one was under or over-dressed (except for me and my red high heels probably). The men were 54-66. The next day I received two emails, one from the second Jewish guy. The other I couldn't really place at all.

I did however find it amusing that the two who bothered to write to actually ask me out were the two youngest men there. Both were 54 and ironically had the same first name. Counting the card from the sailor, the evening had resulted in three legitimate offers. A better than 1 in 3 success rate. Unfortunately I wasn't really interested in any of them. Nevertheless I politely responded to the two emails and alluded to a possible lunch in the next week or so. I know it is kinder in the long run to be rude and ignore, at the very least I should be honest and tell them I am not interested. But I felt sorry for them.

And for me. Single at any age, when you don't want to be, sucks.

# Chapter Eight
## Week 6—The Games People Play

Now well into my second month I have begun to see patterns. These are more than turnoffs and red flags. I offer now for the reader's contemplation their offspring: common cons and genuine scams.

Ladies, beware the emails coming from someone whose "buddy," "friend," or "client" just "happened" to see your profile while the writer of said email to you was online. In the ***Buddy/Friend/Client Con*** the writer (male or female) is now writing you on the buddy/friend/client's behalf with his or her buddy/friend/client's contact info. See, the writer's own membership is about to expire or he/she has found love himself/herself and is now leaving the site, so please contact his/her buddy/friend/client because he really is a great guy. In this con, the person the writer is attempting to set you up with is not into online dating and either doesn't know—or would be furious—his buddy/friend/client is writing you. But he has been all over that buddy/friend/client about you. You know what? If this buddy/friend/client is truly so taken with me, write down my username (jamada), sign up for the lousy $137.94 and do a search. You'll find me. Otherwise, piss off.

Another con is the mass-mailed-oh-so-generic email. In a word: spam. This tact is similar to throwing spaghetti at a wall—eventually something will stick. The ***Spaghetti Spam Con*** entails sending a charming email to numerous individuals with the hope—and intent—at least one will reply. Online dating is a numbers game after all, and this con may be utterly harmless and merely a judicious use of time and effort. Why waste either by tailoring emails to specific targets? Everybody is a stranger anyway. Who is to know? Who is to care? (I do. I care. I don't like being played—even if it is harmless.)

What follows is an actual exchange between a *Spaghetti Spam* con-artist and me. Only his name has been changed. Please note the absence of any personalization.

> *Thank you so much for reaching out. I apologize for my late response. I took my mom to Paris for Mother's Day and only returned over the weekend. How are you and how was your day? I enjoyed reading your profile and would love to know more of you. You are simply charming and irresistible. I'm Tom and you are?*

How about confused? I never sent "Tom" any sort of contact. I didn't "reach out." I have a very good memory for faces and written content. I had never seen Tom or his profile before.

I called him on it:

> *I don't remember "reaching out." I thank you for the compliment if it is indeed sincere and not a generic serial email to anyone who has happened to catch your eye. I don't like this site as is, and sure as hell am not into serial emailers. Judith*

He answered:

*You liked my picture or winked at me 8 or 9 weeks back. I'm matured and not into mind game. Leave me your number and we will text back and forth as we get to know each other better*

I wasn't on the site "8 or 9 weeks back," but decided to let it slide. I also decided to dial back my inner bitch. A bit.

*I honestly don't remember, but I've had trouble learning the site. I won't give out my number until we have actually met or played the text game through the site until we do know each other better.*

Not surprisingly, I never heard another word from Tom, the Spaghetti man.

Very similar to the generic aspect of the emails sent when perpetuating the *Spaghetti Spam Con* is the **No Name Game**. This occurs when the man you are emailing/texting/talking to/or even dating never actually uses your name. Whether in person or in writing, it is always sweetie, honey, babe, luv, darlin'. Ladies, call him on it. Ask him out of the blue what your name is. If he can't come up with it or struggles—you have your answer. Now ask yourself the question why he can't remember your name. The cause is simple. You are but one of many. Another sign he is serial texting and dating is that he doesn't remember details of your texts or conversations. He will repeatedly ask you the same questions. If this does not matter to you (indeed, you may be double and triple dipping in the dating pool yourself), then no harm no foul. Personally, I'd like to believe I merit more consideration from the man I am dating. Fortunately, generic texts and emails are easy to spot. They are generally short in length and lack any detail specific to you—or anything. Consider the difference between "Hi sweetie how was your weekend?" and "Hi Judith how was your visit to Phoenix? I saw on the news the temps were over 100." Granted, men suck at details. But shouldn't he recall some?

A different (and worse) version of the *No Name Game* occurs when neither of you even knows the other's last name. This game—I have coined **Anonymous**— is a phenomenon uniquely characteristic to online dating in general and possible, in particular, because of our 21st century social media- dominating lifestyles. Via "normal" dating practices in previous decades, this marvel of last nameless dating would have been nearly impossible to achieve. People met people through work, friends, church, and school. Even meeting someone in a club or other social setting usually entailed some form of introduction and contact process that would have probably required or produced a full name. I am, of course, speaking here to women my age. So omnipresent and omnipotent are these things today, can we even remember a world absent cell phones, email accounts, Facebook, IM, What'sApp, Instagram, Twitter, etc.?

Trust me, I had more than my share of single dates and even one night stands in my indiscriminate youth. But in not one instance did I *not* know his last name. (Whether I forgot it is another matter.) Nowadays our identities are hidden behind usernames, PINs and log on IDs. People even have multiple email addresses, cell numbers or phones to protect their privacy or to ensure one's public life does not cross over into the private. Last names have become nearly as outdated as calling cards. (I don't mean pre-paid credit cards for placing cell phone calls! In an earlier century, engraved calling cards were the precursor to today's business card. It was exchanged in a formal introduction or even laid upon a silver tray for delivery by a servant to a home's host or hostess when an individual visited—i.e. formally "called.") Via online dating today, men and women (and men and men and women and women) may carry on involved, often months-long relationships without ever meeting face to face. And even meeting face to face may not necessarily result in learning the other's full name.

Believe me, I know whereof I speak. Dumb? No doubt. Dangerous? Absolutely. Does it still happen? No. Not to me. Not anymore. (Sometimes I *do* manage to learn from both my mistakes and my experiences.)

The **Number, Please Con** is a con geared to obtain the very personal contact information we so typically guard in our day to day lives. A red flag should rise immediately with any request to reveal personal contact information, i.e. phone number or personal email address. Classic lines used in the *Number, Please Con* are any of the following excuses cited as the reason why the person can't contact you through the dating site:

- "I don't come here very often."
- "My membership is expiring soon."
- "I won't be on this site much longer."
- "I am getting off soon."

Ladies, (and gentlemen . . . a con can certainly go both ways . . .) regardless of the con, please utilize the tools and safeguards provided by your site. On mine I have the capability to enter a username in the Search function to determine if it is a valid username and to see when last they were online or "active." It will tell me "online now," "active within 1 hour," "active 24 hours," "active within 5 days," "active within 3 weeks," or "active over 3 weeks."

Also, on my site, at the top left is a bell-looking icon. Clicking on this allows me to see who has viewed me. (I have to remember, though, this goes both ways. He can see me checking him as well.) Someone repeatedly viewing my photo raises a red flag with me. Why? It is possible his reason is reasonable. Perhaps he forgot or is verifying something in my profile. I have done this myself. Say, if I forgot whether he is widowed or divorced. (Again, I don't do separated.) I will often see these repeat peekers when I have been given to someone as a mutual match. Just as I check them out, they do me. Their second view of me usually occurs if, when having been given him as a match, I see something that attracts or resonates so I email him. Nine times out of 10 he doesn't actually respond back, but eight out of 10 times he will look at my profile regardless. (Yes. Rejection is so much fun.) My line between reasonable and creepy is rather thin. If I have already thanked you for your interest, but have told you it is not reciprocal, why are you still looking at me? Same for anyone who wrote, faved, liked or winked at me. If I have not responded, I am not interested. Granted, there may be women and men doing just that—repeatedly viewing those who have rejected and/or ignored their overtures. I hear the crazy column is pretty long. Too, it is a numbers game. I'm sure these profiles are recycled, and no one's memory is so flawless as to remember hundreds of usernames and profile photos. Repeat views are bound to occur, I guess.

While we are on the subject of "views" . . . I went back and looked at the 373 men who have viewed me in nearly six weeks now. Seeing how many came up as "active within 1 hr" or "active within 24 hrs," I decided to actually count. I did not take a statistics class in college. Therefore I do not know if my process is correct or if my conclusions are scientifically valid or even accurate. Nor do I know if this figure is as representative for women as men, or for men viewing other women. But on the Sunday afternoon when I counted, I reached these conclusions about the men who have viewed me since I signed up:

- ➢ The vast majority, over 70%, have been online within the last 24 hours, with *24%* of that number actually online *within the last hour* of my tally-taking.
- ➢ An overwhelming majority, nearly 94%, have been online within the last 3 days, while nearly *96%* have been online *within the last week.*
- ➢ Those who have *not* been online for *the past 2 weeks or longer* come in at a measly *4%.*

I might be going out on a limb here . . . but I do believe the preceding percentages and figures pretty much debunk the *Number Please* lines. "I don't come here often," my ass!

The last type of con/scam/game I want to address is the simple out-and-out **lie**. According to those who track such things, 80% of online daters admit to some form of exaggeration or white lie in their profiles. Neither sex skates free nor owns the market on this mini fraud, which is more misrepresentation than malicious. But while honesty and the lack thereof are not gender-specific, the subject of the untruth(s) is.

Lying about height is a male thing. This is not surprising. Since women by far prefer tall men . . . ta-da ! . . . 50% of men surveyed admit to adding an inch or so. Weight, on the other hand is the female's issue. Women typically subtract on average 8 ½ pounds. (Men only subtract 1 ½.) And on the topic of body image . . . men usually will rate themselves as "athletic," whereas women will opt for "average" or "curvy." Age is another "subject"

subject to subtraction. Surveys reveal that "a lot" of online daters round down to the nearest 5. Women especially. Salaries, on the other hand, are rounded up. By men. The so-called experts say that for an accurate accounting, you should probably subtract 20-40% from the typical male profile. Misrepresenting one's job in a dating profile is also a gender-neutral game. Although men do it more frequently, 42%, as opposed to women, 32%.

Knowing I was 100% honest in my profile leaves me with two thoughts:

1.   I am in a definite minority.
2.   I am an idiot.

## Chapter Nine
## Week 7—Oh, Danny Boy

"You *do* know you're *not* going to find someone perfect on this site?" admonished my daughter-in-law.

Two cups of morning caffeine, steaming in Starbucks' "cities of the world" collector mugs, sat on the coffee table before us. I had flown down to Nashville to spend the weekend and catch up. It was the first time we'd seen one another since a couple days after Christmas (and one of the few times she and I had spoken at length, even by phone, since my son's deployment to Iraq in February).

"I know that. They are all crazy, including the one I'm sleeping with," I answered. *And including me*, I thought.

What precipitated this conversation the beginning of Week 7 was an email exchange that had occurred around 1:30 that morning. To explain I need to backtrack . . . The first week I was online "dating," I'd seen among the dozens of site-provided potential matches the photo of a man who had not been an immediate "no." He was okay—nothing to write home about, as my mom used to say. But in scrolling through the other pictures he had posted as part of his profile, I could not help to be enamored of his black lab. A gray-muzzled sweetheart that reminded me so much of a couple I had loved and lost over the years. To that effect, I commented on the photos—which this stupid site tells me is a way to spark conversation. *Dannyyboyy* responded and wrote back that she had sadly died last year. I immediately wrote back with my condolences. He thanked me. And that was it.

Maybe a week or so later, when I was revisiting all my email outreaches that had seemingly been headed in a favorable direction and then died without (to me) a cause, I came across *Dannyyboyy* again. I wrote again. (This was my "give it one more shot" phase.) I explained that I thought I had written him before. I asked if he had considered getting another lab. "I have been there more times than I want to count, but a puppy heals a lot of hurt," I wrote. *Dannyyboyy* never responded—although the site indicated (in red print no less) that he had read my email on May 4th. Fine. Two strikes and I am done.

Yesterday, on June 5th, out of the blue, *Dannyyboyy* writes. He tells me I am "so sweet" I will "surely end up in [his] arms." I found the email odd. Weird in its content and strange in its timing. It arrived late in the evening and without preamble or reference to previous emails. Not only was it (I thought) inappropriate in its reference to a physical interaction between us, it made little sense. Why write such a thing after a month of obvious apathy? The fact he had previously stopped corresponding with me *twice* did not weigh in his favor either. I deliberated a long time if or how to respond. Finally, I answered: "Lol I think I wrote you a month ago." I thought the "lol" would/should relay some degree of humor. My statement was a statement of fact that might have hinted at a desire for an explanation, but certainly was not insulting. (I thought.) His response arrived an hour later: "Gosh. You're counting days? C'mon."

Okay. I know I have a temper. I know I jump to snap decisions and leap to conclusions. I know I don't let shit go. And I didn't.

I was pissed. I believed my statement was a reasonable observation. Should I ignore bad manners, a rude display of apathy and a month of indisputable disinterest because he suddenly—for whatever reason— deemed me now worthy to be in his arms? Not bloody likely! Moreover, I found his remark judgmental and belittling. He included no "lol" or emoticon to mitigate the sarcasm. In his profile he had made a point of stating he wanted no drama. Really? His dumbass snide comment gave me an immediate sense this jerk creates his own drama. At 54 he had never been married. I didn't wonder why.

I answered: "No. Months. A reasonable observation since this site provides the date an email is read in red. Common courtesy might have merely offered an explanation instead of an insulting 'c'mon' comment." I added a postscript a minute later: "Good luck. Good bye." Regardless of any response he offered, this would be going no further. (I have enough drama in my life and men I actually love deeply who hurt and/or ignore me and judge and tell me I'm overreacting when I express my feelings about it. I sure as hell won't take it from an absolute stranger I wasn't even remotely attracted to or interested in.)

*Dannyyboyy's* response came hours later, arriving with a ding that woke me up: "Yikes. Double c'mon. Best of luck. You will require it." Four minutes later his postscript followed: "Waaaa."

*Real mature*, I thought. I wondered if he was drunk. What kind of loser is emailing insults to a stranger at 2:30 in the morning? I figured I must have really gotten under his skin to have provoked a response at all. Men are typically much more inclined and able to drop something. It's we women who will beat a dead horse and want to revisit an issue. I had little doubt he had ignored me for a month because he had found someone worthier of his interest and attention. When that failed, he'd gone back to a contingency choice: me. Well guess what, *Dannyyboyy*? I don't need your good luck wish. I *am* getting laid. And I'm pretty sure you're not—nor will you likely to be.

I shut my phone off and went back to sleep. In the morning, however, I revisited the incident and asked my daughter-in-law her thoughts. She knows much more about online dating in general and male behavior in online dating in particular. She had done it off and on for a year and a half. She thought *Dannyy's* comment might have been less belittling than I had taken it to be. Having been through a similar period of protracted disinterest from my son when they initially began communicating, she was also less bothered by the month-long lapse of contact. Here's how our conversation transpired:

"It's normal behavior," she said. "Let it go. You shouldn't let a stranger get to you."

"I'm not letting him get to me," I answered not untersely I will admit. (Now). "I'm just not willing to let him think his lapse—and me stating fact—make *me* the abnormal one."

"You *do* know you're *not* going to find anyone perfect on this site?"

Make no mistake. I can fall into the crazy column as easily as the next person. I may well overreact to an insult or a snide remark. But reaction does not negate the insult! Nor the issues that precipitated it. All *Dannyyboyy* had to do was own his action and not paint me with all insecure men's favorite tool—the needy cray-cray bitch brush—because I had the balls to call him on it and state a simple fact. (Nothing an insecure man hates more than a woman with more balls than he.) I won't even address his likely frustrated disappointment I did not go all mushy over his pathetic attempt to elicit sexual interest. Fall into his arms? Yeah, right! When hell freezes over and all the little devils go ice-skating.

Ladies, here is a study of types and a portrait of two *very* different men—each conceivably about to be painted as the bad guy by that aforementioned needy cray-cray bitch brush. In one of our text exchanges a few weeks earlier, Z told me he might come over later. After what I deemed to be an unreasonable and mayhap rude interim without follow-through, I texted him: "It's later." Z did not board the D—(for defensive) train headed for Dramaville. He did not respond as *Dannyyboyy* had: "Gosh. Are you really counting hours? C'mon." He simply acknowledged my remark as the statement of fact it was. He offered no excuse nor apology nor explanation. Nor did he make his behavior about my insecurity, pushiness, need, unreasonableness, etc.. He may well have thought all those things. But he did not write them.

"It's later," I wrote.
"It is," he replied.

See? No drama. In fact, he earned major points for the unexpected—not to mention the supreme confidence it relayed. I complimented the response: *"Touché."* He accepted the compliment with a smiley emoticon and asked, "How are you?" "Horny," I replied. He replied with two emoticons—a laugh and a wink. But still he offered no response or address to my "issues." He signed off with his usual "xo." As did I. We were both still interested in one another. Neither was insulted nor threatened. The relationship would live to sext another day.

Consider now the contrast with *Dannyyboyy*—who escalated a truly nothing nothing into a major something. How different it might have gone if he had taken a page out of Z's playbook . . . if, when I wrote, "I think I wrote you last month," he had answered as Z did. "Yes you did. How have you been?" That would have been the end of it.

Gentlemen, I give you the difference via a woman's perspective of an overly assured man and an overly defensive one. Both really are jerks when it comes right down to it. But one will get blown and the other blown off. (Crude. But true.)

Ladies and gentlemen, it's called "defusing." You put out a flame that has the potential to become a fire—you don't throw gasoline on it. A good four point lesson for life in general:

1.  Acknowledge fact when it is fact.

2. Own your actions.
3. Don't attack back just because you feel threatened or guilty or attacked yourself.
4. And finally . . . in the words of my wise-beyond-her-years daughter-in-law . . .
   Let it go.

## Chapter Ten
## Week 8—At Last! A Date

About to start my eighth week of online dating I am discouraged and ready to ditch the entire experiment. The thing with Z has apparently run its course. Or maybe he actually found someone he wants to actually date? (He didn't. The site still shows him active within the last 24 hours. Note: I wasn't stalking. In editing for the last chapter's chronology and content, I went through all of my "views" since day 1. Every man who has ever looked at my profile appears here along with a notation of when last he was active online.) Regardless of the reason why, one day he just stopped texting. (At last! Something about today's high tech online dating that is *exactly* like old-fashioned face-to-face dating—you still get suddenly dumped without knowing the reason.) *C'est le viv. C'est la guerre. C'est la merde*. I wish him well. It sure as hell was fun while it lasted.

Unsurprisingly, the new week brings new matches. At this point they all blur together. All are ridiculously similar in appearance—men supposedly my age, but looking so much older. Some guy sitting in the front seat of his car winks at me *and* sends an email: *Wow you look stunning*. His entire profile is blank except for his age and height, 41 and 5' 5". No thanks. Another wink comes from a guy wearing little round dark sunglasses. He looks like he should have a Seeing Eye dog beside him. His profile comes up "unavailable." Another email tells me I am one of Michael's (not his real name) favorites. He is 54, slightly overweight. His profile does not contain a single capitalized word. He says he is not a reader and that he is ". . . from france and likes ww2 reenactments, loves maine, lake placid and cape may, california . . . " He is looking for a woman 50—59 within 50 miles of his Pennsylvania home, with a height of 3' – 8'11". His only other specified preference is that she speaks English. I think I'll pass. Another email from another prospective match reads, "hello I'm Sean (not his real name) how are you???" His profile tells me he is 56 and that he "would rather talk or text than write a long profile no one is going to read anyway." If I want to know more I am "going to have to send him a wink or a message." I will be doing neither. Still another pm (potential match) sends me a long email telling me he came across my profile and just had to write on "faith and feelings so powerful it's as if some force beyond your control is guiding you to someone who can make you happy beyond your wildest dreams." Too weird, for me. Plus, in a search for his username on the site, it comes back "username not found."

During the course of back-searching the profiles and photos of the six men who have contacted me in Week 7 my cell phone dies. I log on to the site with my lap top. I have never done this before. I am surprised to see the computer site looks totally different from the one on my cell phone. Apparently there are even two different names to designate them: *online dating site* and *mobile dating app.* (Who knew?) I start clicking on icons and learn my profile has been looked at 930 times. (Lovely. A half dozen or so email exchanges actually longer than three or four back-and-forths and a single one month long sexting relationship divided by 930? I can't begin to figure out how low that rate of success is!) The site also informs me I have unseen and/or unanswered 4 likes, 2 Winks, and 3 emails. In that trio of unanswered emails is one from *SCScsponder,* the reporter (whom I didn't exactly decide to blow off, but whom I have ignored). "Where did you go?" he asks. I have literally been out of town since our first and last phone conversation. I am torn now whether to respond for politeness' sake or to ignore for kindness'.

There is also a feature on my computer screen I have never seen on my cell. "Who do you like?" displays two photos side by side with corresponding buttons and instructions. It would appear that I can choose one, both or neither. Pretty straightforward. Neither, neither, neither, neither, neither, neither. All in all, I check only three as "likes" based upon the photos which register on my mental scale as "okay to good." I write down the usernames so I can back-search their profiles later. Oddly, there is no capability to do this now, only the ability to wink or write to them. One profile I look up once I have finished "voting," contains a very clever line about "constructive discontent" inspiring society's upward spiral. He is 53, looking for someone between 37- 52. (Too bad.) I write him and compliment him on the profile's line anyway. Another photo I have "liked" features one of the best profiles I have actually read. It is witty and sarcastic and clever. He states he is not looking for a trophy as he doesn't bowl. His preference is for someone without an STD, not on anti-depressants, and old enough to know what S&H Green stamps were. He asks rhetorically why women would include pictures of sunsets—when they are not in them—and pictures of their pets dressed up for the holidays. (I would wonder that as well. I would love to talk to him just for the purpose of presenting here a man's view!) I write him and provide my qualifications as a ppm (possible potential match: I do indeed remember Green Stamps, have no STDs, have never dressed up my dogs, and am not on anti-depressants. Neither have I included in my profile any photos I am not actually in. (FYI: He never responds back.)

The last man I contact from among these few has a beginning line I actually like. "Oddly uncomfortable," he writes, in respect to this entire online dating process. I can absolutely relate and tell him so. In a few minutes he actually responds to my email—which is in and of itself a hugely rare occurrence! Clearly he has looked at my profile as he specifically references my "strong and independent" line which he says "means fascinating, contagiously enthusiastic and quite sexy." He also tells me I look nowhere near 59. (Gentlemen, a hint—flattery will get you points every time.) He goes on to reveal he has four adult children and a one-month-old grandson. He says he wants to meet me and proposes coffee, brunch, happy hour or dinner. He asks after my schedule for next week and signs off with his name. (Which for purposes here shall be D.) I respond and explain I am on-call, but would very much like to go on a "real" date. Though I probably shouldn't have, I tell him he is the first to really ask me out.

Again he writes back in a timely manner–20 minutes. (Screw you, *Dannyyboy*!) D declares this is his lucky day and that he would be happy to be on-call with me. He would "TOTALLY love" to take me to dinner and says there are "many fine places in Philly." (Screw you, Z!) He needs to drop off a son at the airport Monday and therefore suggests that day would work well. He concludes with his phone number. I tell him it is my pleasure to accept his dinner invitation. (Seriously, it has been decades since a man really asked me out to dinner as a real date-date.) I tell him Monday would be perfect as I live 10 minutes from the airport. I suggest touching base Sunday. Again within 20 minutes I receive a reply. He says he is "honored" I have accepted. He gives me his full name and says he is on LinkedIn if I want to check references. I really do appreciate his gesture and tell him so. (To be fair, Z said I could google him. But I never knew his last name.) I assure D I am equally respectable, having been cleared by the FBI, the FAA and the state of Arizona (via a mandatory fingerprint check for teachers).

Naturally, how this all proceeds remains to be seen. Purposely I do not look at D's profile further or his other pictures. I remember he has dark hair. Certainly from his emails he appears educated and well-spoken, as well as sincere and real. Why jinx it? Or be disappointed because I see or learn something I don't like? At this point in time, just leave well enough alone alone.

Sunday afternoon arrives and my expectations are low—about the upcoming date in particular and online dating in general. During the week while reediting the chapter about cons and scams I recounted all the men who have viewed me since I signed up. Apparently D "liked" my photo six weeks ago. That I never responded doesn't surprise me. I was playing with Z. What does surprise me a little is the fact he apparently viewed my profile last night around 2 am. Was he refreshing his memory? Or reconsidering? Or just surfing the site like I do? Time will tell.

In the afternoon he sends a text and asks if this would be a good time to text or call. He leaves off one digit from his phone number so I check an earlier text. My first attempt goes to voicemail, my second gets a recording "number unavailable." I decide to try once more and then I am done. The call rings through this time. Once again, I don't like his voice. Seriously, even Z's was not that great. I am literally three for three. I am hoping he is nervous given the amount of uncomfortable laughing he does during the call. He asks some questions about my family. Number of children type stuff. He notes mine is an AZ number. We speak maybe 20 minutes. I get the "let's get to know one another a little better" part, but if we cover it all on the phone, what is left to discuss in person? The bright note comes when I find out he has a degree in history. We shall see if this results in anything. We agree he will pick me up tomorrow around 5 and go into the city. I honestly don't care. I feel no spark at all.

**Side note**: Monday morning, the commencement of Week 8, I receive an email. "Refresh your photos," it says. "Give members a clearer glimpse of who you are by uploading more picture-perfect moments to your profile." Helpful and specific suggestions follow:

- ✓ smiling headshot
- ✓ full body shot
- ✓ you doing an activity or hobby
- ✓ you with a pet, close friend or family member.

As always a big blue button labeled "Add Photos Now" is included. Great. I'll get right on it. Not.

Monday afternoon I get ready for my first real date-date dinner date in over 37 years. Three outfit changes yields the winner: a favorite olive green sleeveless dress that hits the perfect spot mid- calf and fits my ass like a dream. (The belly could be flatter, but there was a time when this dress was too tight. Ya gotta take the positives where they are!) My red heels and a chartreuse cardigan complete the ensemble. Hair turns out and make-up too. I am nowhere near as nervous or scared as I was before the Speed Dating thing. I am better one on one. My insecurity rears in crowds.

At about the anticipated time he calls. He is lost. I explain he has driven too far. I cannot help but wonder why he didn't write the address and/or directions down. Not the best start. I go out to the porch to watch for him. Thirty seconds later his car, some box suv thing no longer being sold, comes into sight. It doesn't earn any points. And then he pulls into the driveway.

I shall endeavor to be kind and brief. No.

No spark, no points, no way. Dressed in business casual, grayer than his picture, a cross between Gomer Pyle and Al Gore. Not horrible. But certainly not my type. He compliments me repeatedly on how great I look, admitting he is underdressed. (Ya think?) We are, however, going to a really nice restaurant though, he says. One of the top 35.

(Top 35 where? I don't ask). He opens the door for me and apologizes the car is dirty. As I step over empty water bottles, I can't help but think, "Then why the f**k not clean it beforehand?" The entire 15 minute drive into the city he asks me questions about my job. (Non-airline people are fascinated with the lifestyle.) To his credit, he does have the evening planned: a drink in Center City then dinner at 7:30. We park in a $10 downtown lot and proceed to walk eight freakin' city blocks to a sidewalk French bistro. Once our drinks arrive he asks if we shouldn't just stay where we are. He makes some hokey compliment about how the French fare better suits me than the American grill he had selected. I tell him I am fine either way. Al promptly cancels the 7:30 dinner reservations. (I suspect the bistro is cheaper. BTW: he orders only an appetizer, but does insist I get what I want. I opt for *two* appetizers.)

Gentlemen, glean what you will from the preceding sentences. Ladies, you know the rest . . .

I went. I was pleasant. I made the best of it. The food was good and the conversation not bad. It was like going out with a crewmember on an overnight. And I couldn't wait for it to be over. He paid the bill while I was in the restroom, adding when I returned that he had declined coffee and/or dessert. (I would have liked to have been asked.) He suggested a walk through the park. (Whatever.) We ended up at an over-priced gelato shop. ($6 for a double scoop. I can get better in Mainz for a third the price.) He tried a couple times to hold my hand crossing a street on our way back to the car. Apparently my body language wasn't saying "no" loudly enough, because he then hugged me at my door—a protracted, unpleasant, rubbing my lower back grope that served as a precursor before he dove in for an awkward goodnight kiss. "Great first date," he said. I thanked him for the dinner and said my goodbyes. I locked the door and promptly kicked off my poor heels to see if they still had their rubber tips after sixteen plus blocks of grated and broken sidewalk. All that resonated in my head was a simple single mantra: First *and* last.

The last time I agree to go out with a man after only one phone conversation. The last time I try to make the best of nothing. The last time I think something can come of nothing. The last time I give some boring nice guy false hope. The last time I don't trust my gut. The last time I waste hours of my time and some lonely schmuck's dollars. The last time I don't have that . . . spark.


Postscript:    Al Gomer never contacted me again. No follow-up text, email or phone call. I can only assume he knew he was out of his league. Or he was as turned off by me as I was by him. Either way, a win-win.

## Chapter Eleven
## Month 2—Built It and They Will Come

The actual figures vary, but most so-called experts and consumer reporting agencies agree on two key statistics regarding online dating sites:
1. Today there exist 900-1000 of them.
2. It is a $2 billion plus industry.

In a word . . . wow! I had no freakin' idea! Considering this is a service-providing industry that did not even exist prior to 1995, the above numbers are astounding! So just how many people *are* online dating? I couldn't tell you. Nobody can really. Determining that number is impossible. It is a worldwide industry. Too, many people belong to more than one site. Additionally, memberships lapse and automatically renew—though the person is no longer active—making that data skewed. A common consensus, however, is that in 2015 between 10-15% of all US adults used an online dating site or mobile app. And the numbers seem bound to increase—if the past is any indication of the future.

Pew Research Center interviewed Americans for the first time about their online dating habits in 2005. At that time few Americans had had experience with the activity. Fast forward to 2013 and suddenly 10% of all 18-24 year-olds were dating online. Today (as determined by a Pew survey conducted June 10-July 12, 2015) the number of 18-24 year-old online daters has nearly tripled, to 27%. Their parents and grandparents weren't—and still aren't—quite as into it, but they appear to be headed in a similar direction, albeit at a slower pace. In 2013 only 6% of 55-64 year-olds were using online sites or mobile apps. Today 16% of online daters are over 50. The only demographic group whose online dating numbers have not increased are adults 25-34. (Between 2005-2015 their numbers remained relatively unchanged at around 22%.)

Here are a few more statements and statistics gleaned from a couple more online articles: Universally recognized as the first online dating site, Match.com is credited by *Consumer Rankings* as having 3.2 million monthly visitors. Match's own website claims 10 million success stories and the responsibility for "more dates, relationships and marriages than any other dating site." In *Consumer Ranking's* doubtlessly less biased 2016 report (based upon how sites match compatible singles, the attractiveness of their members, and the user friendliness of the site), Match was ranked as the #2 online dating site. 1st place, with over 1.1 million monthly visitors and one of the largest member bases of all North American dating sites, belongs to Zoosk. OurTime holds 3rd and Elite (a site I had never heard of) owns 4th. Last place on *Consumer Ranking's* Top 5 List goes to eharmony, acknowledged to be ranked #1 in online marriages. They have over 1.2 million members. A different online article on *Consumer Affairs'* website, provides different, but equally impressive statistics. On a more global scale, Zoosk is credited with 27 million members who use an app "available in over 80 different countries"; Match is available in 24 different countries; while POF—PlentyOfFish—can boast 90 million registered users of its "available in five different languages" site.

No matter their ranking and membership totals, all dating websites are peddling the same product—a platform for (and the promise of) potential partner matches. As in any successful business plan, the challenge (and profit) come from the ability to offer what their competitors don't. I believe this is referred to as "carving out a niche in the marketplace." In the business of online matchmaking sites and mobile dating apps, that niche-carving occurs by offering the dating consumer the ability to customize their search according to his or hers individual wants and expressed desires.

All matchmaking sites and mobile apps fall into a few basic types, with the product they offer, ppp (the promise of a potential partner), generated by a search formulated upon one of six criterion:

1. Geographic proximity
2. User-generated preferences
3. In-depth psychological compatibility
4. Demographic similarity
5. Shared Lifestyle
6. Shared Interest

For grins and giggles, I spent just one morning googling the near countless online dating site choices readily available with just a few mouse clicks. What I discovered shocked and amused me.

**Geographic desirability** is pretty straightforward. People are looking for people who live within a reasonable travel distance. As with any criteria, this will vary with the individual. One person may want to drive no further than an hour, while someone with free airline flight privileges may find a trans- coastal trek doable. Matches are arranged by zip code and/or the mile radius willing to be traveled in the search for one's soulmate.

**User generated preferences** are the *modus operandi* for the larger sites. Sheer numbers is the name of this game with a simple premise: the more members the better, because someone is bound to match someone—if there are enough someones out there to draw from. According to Joe Tracy, publisher of *Online Dating Magazine*, these online dating service sites "encompass the bulk of the marketplace and hold the greatest market share." Basically they function thusly: Dear online dater, give us an idea of who you are looking for in terms of general physical characteristic, lifestyle and interests—and we will use our proprietary computer algorithm to find your match. In theory this should work. We all know what attracts us and what we want in a prospective mate. This is the type of site I am on. Eight plus weeks (as of this writing) into it, I can't say I'm too impressed.

**Demographic similarity** is another self-explanatory concept. These sites target specific demographic groups whose members are seeking a potential partner within their same demographic fold—be it race, ethnicity, religion, age, or income. For African-American singles in the US BlackPeopleMeet is the probably the largest of the Black dating sites, while JDate is the premier online dating site aimed at Jewish singles. And no one with a television has not heard of OurTime, a site devoted to 50+ singles searching for their soulmates. There are truly countless other demographic sites out there, sites geared toward Blacks, Hispanics, Indians, Catholics, Jews, Amish, the over 55 crowd, the under 30, millionaires, etc.. There are even sites geared toward the politically like-minded, i.e. Democrats and Conservatives. No surprises here. Though I did come across an interesting side note . . . According to a March 2016 *Washington Post* Wonkblog interview with Stanford sociologist Michael Rosenfeld (who has conducted a long-running study of 3000 online daters), even if they do not choose an online site specifically geared toward their race, online daters on general dating sites still "show a strong preference for same-race dating." One difference, however, between online and offline dating, again according to Mr. Rosenfeld's research, is that online people are "more likely to date someone of another religion." Interesting.

**In-depth psychological compatibility** is based on that—psychological compatibility. People are matched with others whose share similar views and beliefs. We have all seen the television ads for the largest and most well-known of these sites featuring the grandfatherly founder and former psychologist who claims his site has "helped over 1 million people get married." A 2012 ABC Nightline report by Neal Karlinsky reveals the secret to grandpa's avowed success: a 320 question evaluation and a proprietary computer algorithm written by PhDs. My oldest son signed up for this site. He said he spent well over an hour answering a lengthy questionnaire, a time-consuming process which did not generate even a second date, much less the love of his life. Still, their commercials claim 236 marriages a day. Clearly this premise and formula works, especially for marriage-minded online daters who, typically from the onset, chose websites with long profiles and a more intent focus upon finding life partners. (Question: If I start a club whose focus is collecting buttons—though all are welcomed to join—can I truly tout the fact 88% of my club members are button collectors?) Regardless of which of these in-depth personality profile sites you choose, be prepared to spend 40 – 90 minutes answering questions.

The final two types of online dating sites are infinitely more unique and specific. With apologies to *Field of Dreams*, a 1989 fantasy/drama starring Kevin Costner, the motto of these sites and dating apps has to be that movie's most famous line: "Build it and they will come." Believe me, when I say here is where it goes from self-explanatory and unsurprising to "Are you effing kidding me?" These dating sites tune into society's subcultures as far as both lifestyle choices and leisure time interests. They can—and often do—overlap, with a clear line between lifestyle and interest not always easy to discern.

In **Shared lifestyle** you find the expected groups: gays, lesbians, single parents. There exist sites directed toward airline crew—flight attendants and pilots, those in the military, farmers and ranchers, bikers (lifestyle or interest? I'm not sure). Cancer survivors, paraplegics, those who are working on sobriety or living with an STD, the mentally ill, the terminally ill . . . all are groups with online dating sites geared toward them and their distinctive life challenges. Not so challenging, but still unique: nudists, hippies, bisexuals, little people, tall people, big people, beautiful people, ugly people, fit people, retired people . . . you get the idea. No matter the passion or belief, online daters can find a site created just for them. Name it and it probably exists—sites for geeks, goths, virgins, vegans and vegetarians, and people with food allergies, too. And wait! It gets even weirder. Marijuana smokers, polygamists, women in prison, survivalists, clowns (clowns?), and furries (I had to look it up) . . . no group is too unconventional or too marginal to mainstream that they may not like find like-minded folks also looking for love.

And even those not looking for love per se have a place to go. Singles seeking one night hookups, marrieds in the mood to cheat and couples trolling for a third have suitable sites online devoted to their divergent off line quest. Tinder is probably the most well-known of the so-called "hookup" sites. Since its 2012 inception, this free and easy to use dating app claims to have resulted in more than 10 billion "matches." Impressive, I guess. But there are lots more. Google "hookup dating sites," and you will get over a half million results in .66 seconds. With many of these sites the name is a true no-brainer and dead give-away—Mixxxer, Getiton, Passion.com, IHOOKUP and Bootycall. Yet some bear an absolutely innocuous name, for example AshleyMadison, while others seem to want to deliberately mislead, i.e. FriendFinder. Just read a little further. Each site caters to a specific desire. Some are geared to singles, some to "swingers and the sexually adventurous," and others to "sex-crazed couples and singles looking to explore their deepest desires."

With literally hundreds of these lifestyle sites available, aimed to connect people who share a particular conviction or way of living, every sub culture of society imaginable (and some I did not) is probably represented. However, three groups within this so-called "shared lifestyle" category deserve special attention for no reason other than sheer shock value. I call them the **"A" Sites**— sites whose search criteria is based solely upon appearance, age or the desire to commit adultery.

First up are the adultery sites. *Online Dating Magazine's* Joe Tracy contends that ¼ of the people online dating are married. Other estimates put the figure higher, at 30 -34%. I don't know if this figure comprises both perusers and players (those merely window shopping in the candy store as opposed to those actually cheating), but it is safe to say, regardless, online dating is a form of porn. And like other forms of pornography, it is prevalent *and* profitable. According to *Business Insider,* adultery websites in the US alone have 8 million members and pulled in $50M in 2011! Remember that innocent site called AshleyMadison? Founded in 2002, it touts itself as the pioneer in adultery sites. Ashley's Google description says it has 45 million users in 45 different countries—and it's growing. The running tally display on its home screen would bear the boast out. Today when I typed this, it read 46,730,000 users. A UK site called Affairlook vaunts 40 million members worldwide and offers "great tools like married chats and two-way webcams for all your affair needs." The names alone tell their tale—BeNaughty and SweetDiscreet are two of my favs. Clearly, whether one is looking to spice up a boring sex life or simply to flirt, jack off while the missus has a headache or experiment when hubby is out of town, the means and sites are available. As a humorous side note regarding infidelity sites . . . I actually came across one offering the exact opposite— dating services geared specifically for people who have been cheated on in a past relationship. You gotta love the free market system!

Next are the dating sites whose criterion for inclusion and membership entail some issue concerning the physical looks of the participant. These "appearance" sites run a true gamut from gorgeous to gag. Perhaps the most infamous of these sites is one called Darwindating.com, whose tagline is "Online dating minus the ugly people." As one might expect, membership is a strictly monitored affair. (No pun intended.) Existing members of the site vote who is good looking enough to get in. *Business Insider* reports that more than 6M applied in 2011. Only one in eight was accepted. Originally started as a joke (that took off), its archives go back to 2012. I don't know if it is still around. Still around, however, is a Danish-launched site that actually goes Darwin one better. This worldwide site for beautiful people also conducts an online vote by its members of the opposite sex to determine an applicant's acceptance. Yet this site *maintains* its rigorous enrollment standard by also voting *out* and removing existing members who have gained weight, aged gracelessly or in some other way lost their former hotness. With 800,000 members, I guess they didn't miss the 5,000 they kicked out in 2010 for porking out. (Besides, they can always reapply once they've hit the gym or paid the plastic surgeon a visit.)

The amusing opposite of these "only the hot may apply" (and stay) dating sites are those that are intended for the more aesthetically challenged. Seriously! It's actually the tagline for one . . . TheUglyBugBall . . . a UK based site, whose home screen reads " . . . dating for the aesthetically average." And even Ugly Buggers can apparently be outdone. UglySchmucks is a site not only geared toward people who "may feel unattractive or uncomfortable in their own skin," it is one designed specifically "to help them succeed in meeting others who value personality over appearance." Every bit as serious (and exclusionary) as the Beautiful Danes, the Ugly Schmucks have the following Terms of Use Statement: "This website is exclusive to unattractive people. To enforce this, members can vote other members out of the site." Smack dab in the middle of both these appearance-based dating website extremes is at least one site that aims to match people who look physically similar, another that intentionally blurs its profile photos and yet another that forgoes their use entirely.

Beauty may be in the eye of the beholder and only skin deep, but clearly it *is* a commodity in the online dating market. And as appearance-based matchmaking websites and dating apps continue to cash in on the search process for this desired—or not—commodity, I wonder if there isn't an underlying irony in it all. People can claim to prefer an attractive mate, but in reality they usually end up pairing off with people who are similar in attractiveness. Leslie Zebrowitz, a psychology professor at Brandeis, summed it up better: "You might shoot for the moon, but you take what you can get."

The last of the "A" sites are online dating sites and apps targeting people who are looking for a potential partner of a certain age. I am *not* talking about sites aimed toward singles in a specific age range looking for people in their same bracket. Such sites—exclusive to singles 18-24, young professionals in their 30s, busy 40-something-year-olds, the over 50 "sophisticate," retired 55+ seniors, etc.— fall under the domain of the demographic dating websites previously discussed. What I am addressing here are sites for grave and cradle robbers, sugar daddys and sugar mommas, aka *age gap dating*. This ilk of niche sites with names such as AgeMatch.com, AgeSingle.com and AgelesDating.com offer descriptions and mission statements such as:

> ➤ "World's first and largest dating site committed to catering to the needs of those people who would like to meet someone who is significantly older or younger than they."

> "You know what you're looking for. Stop wasting time & get what you want."
> "Recapture some of your youth."
> "Love is ageless."

As a marketing slogan or ploy, any of the above are more tasteful than the tawdry truth. But truth in advertising rarely sells—nor would the tagline: "Looking to date someone who entered nursery school the year after your first kid did? Well here's your site and chance! Register for free!" Granted, with a proven proclivity for men 15-20 years younger, I am no one to throw stones. Besides, age is just a number, right? (Just ask AARP. If nothing else, they'll tell you sixty is the new sexy.) Fact is, many things that once raised societal eyebrows and snickers today cause nary a ripple. In our "live and let live, love and let love" world, May-December relationships are more common and acceptable and less taboo than ever.

Unsurprisingly there are intergenerational dating sites galore for older men seeking younger women and younger women looking for older men. Home screen paragraphs unabashedly, unapologetically and resolutely declare that "many older men like dating younger, vibrant women," while "lots of younger women prefer more mature men." (I'd be more inclined to suspect it's their money and maturing investments that provide the real allure. And if there were ever two things that don't jibe . . . I'll spare you the mental image I get when I think "vibrant" and Viagra.) One site I encountered, called appropriately oldermenlikeyoungerwomen.com, explained that older men looking for younger women are looking for "vitality and life," because younger women possess "a sense of adventure that older women lack that are more set in their own ways." Despite the poor syntax, the between-the-lines meaning seems pretty clear to me: A young hottie will go where the vanilla matron won't. (Of course she will! It's called symbiotic.) You "treat" her nice, and she'll return the favor. It says so in the same passage that clarifies how mature guys "always know how to treat their women" and younger women "want the financial stability and long term security." One site makes no pretense of this understood financial arrangement. Utilized by college students as a means to finance college it goes by the fitting name of Sugardaddie.com.

But the "no fool like an old fool" adage is hardly gender specific, especially in the worldwide web world of online dating. I counted at least a half dozen cougars and cubs websites: MyCougarDates.com, CougarPassions.com, GoCougar.com, Cougardate.co.uk, Cougared.com, CougarLife.com. Out of curiosity, I actually signed up (for about twenty minutes) on one of the cougar-centric sites. The home screen looked tasteful enough: an attractive mature woman and a tagline about women and fine wine aging similarly. Registration was free and easy, entailing the prerequisite age and zip code questions and a photo request. As cub pictures proceeded to pop, so did my balloon. When they said "cub," they weren't kidding! The site's sugar momma-seekers ranged in age from 18-28, with a clear majority in the 19-24 bracket. Many were sans photo and those with were mostly young African-American males in the New York City area. More than a few had crude or crass user ID names that left nothing to my imagination. Christ! I want younger—not barely legal! I hit the unsubscribe button and took a shower, feeling equal parts sleazy and foolish. Yep, no fool like . . .

The sixth and finally type of online dating sites and apps are the **Shared interest** websites. These dating platforms are less about finding a partner who lives a similar lifestyle and more about locating a person who likes to do what you do. These sites are all about sports, hobbies, leisure activities, personal tastes and fixations.

Sailors, hikers, scuba divers, golfers, bikers, cyclists and horseback riders, as well as travelers, cruisers, Star trekkies, video gamers and vampire enthusiasts can all find a site where they may find a potential partner similarly obsessed. There are sites aimed specifically toward men who like "curvy" women and women who prefer "big boys." All euphemisms aside, if a particular body part or physical feature floats your boat, this is the category in which to look for a date who owns it. Big butts and chesty chests, bald heads, lovers of moustaches and mullets (I'm not kidding!), to name a few. Lovers of sci fi, cats, salads, and hot sauce may find a similarly inclined mate, as may those looking to find someone with comparable tastes in movies or music.

At first glance this last category appeared (at least to me) to be fairly bland (with maybe a dash of odd): golfers looking for other golfers, hikers wanting hikers, trekkies or aficionados of hot sauce seeking the same, etc.. Even men with a penchant for "the bigger the cup size the better" casting their hooks in a site where well-endowed is the name of the fishing hole didn't seem particularly strange to me. Different strokes . . . Then I came across a website specifically for people who like to wear diapers. Bland suddenly bypassed odd—and even bizarre—and jumped straight at warp speed to kink—and beyond! Foot worship, pet play, rope play, water sports, spanking, bondage, BDSM, CBT . . . pretty much any fetish or perversion you can think of—and some you'll never believe. Trust me on this one. If you have to look it up, you don't want to know. But again, different strokes . . . I guess.

All sarcasm and mockery now aside, regardless of the type of site or the criteria an online dater seeks to have met, an inherent problem exists. It is the problem of human attraction and interaction itself. We want chemistry, while also wanting a partner with shared interests or a similar background or lifestyle. We believe this will make us better suited to one another, which will lead ultimately to a better relationship. And so, especially online where choices abound and we are meeting and greeting, considering and dismissing based sometimes upon a single photo, we laser in on our target, focusing on qualities we *think* are important in a potential partner—while neglecting the ones that actually *are*. Traits such as kindness, fidelity, honesty, dependability and generosity are often overlooked in favor of sparks and spice. Too often we forget: Both can burn.

# Chapter Twelve
## Week 9—Hacked In, Locked Out & Pissed Off

A couple days into Week 9 I received an email from someone whose username I recognized. While the photo looked vaguely familiar, I couldn't place him. His message was definitely however red flag-worthy:

> *Hi, do you know what? I just uploaded some private pics on xxxxx but not everyone can see it. I guess you might like them. You can sign in and view them through my xxxxx private photo page on http://myxxxxxphotos1.weebly.com. Let me know what you think okay?. No lies please ..lol*

The fact he didn't use my name said *Spaghetti Spam* to me. But in trying to give him the benefit of the doubt, I thought best case scenario instead: Maybe he was one of those wannabe photographers I had come across lately. (Is it a mid-life crisis thing? There seems to be a lot of men wanting to do this—turn a hobby into something more.) Of course, I had to be realistic as well. Worst case scenario might give me a *really* good chapter—as I'd not as yet had the pleasure of either the aforementioned "cock shot" or the supposedly pervasive "dick pic.") I clicked on the link which directed me to sign in to my own account. I tried. It didn't work. The pictures didn't load. Whatever, I thought. But curious then as to who the sender was, I went to my email list to look for *vstate123*.

He had originally commented on a photo of me with my son at his wedding. *Vstate123* had written that my son was a very good-looking young man who looked a lot like his mother. He had insisted this was not a line, but a genuine thought he'd had the minute he saw the picture. He asked if my son had returned safely. I wrote back. I thanked him for the compliment and told him yes, my son had returned from Afghanistan, yet was now redeployed in Iraq. He wrote again, expressing his gratitude for my son's service, explaining that he had friends and family serving as well. He offered a few words of support for which I thanked him a second time. That was it. I didn't write again, nor did he. Until now. Considering we had exchanged several emails of a more personal nature, I thought he could have at least used my name in this one. I decided it was an enhanced version of the *Spaghetti Spam*. (Oh, goody! This see-what-sticks schtick has pictures!)

Then I noticed several recent emails I didn't recognize. The date and time sent indicated they had come *from me* just a few minutes ago. Ah, no! Moreover the recipient usernames were all female. I started clicking. And became quickly furious. Right there to the left of my profile pic was a load of crap that appeared as if *I* had sent it! I should have copied it down right then and there, but didn't. The gist of it follows:

> *Hi I'm Judith. Sorry to bother, but I just felt the need to reach out. I have this friend who isn't on xxxx, but was watching me do it and we came across your picture. He thought you looked like someone he would really like to know. I know this is weird, but I promise. His name is Josh, he is 5'11" and really a good looking guy and super*

*nice. I told him I would try to reach out to you. If you got a hold of him through his private email josh_mcxxxxx@aol.com, I'm sure you won't be disappointed.*

Crap. I'd been hacked. I had heard of this happening, but never thought it would happen to me. (Big mistake.) Someone had hijacked my name and account to spread spam. I immediately started emailing the women, telling them the previous message had not come from me and that my account had been hacked. The more women I wrote, the more women appeared in my inbox. At first it was faintly amusing to see my competition. All in their 40s, most were average to frumpy. Though there was a brunette with a great smile who reminded of Brooke Burke. Two of the women actually wrote back and thanked me. One wrote me before I got to her and told me "to go spam someone else." I still wrote her to proclaim my innocence. By the time I got disgusted and just quit, I had emailed over twenty women. Come business hours tomorrow I would be calling this damn site!

In the morning I tried to log in. I wanted to copy down the spam message verbatim. Instead, I received a message that there was a problem with my account (ya think?) and that I needed to contact customer service. When I tried to log in through the mobile app, I was informed that my account had been locked and I should have received an email from xxxxx. (I hadn't) They provided an email address to their resolutions department. Oh hell, no! I wanted a person to bitch to! I called and was informed by a recording I had called outside of their normal business hours. (I'm east coast. Apparently they are on central time.) Then I checked my inbox again to see if their email had arrived. It still hadn't. Instead an Asian woman with major second language grammar issues had emailed me thanking me for contacting her. Great! That's all I need now. My inbox continued to fill with women who believed the spam. One she-dater, however, was far more shrewd—and more than a little fire and brimstone retaliatory. She wrote back, calling me a scammer and telling me God will punish me for taking advantage of women on this site.

On the dot, at 8am central, I called. I followed the prompts and immediately obtained a real person. So much faster than when I had followed the "I want a refund" route months ago! I had been on hold then for 20 minutes. Doesn't that tell you where they see a staffing need—and not! The young man who answered was clearly an English as a second language speaker. I had to explain the situation twice. He admitted their system had "detected" a problem and that was why I was locked out. (Duh!) He wanted to re-enable my account and provide me a link to change my password. I wanted an explanation how this had happened and some reassurance not more than my name and user ID had been stolen. Did they have my personal email? My credit card information?

The poor guy was in over his head. All he could do was spout canned phrases and promises to contact and report my situation to an account specialist. After a two minute hold he came back on the line and gave me an explanation that made little sense. He could not tell me how this had happened other than it does. He assured me my information had not been compromised. I told him his site's security sucked and so did the site for that matter. He honestly didn't know what to say, and I felt bad venting and dumping on some minimum wage call center flunky. I apologized and thanked him for his help. To say he was relieved to get rid of me would be an understatement.

I followed the link to reset my password. Can I tell you how annoyed I was by the message that popped up?

"It's ok to forget." (I didn't forget, assholes. Your lousy site let my account be hacked and my profile stolen.) After the reset was complete I received an even more irritating message: "Now go have some fun." (Screw you, xxxxx!)

I logged on to see if the spam message and all the emails to all those women were still there. They weren't. Then I went back to see if I could see *vstat123*'s photos. (I was still curious.) I entered my email and new password and got to the same place as before—a "site" site that looked like it was part of my site, with a message that if the photos did not load to try and log in again. I started to and then saw that the word "password" was misspelled "pasword." Realizing this may have been how they hacked me before, I immediately went back to the link and changed my password a second time. It remained to be seen if this was over.

Apparently not. The woman who'd called me a scammer wrote again, even after I wrote her and explained I had been hacked. She sent the same message. Then I received a message from a woman my age, who looked 10 years older. She wanted to know more about Josh. Was he employed? What was his race? Was he tall? A former teacher, she said she was new to online dating and didn't want to proceed without being more certain. I felt so sorry for her. I can't imagine any man looking at Ms. Frumpy McFoo's photo and being so charmed that their "friend" had to write. I wrote and told her it was a scam and to be more careful and never to respond to such an email. I think I prefer being told I will rot in Hell as opposed to having to be the one to stick a needle in another's woman's hope balloon.

Ladies, I don't know how to caution you to prevent hacking from happening to you. It's a feeling of being violated and falsely accused and guilty for being even an unwitting part of it, all at the same time. My best advice is to be vigilant. Know that it does happen. And it *can* happen to you. But don't make it easy for the bastards! Watch what you click on. And don't click on shit ON the site—unless it comes FROM the site.

# Chapter Thirteen
## Week 10—My Inexpert Opinion & What the Real Experts Say

My age group, the so-called "Baby Boomer" generation, is at a distinct disadvantage when it comes to online dating. Three issues are at play.

First is the mechanics. The whole internet site/mobile app world is foreign—and hard for us techno-idiots to negotiate. And why wouldn't it be? We grew up with rotary dial phones for Christ's sake! A web site was where Charlotte spun her freakin' spider web. Remember the old woman in the television commercial "posting friends" by hanging their photos on her living room wall? Funny—because it's true. In fact, there is actually a web site called MyLonelyParent where children can set up dating profiles for their older parents who don't have an internet or computer clue.

The second, even bigger problem for middle-aged plus Boomers is that ours is what sociologists and other self-proclaimed dating experts call a "thin dating market." In other words, we are fishing in a pretty depleted pond. Many of the opposite sex are already paired off. Hell, the divorce rate has actually been declining since the early 1990s! And people of both sexes are living longer. Disease just doesn't kill like it used to. All causes for celebration, to be sure—until you as a single at sixty dater see the big picture through a self-centered prism: Crap! Divorce and death both down? Don't tell me . . . Yep, less divorced and widowed folks looking for another partner.

A particular problem for Boomer men online (or off) looking for a committed relationship, be it marriage or not, is that many Boomer women are not looking to be tied down again. Been there, done that, is their mantra. They are loving their independence—perhaps the first in their lives. Moreover, they are financially secure, with a lifetime of earned assets they very much intend to keep un-co-mingled. They want to just date. As many men as possible—and on the schmucks' dime, according to the guy I met Speed Dating.

Women in the Boomer bracket, on the other hand, have their own particular issue: widowers in the Boomer bracket. Most claim to have had wonderful marriages. Lonely and domestically challenged, they are looking for a repeat/replacement. Here's the rub . . . not only are they are often helpless (what they really are looking for is a maid, cook, nurse, laundress, accountant, etc.), they are usually hopeless—hopelessly still in love with their dearly departed. Good luck, ladies, going out to dinner with your new beau and the ghost of his dead wife! A colleague was in such a *ménage a trois* for nearly a year. Everything she did, wore and said was compared to Susie-the-Dead-Spouse. (Do I have to tell you who was always found wanting in *that* comparison?)

The third and final issue is not exclusive to Boomers: the perceived stigma of online dating. It is a perception that crosses most generational lines, yet is one that also appears to be diminishing. In a 2005 study conducted by Pew Research, participants were asked to agree or disagree to this statement: "People who use online dating sites are losers." 29% agreed. Ten years later the number of participants agreeing had gone down to 23%. Another statement posed in 2005 and again in 2015: "Online dating sites are a good way to meet people." Initially, 44% of the Pew's study guinea pigs agreed. Fast forward a decade, and that number had climbed to 59%. In fact, Pew contends that half of all Americans know someone who has met their spouse or partner via online dating.

While the stigma may be less and the practice more accepted than ever, it is important to recognize that the VAST MAJORITY of relationships still begin OFFLINE.

Again, according to Pew in 2015, 88% of the couples in America *together less than five years* "met without the help of a dating site."

There also exists the question if online dating might not actually be harmful to society in the long run. Remember Michael Rosenfeld, the Stanford sociologist and his long-running study mentioned in Chapter 11? Given the length and breadth of his research concerning the dating habits of 3000 online daters, he's about as expert as one can get. Interviewed in 2016 by *Washington Post* wonkblogger Robert Ferdman, Mr. Rosenfeld served up a pretty credible overview of this twenty year phenomenon. Sharing both statistics and conclusions comparing on and off line dating, he also responded to the most common criticisms and concerns about online dating.

Whether it works is a proven given. YES. IT DOES. But one needs to define what constitutes *true* success. Dating sites would like you concentrate on statistics, such as this from Match: "33% of singles met their last first date through online dating, while 26% met their last first date through a friend." Their TV ads also tout the fact they have more second dates blah blah. So here's the rub—and the question each individual dater must answer for her/himself: What is "success" *for me*? A first date? A second? A relationship? Marriage? Nowadays the estimate is that 1 in 4 straight couples and 2 in 3 gay couples meet online. But do the math. As high as 1 in 4 may sound, it is still only 25%, thereby making so called "traditional avenues," such as friends, family, work, church, bars and other social settings, still responsible for how *75% of all straight couples* meet. For gay couples, however, the percentages are nearly flipped, with *66% meeting online* and only 33% meeting off. Because it is harder for gays and lesbians to identify potential partners offline in a world majorly straight, Mr. Rosenfeld calls online dating "tremendously beneficial for gay couples." In fact, based upon his study,

Mr. Rosenfeld recognizes a twofold advantage of online dating for *all* daters: sheer numbers and access there to never before possible. Think back (or flip back) to Chapter 11 and the membership totals provided there.

As I have previously stated, the online dating is an industry that DID NOT EXIST before 1995! (The very first online dating site, match.com, was founded in 1993 by two men [told ya!], Gary Kremen and Peng Tong. In 1994 they hired a woman to make the site friendlier and more accessible to women. In 1995 Match went live.) Twenty years and 1000 imitators and competitors later, and today's online sites and mobile apps provide today's online daters with a dating pool of literally millions of perfect strangers. (Disclaimer: I refer to "perfect" in the sense there is no way you know him/her, not perfect as in without faults.) With a pool this deep, a dater can easily select the specific characteristics he/she knows they like and/or want. Not only does the internet make this access possible, it is an access highly improbable *without*. Consider this statistic: 75% of people who meet online would have *never* met otherwise! They have no prior connection of any kind, no common friends, for example. Without the internet it would have been nearly impossible for their paths to have crossed.

Another recognized advantage of online dating over off line is both advantage and disadvantage. This boon *and* curse is the excessive communication that takes place before an actual face to face meeting. In the form of emails, progressing to texts, progressing to phone calls (and even the profiles to start, for that matter), this systematic exchange provides not only a social activity, it also serves as a means to streamline and fast track the process of information-gathering and person-learning good old-fashioned courtship was meant to achieve. In the long run, this results in less wasted time, energy, money, and emotional investment in a relationship not destined for any real future.

No doubt this is why that all important "second date" milestone is so touted in television advertising. By the time you actually go out on the first date, you know pretty damn well this is a person you are really interested in—ergo the second date is a no-brainer. Indeed, if I *had* adhered to the formula and followed the systematic steps (and had actually spoken more than ten minutes on the phone to Al Gomer), I would have *never* have gone out with him.

Critics of online dating wonder if "millions to choose from" and "a fast track system" are really good things. With so many options available might people be inclined to break up more easily and quickly if they believe a replacement is just a few mouse clicks away? Mr. Rosenfeld says no. His research has shown that "online meetings are no more likely to lead to break ups than offline meetings."

And what about the "grass is always greener" trap we humans have a tendency to fall into? With infinite choices out there, how can we truly know there isn't a better one? I have a friend who thought she was in a happy relationship—and then she discovered her significant other online searching.

The belief that online dating creates serial daters is a common one: Not only are people more apt to date several people at once with online dating than off, they are putting off settling down with one person in an exclusive, committed relationship. One article I came across stated that 31% of online daters concur that the plenitude of options keeps them from settling down. My own anecdotal evidence would bear this out. I cannot count the number of profiles I have read in which men stress (and I *do* mean stress) they are looking for a committed, no drama, no game playing relationship with a loyal partner interested in spending the best years left together traveling and/or cuddling on the couch. Given their capital letters'

121

emphasis, I can only assume the women they are encountering are *not* interested in the same. But then again, to play Devil's advocate . . . I once had an employee on a flight using his free flight benefits to date women literally all over the country. He was, he freely admitted, having the time of his life. Can he be blamed? The curiosity "to see what else is out there" is powerful and the thrill of a new, as yet unknown, just beginning encounter can be addictive. There is no other rush like the first time.

And what about that formula of electronic communication? Are we in essence creating a new reality in which people are–willingly or not—avoiding real-life interaction? Remember what I wrote previously about the honesty paradox? The anonymity of online dating allows anyone to be anyone and anything. In 2007, country singer Brad Paisley co-wrote and released a song entitled "Online." Its protagonist was a short chubby geek living in his parent's basement, while his online alter ego was a tall, six-pack-abbed international man of mystery. Satirizing the online world, the song's lyrics are hysterical and its chorus line so, so true: "I'm so much cooler online." We all are, Brad. We all are.

I once spent a very enjoyable evening sexting Z in raggedy-ass sweat pants, no makeup, hair in a topknot, without contacts in or teeth brushed, sitting on the couch watching *Blue Blood* reruns and eating a local delivery peperoni and black olive pizza.

*Want to come be loud with me?*
*How loud?*
*As loud as you like*
*What else?*
*Whatever either of us likes*
*Like what?*
*Use your imagination. I can be very bad*
*How bad? Tell me more*
*Naughty bad*

*Promise?*
*I do*
*You are sexy Are you in bed?*
*Yes*
*Naked?*

I'm sure you get the drift and can imagine the rest. And I was perfectly content. As was he, I imagine.

So again, that question about online dating versus offline: Does it create, foster and encourage unhealthy habits? Do we live more contentedly on our phones and computers than we do in our offline lives? I don't know. I do know digital technology and smartphones have transformed our lives in general, and certainly how we seek out and establish relationships in particular. But just what the societal implications and psychological repercussions are of this transformation is a question whose scope goes well beyond a few paragraphs about online dating.

I do however want to stress now (because this *is* treatise on online dating) the magnitude of the change the internet has brought to dating and male/female interaction. IT IS HUGE. And my opinion is one shared by experts far more qualified than I. Justin Garcia, a research scientist at Indiana University's Kinsey Institute for Research in Sex, Gender and Reproduction offered the following in a 2015 *Vanity Fair* article by N. J. Sales, entitled "Tinder and the Dawn of the 'Dating Apocalypse.'"

> *There have been two major transitions in heterosexual mating in the last four million years. The first was around 10,000 to 15,000 years ago in the agricultural revolution, when we became less migratory and more settled . . .*

*And the second major transition is*
*with the rise of the internet.*


Clearly this evolutionary change in the way we do our dating business today is a transformation universally acknowledged. But has the change resulted in actual damage? Just because the world of dating is different does not equate to it being a bad metamorphosis. Or does it?

In his interview, Mr. Ferdman posed several questions as these to Mr. Rosenfeld. Most mere observers of life would posit it is easier online to find what we are specifically seeking. It falls then to the "experts" to answer if our expressed preferences are truly in our best interests. Does this ease of finding super special specific lead to what Mr. Ferdman calls "a pattern of regular hookups that doesn't lead to relationships?" In other words, "Is online dating ruining relationships?" Mr. Rosenfeld says not. People online actually progress to marriage faster, he says. To back up his claim, he offers the following data: ½ of online couples are married by year four of the relationship, in contrast to offline couples who require ten years to reach that same ½ statistic. This is not to say either that online dating does not make hooking up easier, he concedes. It does—because it's easier to meet *and* easier to end (less time invested and ability to block unwanted contacts after the fact).

And yet, according to a previously referenced 2016 online post by Pew Research based upon 2015 data, 1/3 of online daters have *never* actually gone on a real date with someone they met online. But that's not to say there are not those internet daters who do indeed "hook up" without actually ever going on a real date. (I know of at least two.) That people are delaying "settling down" is a consequence of modern society, Mr. Rosenfeld contends, not online dating. I would certainly agree. Women have options.

Depending upon their generation (Millennial, Gen X), both sexes have seen their parents divorce at the highest rates in history. Many have seen their parents struggle financially to raise a young family. That they want to be sure and secure before they themselves commit and marry is not a surprise.

A real problem with trying to determine internet dating's harm to and/or impact upon relationships in particular and society in general is that the target group affected is far from homogeneous.   I don't believe adequately specific studies exist to gauge or glean more than an overall general impression. What an 18 -24 year-old online dater is seeking is far different from a thirty-something-year-old professional looking to settle down. And both are groups a world apart from the 50-70 year old widowed, divorced, retired "our time" crowd.  The dating sites might exist that cater to each, but as far as experts being able to determine if the online experience is hurting, helping, impacting or changing some end result, the studies don't. Not yet. Or at least not yet in sufficient depth as to offer a pretty solid inarguable result.

By far, the biggest criticism of online dating is its superficiality. Everyone is "so focused on appearance," said the guy at Speed Dating. But this is not unique to online dating. Judging one another first by looks is "not an attribute of technology—or even modern society," says Mr. Rosenfeld, "Dating has always been a rather superficial endeavor." Again, I agree. I have two names for you: Henry VIII and Anne of Cleves.

In considering a potential date or mate, we are primordially hardwired to evaluate the other's suitability, subconsciously or not.  The whole reason men have a thing for boobs is supposedly an evaluation as to her ability to nurture children. And her fondness for broad shoulders and huge biceps?  Tangible proof of strength and power and a good indication he can defend his family.

Mr. Rosenfeld agrees the actual attractiveness of the photo is a primary factor. (Duh! I could have told him that!) Social class is a secondary factor. Online versus offline statistics for socioeconomic factors, education and background are pretty much the same. Though he concedes a "slight tendency for women to prefer people who claim to make a lot of money." (Again, duh?)

An unexpected discovery along this line of attractiveness is that the preponderance of men over women has apparently given women a stronger sense of value. Women who in the real world might be a 5 or 6 on a 1-10 grading scale find themselves online being a 7 or 8. From what I gather reading online responses to blogs and online articles, the men don't like it. Suddenly they are being rejected by women they think now think they are too good for. It's simple supply and demand, boys. Online is no different than any male heavy environment—the military, frontier towns in the Wild West, California gold rush mining camps, Alaska to this day—the minority gets to be pickier. Maybe the average Janes are judging too harshly the looks of the men they encounter online. And maybe they really are holding out for a stud, but some might call it "turnabout is fair play." Women have been judged always by their looks. Welcome to our world, boys. It sucks, doesn't it?

That online dating is losing its stigma and becoming the norm is backed by solid data. And why wouldn't it? These days we live our entire lives online and connected. In a world governed by Google, who can remember the last time they used a library card catalog? (If such a thing even exists?) Maps, restaurant guides, clothing catalogues, movie show times in the newspaper—hell! newspapers themselves—are all going the way of spinning wheels and butter churns. Streaming, downloading, apps for everything . . . My neighbor recently had a web appointment with a doctor during which she held her smart phone to her wrist so he could check her heart rate. And the last time I bought a watermelon, I used an app on my cell phone to pick it out. Seriously! There's an app for that. Small wonder there'd be an app (or two or twenty or a hundred or a thousand!) to pick out a mate. 72% of Americans are active online. So aside from the fact we do nearly everything online today (so why not date?), there are several specific reasons and incidents when it makes perfect sense to at least try. Some circumstances are universal and apply to all ages, while others are more unique to a particular group.

So when is online dating most beneficial? When the person has

- ✓ been focused on other things, i.e. military service, completing their education and/or starting a career (mid to late 20s)
- ✓ had little opportunity to pursue more conventional options, particularly if theirs is an all-consuming career (30s-40s)
- ✓ recently relocated to a new city (all ages)
- ✓ found themselves recently single after a long-term relationship, particularly widowed or divorced (40-60s)
- ✓ discovered theirs is a thin dating pool because most everyone is paired off (late 30s-70s)
- ✓ struggled to meet someone for whatever reason (all ages)
- ✓ been suckered in by advertising (all ages)
- ✓ actually known someone it has worked for (all ages)

The bottom line is one never knows. The experts can conduct studies and interviews, surveys and experiments. At the end of the day it comes down to two people. How they meet is immaterial. Whether online or off, if they click a relationship is born. If not, take the guidance of Scarlett O'Hara, fiction's serial dater/mater of all time: Tomorrow is another day.

## Chapter Fourteen
## Week 11—You Better Shop Around

By the end of Week 10 my disgust with this entire process knows no bounds. Since the hacking I have received no emails from my site—no daily matches (when I used to get 24 a day?), no progress reports, no winks, likes, favs, and not even offers hitting me up for additional services (for additional  fees). I wondered if, with the reactivation, something got hosed or turned off. I could still log on and see the list of losers they are giving me—a list that was getting WORSE! Older, more men not in my race preference or beyond my age range, and more for whom I was not in their desired age range. Lots of repeat faces as well. Wtf?

I called customer service and at least reached someone with a passable proficiency in English. She put me on hold to check, then came back to tell me my email had not been deactivated. Yet she couldn't give me an answer why I was no longer receiving the emails I once did. She said she would forward my problem to their Resolutions Department and they would be in touch. She gave me a resolution case number and told me I should hear via email in 24-48 hours. If not, I could email them "because that department doesn't take live calls." Wonderful. (As of this writing, it's been over 72 hrs. Zilch.)

Suffice it to say, at this point between the no-action taken on technical issues and the lack of viable prospects the honeymoon with XXXXX was definitely over. Given the bad to worse matches I was receiving, I was convinced they were scraping the bottom of the barrel. The last wink I had received was from a 24-year-old kid! (I did write him back and asked if he hadn't made a mistake. I thanked him for the compliment regardless and then told him I have three sons older than he. He wrote back and said it hadn't been a mistake. Really? (I don't even want to go down his mommy issues road . . .)  So back to my dilemma . . .

Quitting wasn't an option. I was determined to stick this out. But considering the abundance of options out there and the fact this *was* supposed to be an exposé on online dating sites, maybe it was time to branch out and try a different type of site? I decided for the sake of presenting a broader picture of my experience (if nothing else), I would avail myself of another dot com dating site—but one with a narrower age and income focus.  If this one didn't work, I swore I was moving on to another cougar/cub site! Maybe the 24-year-old had a cuter, slightly older brother? (Just kidding.)

In my research I had come across numerous articles, not only discussing the various types of sites out there, but also evaluating and ranking them with a specific criterion in mind—best for singles 18-25, best for retired folks, best for those looking for marriage, etc.. One of the sites consistently appearing in the top ten lists is one that touts itself as a site for more educated, intellectual and sophisticated daters. Their ad states "You have every right to be demanding." They claim 18,000 new members a week, with someone finding love every 8 minutes through their services. Their niche in the online dating market is single professionals 50+. I realized this flew in the face of my younger man preference, but I decided to go for it anyway.  Besides, they had a free sign-up offer. What did I have to lose? (Famous last words.)

Ever hopeful, I registered for my Basic FREE membership. I was asked the normal age, occupation, height, race, smoker or not and did I want children questions. I provided an email address and a password so I could log in to my account in my "first step towards finding a fulfilling long-term relationship!" Next I answered most of the same questions for my desired partner—age, height, race, smoker or not, children or not. So far, so good.

Then came screen after screen after screen (!) of personal questions and/or statements about me. The answer to which—or degree of applicably to me—I was to rank on a scale of always, most of the time, sometimes, seldom, hardly never, not ever. Obviously these questions were a personality test of sorts. And it got old. Quick. Just when I thought I had reached the end, I was asked to describe myself in four words. I was asked what I dislike, what makes me laugh, where I feel most at home, what would I not part with, what was I most grateful for. Finally, lots of questions and choice selections about my hobbies and interests.

I realized rather quickly, I'm pretty damn boring on paper. I have no interest in water sports (not of the kink variety! but rather surfing, sailing, waterskiing, etc.) nor winter sports, racket sports—no interest, in fact, in any of the probably 20 they listed. What do I do in my leisure time? Read, knit, write. Exciting. What am I passionate about? Travel. Not being bored.

When it came time to describe my partner, there was another series of questions and options and another sliding scale system. Then more short answer boxes to fill in. They are called "free text fields." And I'm told they are important, so I should spend some time on them. What should my partner know about me? How would my friends describe me? What would I wish for? What am I seeking in a relationship? ("Laid" is probably not an acceptable answer—although it's the main reason I'm seeking.) At last I was asked to download some photos and submit the whole profile for approval.

Almost instantaneously I received five faceless profiles of potential partners selected for me. They listed name and hometown and age. Every one of them was 60 or older. Apparently "sophisticated, educated, intellectual" only occurs after one's 6th decade on earth? A green button indicated I should click here to "view profile." Doing so revealed occupation, height, race, and whether or not they were a smoker or wanted children. (Really? How is this truly an issue at this age?) I could even read their self-introductory paragraphs. Obviously, however, if I wanted to see or know more though, I was going to have to become a paid member. My thought was: No thank you.

But then I started to get more emails from the site, telling me Doug (not his real name) was interested and requesting a photo. Or Michael (nhrn) had just viewed my profile. Rick (nhrn) was intrigued by my profile as well, and like Doug, he was requesting I upload a picture "to get a better idea of the person behind the profile." Each message contained a green button so I could discover my visitor. I realized I actually liked the use of names rather than stupid user IDs. And I had to admit without a photo, I was giving the profiles a closer look. A couple didn't read bad, but I was put off by the ages—most were well over 60, a lot of retired and semi-retired. (Oh lord, my dating pool is full of floaters and half floaters! I need a swimmer. I can't do "retired.")

And still more emails came, enticing me to shell out for a premium membership so I could view all the profiles and photos and contact anyone I wanted and have alerts when my messages were read, blah, blah, blah. (With my old site I had just signed up from the get-go, so I have no idea if they do the same tease. I'm sure they probably do.) The emails continued:

- *Your profile is very popular with other members! Find out what in particular Rich, 64 from XXXXXXtown liked about you.*
- *Your profile has just been visited by Carl, 57, XXXXton!*
- *Mark, 58, XXXXXXfield, sent you a smile!*

131

- *Discover your new matches and find out who could be that exceptional somebody for you!*
- *Your profile caught the attention of other members. Become a Premium Member now and discover who wants to get to know you better.*

I'm ashamed to admit it, but I was suckered in. I didn't know if the men themselves were an improvement, but their occupations were a definite step up. I counted an architect, two physicians, a psychotherapist, a professor, an interior designer and four directors and/or executives from among the dozen and a half men who had viewed my profile. (The rest were listed as retired or semi-retired, with a couple as young as 54 and 56!) I figured what the hell. I'd take one for the team and spend another $100 for the cause of comparison shopping and further chapters. I clicked on the appropriate green button and chose the cheapest and shortest option: $29.65 for three months. I entered in my credit card info and hit the pay button. An immediate email appeared in my inbox: *Congratulations! You've taken the first step to finding true love.* My thoughts were closer to: "Congratulations, dumbass. You've probably just flushed another $90 (give or take) down the drain."

Yep. Down the drain. The first green "Discover" labeled button I clicked led me to an "oops! page not found" screen. The next "View" button revealed a front seat selfie of a bald, moustached guy who listed no occupation, ethnic background or religion. He is a non-smoker, however, who spends his leisure time "sports, music, camping, tv, home." In relationships he looks for honesty. He doesn't like "dishonest, drunks, drugs, laziness, dirty" and is most grateful for "being born, healthy, happyiness[sic]." Yeah, I'll pass.

One of the physicians came next. This one was 58, balding, 5'9", and retired. He stated that his ideal day was golfing. In fact, the word "golf" appeared four times in his profile. He wrote he has a "great capacity to give in a relationship emotionally and materially." Another pass.

Paul (nhrn), 59, from XXXXport is also retired and balding. He stresses twice within six fields he is honest and doesn't like games or being used. He uses the word "loyal" three times. I think (besides obviously needing a dictionary of synonyms) Paul was really betrayed and scarred in a past relationship. Either way, I passed on him too.

In all, in the first two days with my new site, I passed totally on 17 of the 18 men who viewed my profile. However three of the 18 sent me a smile and three wrote. The first was a physician. He sent a really long message telling me how intrigued he was with my profession as a pilot. (I had typed "flight attendant," but it had posted "flight deck crew" on my profile.) I wrote him back merely to set the record straight. The second was another physician, this one heavy set and divorced four years. He sent a generic message introducing himself and asking how I was doing. Since this site provides my name, I should think he could have at least used it! Whatever. I didn't bother to write back. The third guy's email to me was a really detailed reaction response to my profile that was kind of witty.

The one guy I didn't pass on, I wrote to. With a full head of dark hair he was a definite standout from among the bald and balding. Younger at 48, he copped to Italian roots. Of course I never heard back. *Quid pro quo,* I guess: I ignored the fat doctor who wrote because he didn't do it for me, and the good-looking Italian ignored the decade older broad who didn't do it for him.

A couple of days later I noted a profound shift in the matches I was receiving. (Ok, this site calls them partner proposals—potato/potahto.) I was seeing less white collar, more pale blue, and some definitely (definitely!) dark blue. The first few days there had not been a single man with a profession that would dirty his hands. Now I was getting tractor mechanic, truck driver, maintenance man, and laborer . . . not that there is anything wrong with any of those jobs! But I found the abrupt change odd considering the site's home screen states that 82% of their members have either a Bachelor's, Master's or Doctorate. (BTW, they also state that 56% of their members are women and 44% men—great! Leave it to me to choose a testosterone-short site in a marketplace supposedly loaded with it.)

I also found it odd that suddenly there was a marked absence of photos appearing above the names, ages and hometowns. During the first couple days of the new member/fresh meat blitz there had been only three photo-less proposals. Now come Day 4 (and beyond) and I'm counting upwards of two dozen *sans* photos—meaning they are window shopping for free. To be fair—and honest—these men were absolutely age appropriate. (Not that I wanted age appropriate!) The vast majority were 56-59. In fact, during my first 5 days on this site, out of 70+ proposed partners "selected for me from 1000s of singles," only 6 were older than 60 and only four in their 40s. (You might think I made up these numbers—6 in their 60s, 40 in their 40s—cute. But I didn't. Promise.)

The week ended with another twenty or so men having appeared in my inbox. All were in their 50s, two were retired, one claimed "golfer" as a profession and one was a caregiver. The rest were bona fide white collar professions. The problem was—now that I had shelled out the bucks to become a premium member and could actually see their photos—I was unimpressed. In fact, out of nearly

100 men provided as possible matches, I was motivated enough to write only a couple more. (Ok, it was three more. But in all honesty, one of the three I wrote between days 3 and 7 didn't really count—he was a law enforcement officer without a picture. Given the recent spate of attacks on LEOS, I wrote merely to thank him for his public service and to express my support.) So that said . . . who were the two I found email-worthy? A 58-year-old gemologist and a 57-year business manager. And . . . wait for it . . . the number who responded back to me? ZERO.

Of course I was also guilty of the same crime. In my first week on site #2 I had received one wink, three messages, three smiles, one photo like, and one 5 question contact. The 5 question contact is a feature unique to this site. Basically you select 5 prewritten questions to send to a person you want to make contact with. With multiple choice answers for the recipient to select and send back, the site explains this exercise allows for comparing likes and dislikes. After which they recommend you create a personalized message and send it. They even provide little picture icons for each step (which they helpfully number 1-5—in case you can't keep the order straight). This contrived cartoon-augmented question/answer ice breaker is an insult. But I guess it's a must for those idiot individuals who don't know how to write something themselves. Silly me. And here I'd thought this was a site for educated professionals?!?

## Chapter Fifteen
## Week 12—A Tale of Two Sites

Thus far I have received another 50 or so partner proposals from this new site. A half dozen provided no profession, another five listed "retired" and four claimed "self-employed" or "entrepreneur." For the most part, the occupations are undeniably professional. A lawyer, journalist, geologist, engineers of every variety—civil, software, electrical—all requiring a university degree. Whether it's their ages or egos, I am also seeing a hell of a lot of titles: four "executives" (marketing, entertainment, financial and construction), five managers (engineering, telecommunications, program, sales and retail), two directors (construction and just plain director) and one foreman (construction). Rounding out the bluer end: a couple clerks, a driving instructor, a security guard, a coach, a taxi driver and two maintenance men. The rest are either in banking or real estate. Only a few are not my race preference. And yes, they are age appropriate, following my new—and more stringent—50-59 preference. Only one is 61, the rest range from 59-51, with 70% being either my age exactly or a year or two younger. It runs about 50-50 whether they have a photo. The ones who do are absolutely less outright icky than my old site—none look like felons, ex-cons or pedophiles.

But there still are no winners in my book. (Unless I count my favorite loser line for the week: A 59-year old Jewish banker, who wants to find his soulmate and writes "she must be exciting and entertaining.") They all look older than they claim and most are bald, balding or really thin on top. I have also come to realize that most—despite the site's admonition to the contrary—did not bother to spend much time or effort on their profiles. And one other unusual thing . . . most post only a single photo. Probably a judicious decision, since the photo(s) pretty much eliminate them from my consideration anyway. Thinking it might help to cast a wider net, I up the miles I'd be willing to travel from 50 to 100. BTW, I sent one message to a 57-year-old and shockingly got no response.

Meanwhile on my original site it's next to no business as usual. In total my profile has been viewed by 23 men this week. Two sent a wink and one an actual unsolicited email. (Another also wrote, but he doesn't really count—he was just finally getting around to responding to an email I had sent him 2 or 3 weeks ago. More on him later.) Do the math. That leaves 20 men who, after viewing me, were not interested enough to pursue anything further. In other words I was rejected by

- 5 retired widowers ranging in age from 60-63
- a 58-year-old African American
- 2 chubby/stocky 63-year-olds, one of whom wrote *a lot* about his 85-year-old mother (In a dating profile?)
- a 42-year-old musician touting his new album on iTunes
- a 59-year-old who enjoys "dinning {sic} out" and is looking for the "whole package." In 13 lines he mentions the word "sexy" five times. He says smoking is a real turn off. Oh, and he has no photo.
- a 50-year-old also without a photo, who writes he is not "looking for the flavor of the month." He brags he is a "tell-it-like-it-is guy" with a sarcastic side.
- a 68-year-old separated, self-proclaimed romantic whose only photo is a nightscape of some large

Asian city. His username? girlwatcher517 (Did I mention he's 68! And separated! Seriously, who separates at nearly seventy?)

- 4 divorced men in their 60s (60-66) who don't stand out at all
- a 47-year-old "Ivy League-educated athlete" with an 8-year-old son
- a 56-year-old-PhD who writes "if you are really interested in talking or want to know more send a quick email."
- a 45-year-old soldier looking for 35-45
- and last (but not least) a 35-year-old who "prefers a mature woman that appreciates a youthful man." He has no photo, but does claim to have a Graduate Degree.

Yep, intoxicating stuff—to know that 87% of the men who examined my photos and/or read my profile passed. A real ego booster.

But you might be wondering about the three men who wrote or sent winks? After all, if you're a "as long as there's anything in the glass at all, it's not empty" type of gal, that equates to 13% who *were* interested. And never forget. It *is* a number game—and it only takes *uno, un, en, eins* to win! Well, one wink came from a stocky 53-year-old never married former high school hockey player. How do I know? By his *hockey3563* handle and the 35-year-old yearbook picture he posted. The other came from a 54-year-old government/military/ law enforcement type who is searching for 35-55. Salt and pepper hair, goatee and really stunning blue eyes, he was a definite keeper—even with his introductory "I am spantanious {sic}" line. (He spelled it correctly later on.) Johnny o' Blue Eyes actually lives in the same small enclave suburb outside Philadelphia that I do. I responded to his wink with an email that mentioned how small the world was. He never responded. (I checked a week later and my email still does not show as having been read—though the site says Johnny has been active the last 24 hours.)

Speaking of not responding . . . the unsolicited email I received came from a 49-year-old Pakistani physician from Philadelphia. (What's with me and physicians?) He wrote that he liked my photo, I had a charming smile, and he asked if I would like to exchange messages. He really didn't appeal to me, but I wrote back thanking him for the compliment. For some reason the email didn't go through. I chalked it up to "meant to be" and didn't write again.

I did, however, write to the 35-year-old who was looking for a mature woman. I was curious. I also asked why he had posted no photo. He did not reply either. Nor did Mr. If You Want to Know More Just Write. He had written at length about his rescue dog. I'm a sucker for dogs and wanted to know what breed he was. Again, no response. (I guess to get a reply I needed to want to know more about the rescuer—and not the rescued.) I also wrote to the guy vaunting his sarcasm and tell-it-like-it-is trait. I told him I had seen that he had viewed my profile and had obviously passed. "Such is life," I wrote, "but from one sarcastic to another," I wished him well. I also wished the soldier well and thanked him for his service.

Mr. Sarcasm read and ignored my email. Soldier Boy, whose profile is now hidden, shows to be inactive the last 5 days. (Follow-up checks indicate it was never read.) No less a sucker for the have served as for the currently serving, I sent a photo comment to one of the widowers who mentioned a marine background. I told him I could see it in his photo. Once a marine . . . (He wrote back and thanked me for my note. Score one in the common courtesy column for the jarheads. *Semper fi* and hoo-rah.) Oh, and I also wrote to the guy with the 8-year-old son. According to his profile, he is a fiction writer rather active in publishing. I told him I was interested only in establishing a professional contact. I provided my full name and the title of my best selling romance. I hoped 125,000 copies would earn me some gravitas—even if it was 20+ years ago. He has yet to respond.

Which brings us now to my solicited email: A 43-year-old New Jersey lawyer who is big time into genealogy. I had written him a couple weeks earlier. I was out of his age range (and as a blond WASP he was definitely out of my type range), but I found his family tree interesting. And told him so. A descendant from the original *Mayflower* folks, he has a great-great-great-great somebody who signed the Declaration of Independence! As a former American history teacher I found that cool as hell. We ended up exchanging a half dozen lengthy, detailed emails. He was as interested in my medieval history/romance novel background as I was his Plymouth Rock connection. Turns out, he can actually trace his family back to England's Henry II who was a secondary character in my second book. We sort of open ended it, mutually agreeing it might be fun to meet some time over wine and talk history.

During this same timeframe I actually received a much more concrete invite for conversation and cocktails. The doctor from Site #2 who had thought I was a pilot wrote back after I set him straight. He said he would enjoy meeting me and thought I was attractive and interesting. He thought "if we met, we'd have a very nice conversation and a good time." He would enjoy meeting me for happy hour. He provided his cell number and asked me to text or call. Shortish and bald on top (the monk tonsure is *not* a turn-on for me), he was a bitter pill to swallow after Z. (Isn't there a rule written somewhere that imposes a limit on just how far down the looks scale you should go after getting dumped? From a 10 to a 5—and 16 years older to boot—just seems too far to fall!) I decided to sleep on it.

The next morning he wrote again. He said he had once dated a flight attendant so he was familiar with my erratic schedule, nevertheless he really hoped I would be free to meet him during the week. Again he said I "would be so fun to get to know." Then he crossed the line. "Since I sold my practice I can up and travel on short notice and you would be so fun to do that with." Besides benefitting from a thesaurus, he needed a copy of Emily Post. I hadn't even talked with him and he was proposing traveling together?

A girlfriend admonished me to give him a chance. What harm was there in meeting him for a drink? I relented and against my better sense texted him. I had a flight to Frankfurt over the weekend but could meet him for happy hour Thursday evening in a nearby town known for its vibrant downtown and eclectic restaurants, bars and outdoor cafes. I asked that he select the time and location. We exchanged a couple texts. He was *so* glad I had agreed to meet. He was *so* looking forward to it. He was *so* sure we would have a fun time. Blah blah blah. The next day he called. I was in the shower and didn't hear my cell. He left a voice mail telling me he was *so* sorry he had missed me. He also left a text, saying the same. An hour later he called again. This time I let it go to voice mail on purpose.

I was beginning to have serious reservations. He was giving off an over the top needy vibe. He left another message, telling me he thought we might meet around 12:30 at some Mexican place, have a margarita and explore the downtown together. How the hell did meet for a happy hour drink turn into an all afternoon affair? A couple hours later I was expecting a call from my supervisor, so when a PA area code popped up on call ID, I answered. Oh dear lord, it was *him*!

I hated his voice! High pitched New York accent and he talked a mile a minute. He gave me more details about the Mexican restaurant and went on and on about how much he was *so* looking forward to meeting me. He again talked about the flight attendant he had dated and asked questions about my flight schedule. And again he mentioned how he was free to travel. I think the call lasted about 5 minutes. I spent the rest of the day trying to decide if I was going through with it. When he texted again that evening he made up my mind for me—and sealed his fate.

The next morning, D—as in date—day, I texted and canceled. I told him I had had a family emergency and was very sorry, but I was not going to be in a mood to socialize. (True, actually. My middle son was being admitted into a medical facility in Phoenix.) Of course he tried to call me back. Of course I let it go to voice mail. He left a text expressing disappointment and sympathy and his hope all would be okay.) A few hours later he texted again and said that if things should work out and I could meet him that evening, he would still *so* love to get together.

At that point I had had it. I texted the Stalker Doctor and told him exactly what was wrong with my son. It was serious, and I would be headed to Phoenix after my Frankfurt flight. While I did not want to be rude, I would very much appreciate it if he would respect my wishes, give me space, and not contact me again. Again he texted me! Twice. As a doctor he had had experience blah blah blah. He would be happy to walk me through what I needed to do blah blah blah. Dude! Get a freakin' clue! I did not respond, and he finally stopped contacting me.

Maybe it was me. Maybe I wasn't being realistic. Seriously, did I truly think there was another TDH (tall, dark, handsome) 42-year-old in my future? Maybe short, bald Stalker Doctor was as good as I was going to get? Maybe I didn't give him a fair chance.

And maybe, ala Rhett Butler, I really don't give a damn any more.

## Chapter Sixteen
## Week 13—Batter Up?

I hated dealing with *one* online dating site. Dealing with *two* is a real pain. Twice the effort, twice the time-suck. Twice the frustration. And twice the rejection. As the rejector—and the rejected. Week unlucky #13 began with another group of 50-something-year-olds from Site #2. I will give this site credit for one thing: They do keep my potential partners within my stated age range preference. This week they were 59-53, with only 2 exceptions—youngsters 48 and 40, a trainer and construction worker respectively. Professions run the same gamut as last week: a number of retirees, a few who list no occupation, several engineers and managers, a couple directors and an analyst. Thus far, the bluest collars this week belong to a detective and the two forty-something-year-olds.

During this same week my cell phone had started acting up, dropping calls and connections and crashing. So when I received an email message from Site #2 that a couple more Tom, Dick or Harrys had viewed my profile, I forwent the frustration of trying to log in on my phone and went instead to the computer to check them out. I guess I hadn't paid attention on the small cell phone screen, but on the computer it was rather hard to miss. Site #2's home screen—a slick layout in hunter green with a background replete with zillions of tiles of smiling, good-looking and *young* people. Men and women alike, all in their obvious 30s and 40s. WTF! I want to sign up for this site! Because it sure as hell is *not* the site I signed up for. I'd expect such slanted advertising from Site #1, which is a general all-ages dating website. But Site #2 is supposed to be for 50+. Not one guy have I seen, from the literally hundreds of partners, matches or whatever-the-eff they call them, has come even close to making the cut to be on this wallpaper. Talk about bait and switch!

Once I'd had my temper tantrum and had sneaked at peek at Tom, Dick and/or Harry (no, no and no), I logged off the liar site and went to Site #1. There I sent out my usual 3-4 emails to my usual 40-something-year olds. This time they were one 42 and two 45-year-olds. One of the 45-year-olds speaks Russian (I have a Russian minor). After I hit send, I went to look at my email history to see if the three messages I sent last week had been read. One (who still doesn't show to have read it) now has a hidden profile, one hasn't read it, and one read it and looked at my profile and never responded. Par for my dating course.

Now you might think a rational woman would read (instead of her email history) the writing on the proverbial dating site wall. Clearly I'm having no luck with the 40-year-olds. But on the other hand, I'm having the same success with the 50-year-olds. If I'm going to waste my time, I'm going to waste it on what I really would prefer. Besides, I did catch one—actually maybe two. The genealogist/lawyer and I have been in contact this entire week. Texts led to phone calls. He has the best voice so far. No Barry White or James Earl Jones, but listenable. Two nights in a row the conversation lasted over 3 hours. He's definitely interesting—at least on the phone. The second night we had started with texts that veered somehow into word games and sexual innuendo/baseball analogies. He is not as raw and erotic as Z was, but he does have a sharp wit. The conversation ala text started when he asked about my day and I admitted to sleeping in til 9. (We had been on the phone the previous night until 1 am.)

*Hmmmm. I was up early . . . forgot I
had things to do. Glad you got to sleep in :)
Looks like you owe me one... lol*

*Lol*

*No comment? Lol*

145

*Pleading the 5ᵗʰ*

*Well that is certainly within your constitutional rights... ☺ But I am surprised... lol You don't seem like a woman that would let a cat take her tongue...*

*I am also a woman who knows discretion is the better part of valor ☺*

*Nice...Touché*

*Oh points, counselor! One of my favorite repartees. Used it in Book #1, in fact. One of my favorite scenes. It's called building sexual tension in the romance biz... I'm by the river. The tide's coming in.*

*Thought you would find my banter amusing ... lol I see ... interesting...Don't get yourself wet.*

*At least not that way...*

*My point exactly ☺*

*☺*

*Thought you would get the gist of what I was talking about. With you I did not have to drive the point home ☺*

*That can be rather pleasurable however, driving the right point home*

*Understood...however there are several ways to get a point across. It all depends on what area or areas you wish to concentrate your efforts on ☺*

*Very true. But the most bang for your buck is usually a good choice.*

*I am a man that likes to cover all my bases...Not spreading myself too thin but covering all the bases...*

*That'll work too. But sometimes you gotta swing for the fences. Ok I think I've exhausted my baseball analogy repertoire now...*

We ended up speaking for a couple of hours more, the topic departed baseball sex parallels to end up upon my family background and ancestors. He started a family tree for me. I found out my Russian great-grandparents' names and the fact my maternal grandfather had served in WWI. I had asked him previously if he had suggestions for a day trip. I had considered driving to Lancaster to visit Amish country. He suggested instead going to the shore. I took it under advisement, and we called it a night. It was again past 1 am.

The next morning I was back on the computer, writing this chapter and perusing my potential partners *again.* Site #2 sends about 20 a day. I never thought I'd say this, but I prefer my original site. This second site doesn't indicate what time a message was sent or if it has been read. (Unless it's the green check mark to the left?) And I have a difficult time even pulling up old messages in order to keep track here for the chapter. (Yes, I know techno-idiot . . . monkey at the keyboard) I wrote only one other after the Stalker Doctor episode. I was trying to be a good little almost sixty-year-old dater and look for men my age. One gentleman with a gray brush-cut type hair cut looked really good in a white dinner jacket and black tie. I told him so. He responded (imagine that!) and suggested meeting casually the next time I was in NYC. I didn't plan to be and so wrote back, suggesting we might meet halfway. He wrote again, (shocker!) asked about my family and suggested the Jersey shore. Then he asked, "Can you at least text?" He provided his number.

I'm not sure why, but it turned me off. I ignored his request and answered his question about my sons. I also ignored the shore suggestion. He wrote back again and asked if I wanted "to come for nyc fun? Jersey shore?" Once more he said it was best to text him. I looked at his profile again. He seemed older than before and is really into Argentine tango. I'd love to learn and like watching it, but I just couldn't see the two of us in step. A four hour round trip drive to meet a stranger for lunch would just be a waste of gas.

Meanwhile back at Site #1 there had been a little action—of sorts. After not having been looked at for over a week, my profile had suddenly garnered 20 viewers, including the baseball-innuendo loving lawyer. Of course the vast majority of the other 19 lookers had done nothing more than look. One had, however, actually written. He stated outright that he knew he exceeded my age requirement, but after viewing my photos and profile he'd had a strong sense we matched up well. He went on to state how difficult it is to meet someone with like interests and values. He invited me to read his profile and, if I was interested, perhaps we could talk and learn more about one another and hopefully meet for lunch or just coffee. His email was well written and articulate.

Of course I looked at his profile. He is a 67-year old widower. Alright looking, but no fireworks, to be sure. And his age was such a turn-off. Yes, I know. Shallow, judgmental, unrealistic. I wrote and thanked him for the compliment and suggested we might try exchanging texts to see if we had anything in common beyond our profiles. I explained a bit about my family and told him I had a flight Saturday. He wrote back with another thoughtful, articulate email, providing further information about himself and his family. This time he provided his cell number with the hope we might talk again through email or text. I was torn and decided to not reply immediately.

Apparently Mr. Baseball was similarly torn and/or having second thoughts. That third night I didn't hear from him. I figured it was a good thing, to take a breather. I had looked at his profile again and had had mixed feelings. He definitely was not my physical type. I needed to decide. And so did he. A seventeen year age gap is a wide one—especially if there has been no physical in the flesh fireworks. Phone flirting just ain't the same. A seventh inning stretch was in order.

To keep the baseball theme going . . . By writing me back and engaging in an exchange of emails he had merely separated himself from the other bench-sitters. But once we started texting offsite, he left the dugout entirely. Two evenings in a row of loooong phone calls had then served to put him right square in the on-deck circle. As far as I was concerned, the word play and dropped hints had actually moved him from on-deck to at bat. I figured the next couple days would tell how he did in the box. Would he step up to the plate and take a swing? Would he ask me out?

Friday came and went with again no contact. So did Saturday. Now it's Sunday. A blind ump could call this one. Striiike three! Go figure. Mr. Baseball was the one at the plate, but I'm the one who struck out? I think he either lost his nerve or found his sense. Either way, I'm actually good with how it went. I never liked baseball anyway. Besides, I got a family tree out of it.

# Chapter Seventeen
## Month 3—Mirror, Mirror

In May 2016, *New York Post's* Stephanie Faris posted an article detailing the worst things a man can put in his online dating profile. Based upon her interview with April Masini, a New York City-based relationship expert and psychotherapist, Ms. Faris contends that the top three phrases women most hate to read are:

1. *no drama* (an implication that he wants no baggage, no history, no issues, i.e. a clean slate; women interpret this as "Be perfect or move on.")
2. *looking for someone physically fit* (infers he's shallow, plus it triggers every woman's insecurities about her body image)
3. *I enjoy kissing, hugging and touching* (an instant hook-up alert, suggesting he's only looking for sex)

Other so-called experts have weighed in with other so-called "deal breakers." Use of the word "sorry," sounding desperate, complaints in general and negativity in particular, and all reference to the "stigma" of online dating are supposed "no-nos." Another no-no is any reference to sex. (See # 3 above.) In fact, according to Ms. Faris' article, the word "cuddle" gets 48% fewer responses than a comparable profile that omits the word. (I knew I wasn't the only one that cringed every time it appeared!) Time and time again professional profile writers (yes, they exist!) stress the need for correct spelling and grammar as women report the lack thereof to be one of their biggest complaints.

Apparently text message abbreviations are also an issue. But I think this is a generational problem. With the exception of "lol" I've not seen a single text truncation from a 50-60-year old.

Whether for a fee or free, hints for success are not hard to find. Avoid discussing the past and come across as confident, playful, interesting and fun are the most commonly cited suggestions for men. (I might also add here: *do not come across as cheap*—even if you are. True example . . . This description of his ideal mate was lifted from the profile of one of my proposed matches, a 62-year-old claiming to earn 75-100K, ". . . we both bring income to support our flow of when and where[sic] ever we go . . . don't need the earthly trappings to define your-self [sic].") For women, spunk and sarcasm are good things, but coming across as too sophisticated will derail most men's interest. Or so the experts claim.

But once again I feel I should quantify a simple fact. Most of what is written and/or researched about online dating is *general*, one size fits all. I strongly contend (perhaps incorrectly) that generational dissimilarities might produce different results. What works for—or turns off—a 20-30-year-old dater may not have the same effect on a 50-60-year-old. Two cases in point . . . The *only* reason I initiated contact with Al Gomer was because I *liked* his line about how online dating was an "oddly uncomfortable" process. And 43-year-old Mr. Baseball made a point of telling me my *de rigueur* selfie comment made him laugh.

Regardless, I think most would agree the following is a perfect example of what *not* to do. Mr. No Doubt Wondering Why He Can't get a Date is a 59-year-old retiree who describes himself as down to earth with "realistic expectations." (So far so good) He states he is looking for a woman 50-60 (reasonable) who "should look good in a swim suit." (Ouch!) He prefers "a slim, slender or average woman" who is "affectionate, caring and love [sic] to make love." (Double ouch!) To his credit he then adds an aside in parentheses stating he is just being honest. His one wish would be to have the love of his life and best friend (whom he names by name) back in his arms. Apparently his wife of 30+ years has Alzheimer's, and "as her life has ended," he's looking "to move on to the second half of his life" and hopes "with god's blessing to find his next life partner."

Sad, really. But seriously? Ladies, are you going to sign up for that gig? I, for one, do not want to compete with a dead spouse ghost—much less one still living. He's in reasonably good shape for his age, bald (as nearly all at this age seem to be) and not really an immediate turn-off. Except for his profile. Maybe he's trying to be honest, and I can give him credit for that. But to hang all of it out there? Some shirts and socks and sheets, okay. But what he clothes-pinned on the laundry line was some pretty intimate apparel. I saw skivvies with streak marks that hadn't come out in the wash. Maybe there's a woman out there willing to give it a try with elbow grease and a good stain-fighter. But it ain't I.

New topic. I am halfway through this experiment experience. If nothing else, it has been entertaining. Working on this treatise/memoir has filled idle hours and re-ignited my love of writing. I've actually learned a lot, and not just about the online dating industry. I've learned a lot about myself. Some of it good and some not so good. (The next chapter will delve into my flawed character in more detail.) Truly, before I started this, I would have never imagined to where some legs of this dot com journey would lead.

I've reached a level of self-awareness, personal honesty and physical intimacy with absolute strangers *I've never laid eyes on* deeper than anything I could have ever believed possible. Indeed, had I been told beforehand that some of what I've experienced, said and done would occur,

I would have called you bat-sh*t crazy. This *über* honesty is a phenomenon that exists uniquely in virtual reality as opposed to actual. Entire books have been written on the subject. But the bottom line is this: People will type and reveal online or in a text what they would *never* expose otherwise.

Conversely however, this process of interacting solely from photos and paragraphs and voices on the phone also acts to nullify each participant's humanity. The person at the other end of the email, text or cell is not a real person. He or she is a user ID or a number, one of 20 (or more) photos we might look at in a day. And we act accordingly—inhumanely and crassly. We are deleting an *email*, ignoring a *text*, dismissing an *outreach*, opting not to respond to a *message* or letting a *voice* go to voice mail. In other words, we are not dealing with a *person*. Except we are. At the other end of that text, email, voice message, wink, smile, thumbs up (or whatever) is a living, breathing, feeling individual.

I'm not saying that in order to preserve our humanity we should therefore respond to every outreach and feign interest where there is none. But I am saying we need to remember action has consequence. Websites and dating apps have made us think of one another not as people but as profiles—pictures to swipe or ex-out or vote no on and paragraphs to dissect and critique. I am as guilty or even more so. I've written pages and pages here poking fun at lonely men who can't spell or fail to meet my appearance, education, income or age requirements, men who are mourning lost loves, men merely looking for companionship. But online dating has made me see them not as men, but rather as men-u. They are items on a *carte du jour* to choose—or not. After all, the Chicken Piccata doesn't care if I opt for the Steak Milanese instead. Nor will the free sample of tonight's featured Shiraz be hurt or offended if I ignore its special price and still order my favorite Malbec.

For the purpose of this chapter I am not going to berate myself—or anyone else—for ignoring someone's initial outreach. A wink, a like, a fav, even an email is no different than a wolf whistle. Flattering sometimes, but sometimes just an annoyance, an expression of unwanted attention best to ignore. My issue here is when the initial contact *is* returned and then later, whether after a couple of exchanged emails, several phone calls, an actual face to face meeting or even several dates, one of the two people involved simply disappears. There is a term for it in online dating—actually two: ghosting or fading. Everything seems to be progressing nicely—and then POOF! The person is gone. They no longer respond to texts, calls, messages. It's like they never existed. Obviously the reason is clear. They've lost interest and have moved on—leaving hurt feelings and confusion as to what went wrong.

It's happened to me multiple times and at each end of the online dating spectrum. I've exchanged a series of emails or texts with a guy and everything seems to be fine. He has even perhaps indicated we should meet. And then suddenly I never hear another word. The best (worst) example was *derek425*, 58. He wrote me first. Judge for yourself and see if you can determine where it (I) went wrong.

> *Strong profile...nice and beautiful pics...your[sic] very beautiful, just thought i would let you know*

> *Thank you for the kind words. They were a wonderful compliment. Judith*

> *Your[sic]welcome...Judith...great name too...a rare Judith... i like*

154

*Thank you:) curious. Where was the photo taken with the lilies in the wall vase? Nice photo, by the way*

*Thank you! It was taken at the XXX Resort in XXXXXXXX this past winter. i grew up in Philly but moved out to Lancaster county 30 yrs ago. live right in the heart of amish country. Love the city as well but prefer the beauty and ease of living out in open spaces*

*I am an Arizona transplant to Philly since Sept. (flight attendant for US Airways) I transferred bases 3 years ago to do international and couldn't take the commute from Phx any longer. Originally east coast born. I've returned to my roots lol. I hated the desert for 36 yrs. I would love to see the Amish country. It's definitely on my short to-do list.*

*That's funny...I considered retiring to the southwest, never been there...maybe i should talk to you first, lol, going to my daughter's college graduation this morning, hope we can talk more*

*Congratulations, dad! Have a wonderful time.*

And that (as the cartoon says) was all, folks. He didn't write back and I didn't either. It didn't matter a whole hell of a lot. It wasn't like we'd slept together or anything . . .

*That* would be Z . . . one night he is over after work, showering at my place and sipping ginger ale on my couch.

155

Two days later his daily "Hi/Good morning/hello, sweetie" texts abruptly stop. Sure, he responds if I text him, but only minimally. For a week his responses get shorter and shorter, until finally, after another week passes, he simply doesn't respond any more at all. With no explanation he pulls a Casper. Believe me. *That* one hurt.

Maybe it was karmic payback. After all (minus the showering part and 700 exchanged texts and sexts—give or take) I'd done much the same to more than a couple men. A few times, as with the two from speed dating, I exchanged emails to be polite and then put them off with a "I'm going to be out of the country for a couple weeks" excuse, figuring it was a kinder kiss-off. Other times I would begin to correspond with someone I found initially interesting, but then when my interest waned or theirs waxed, I bailed. I faded. I disappeared. I ghosted. I ghosted the reporter, be sure. I just didn't know otherwise how to end it. In a way I feel guilty, but then I don't. He might not have deserved it, but he earned it.

Not so the case with a guy I really do still feel guilty about. I encountered him fairly early on. He was 61, seeking 45-65, a reasonable preference. He wrote me a very positive and articulate email, with good, thoughtful content and grammar well above average:

> *Hello! I really enjoyed the strength and confidence radiating from your profile. Like yourself I have family members who are active military as well as retired military. Thank you for your son's service. I invite you to visit my profile and I would enjoy hearing from you. David (nhrn)*

Honestly, it was one of the better emails I had received in six weeks. His profile was also good. He was well-traveled and college educated. But in the spirit of full disclosure, I did not want to pursue it because of his race. Nevertheless, I wrote him back and thanked him for his lovely email and the military service of his family.

He thanked me for taking the time to reply. He stated that said to him I was "a classy person," as a number of women whom he had encountered on the site "seemingly forgot the manners their parents taught them." He asked if I would like to continue our email chats and looked forward to hearing from me. He explained that he liked interesting people and not every encounter needs to "lead to romance." (In theory I absolutely agree. In practice, however, between a man and a woman, it usually is another matter. Still, I was willing to give it a shot.) I wrote back, and an exchange ensued.

After several very pleasant email back and forths, he asked if I would like to exchange phone numbers so we could text and chat sometime. He said he wasn't trying to be pushy, but was "really enjoying our 'e' conversations. I avoided the whole phone number comment and mentioned I would be heading to Frankfurt the next day. I really needed him to back off the wanting to exchange texting for calling. But he didn't.

> *Very nice to hear from you. I certainly understand how your schedule can work. You are an interesting person and I would enjoy talking with you. Let me know if/when you'd like to exchange phone numbers and we can set up a time to chat.*

I might have simply said I wasn't ready to go there, but instead I started to fade. I didn't reply for several days. When I did, I simply apologized for not replying sooner, reiterating I had been out of town. He responded, saying he understood. Again he wished me safe travels and said he looked forward to hearing from me soon. I never wrote again. Neither did he.

As I stated previously, I still feel guilty. I was afraid he would want to take it where I didn't. I told myself at the time I was being kinder, breaking it off before it went further. Even now, writing this, I think about writing him and apologizing. But to what end? To make myself feel better for being racist? (One of the many definitions of racism is the mere holding of an irrational bias, either toward or against, which leads one person to treat another differently for no reason other than their race.) I suppose I could argue again than a racial dating preference is not a racist one. But isn't it?

At the midway point I can't undo anything that has occurred. I can't make Al Gomer more appealing to me any more than I can reignite Z's interest. Those I have hurt, offended, angered, or snubbed shall remain so. The past is the past. All that I can do is to learn from it and move forward a better person. Now I said *better*—not *saint!* I'm not going to turn into Mother Theresa of the Convent of the Dot Com and dole out charity dates in the spirit of equality and brotherhood among all. I will continue to not respond to winks, favs, likes, smiles and messages from men I am uninterested in. But *if* I take the step of replying, the rules change. If and when I want to end it, I will say so. I have no doubt ghosting will still be in my future in the next three months. But I will be the ghostee. My Casper days are over. So . . . enough of the *mea culpas* (for now).

Before I conclude this chapter, I would like to offer a few random self-reflections and other realizations reached at this juncture in my journey:

- I don't want to play house or have sleepovers. (see below)
- The longer I am alone, the more I prefer it. (see above)

- Online matchmaking and online dating are not one in the same.
- I still want fireworks.
- Be nice, but be honest—especially with yourself.
- Know when it's time to call it done, and do it with courtesy toward the other.
- Everyone looks better with sunglasses on.

## Chapter Eighteen
## Week 14—"I Make Bird Houses"

While seeking, sifting and searching through literally hundreds of matches and partner proposals this week, I encountered a sentence that made me laugh. "I make bird houses," was what some guy had supplied as his answer to either the profile question concerning what he is passionate about or the activities he most enjoys. A 58-year-old carpenter, he had no photo posted—a good indication he was a free trawler. The rest of his profile was as short and simple as his opening line. "What could he not do without?" Answer: his kids, his health, his dog. The remainder of the site's proprietary personality test type questions remained blank with no responses at all.

No photo and no profile to speak of, on top of a statement like "I make bird houses" for fun . . . I didn't see how this guy was going to get much—if any—attention in the Dot Com Dating Realm. At least not from me. Sir Simple was merely that, SIMPLE. And as far from the sophisticated Dark Knight of my personal romance fantasy as any country bumpkin could be. I laughed again and clicked on to my next prospect. A construction contractor—doing duty in the same field as Sir Simple, but with a loftier title. He was tall and really not bad looking. A photo of him with a yellow Lab earned him a few more points. So, too, a third photo that indicated that even at 59, he had a chest and set of shoulders worth a second look. I wrote to him, logged off and proceeded with my day.

Funny thing though . . . I kept thinking about the carpenter. Not him *per se*, but rather his guileless, honest response: "I make bird houses." Four words. Subject, verb, object. The sentence could not be less complex—nor the man who wrote it probably. Yet he haunted me. Unpretentious, unrefined, uncomplicated. A good man, a common man, he loved his kids and dog. He worked with his hands. Salt of the earth. Yet I had judged him lacking and unworthy of my attention.

As the day went on, my discomfort grew. I could not get Sir Simple out of my mind. "I make bird houses" haunted me. As did my conscience. In all honesty . . . which one of us was the deficit individual? He (who was probably a better man than most who touted their many sports and multiple hobbies and divergent interests) or me—judgmental, snide, smug, condescending . . . And what the hell had *I* written? I read, knit and write. Whoo-hoo. Not any more exciting than making bird houses. And BTW, what kind of bird houses *did* he make? Simple, flea-market variety scrap wood, four-sided boxes beneath a pitched roof with a hole and a peg was what I had initially pictured. But maybe they were elaborate works of design craftsmanship and woodworking art? Yet I had instantly assumed the worst/the least and formed an opinion based upon the smallest information. Moreover, I had formulated from a drop of data an entire person whom I then proceeded to dismiss.

So much for the previous chapter's clarion call to kindness, compassion and courtesy!

However, in Chapter 17 I addressed more the issue of *behavior*. Whether it was a callous *action* (i.e. swiping, x-ing or no-ing based upon a split second glance at a photo and evaluation of appearance) or a crass *inaction* (i.e. abruptly ghosting some poor schmuck who suddenly started to bore or bother me), I was *doing* something that made me ashamed. Now, with Sir Simple the Birdman, I had sunk even lower. I was *thinking* in a manner that mortified me. And it bothered me—a lot.

I know I am a better person than that. I have always been proud of my inner self—the soft, mushy, sentimental, root for the underdog heart hidden (perhaps too well) beneath a strong and hard, necessary exterior shell. My own sons have called me The Ice Queen. And I am. When I need to be. And I make no apologies for it. Navigating the tragedies and trials of life is like being in a small boat tossed about on a tempest sea. While everyone else is hanging their heads over the side and puking, someone has to swallow down their own bile and hold the rudder to steady the course. My boys call it "going cold." I call it going on auto pilot. Do what needs to be done now—and fall apart later. But traversing a damn dating site is not dealing with disaster! So why was I now comporting myself like such a shallow, belittling bitch? It was time for some serious soul-searching . . .

I believe the answer may lie within both the concept and the process of online dating. Dot com sites and mobile apps have turned a very emotional action into a very mechanical reaction. When I was teaching high school English many, many years ago, we hammered home the 5 Universal Conflicts in literature: man vs man, man vs nature, man vs self, man vs God, man vs machine (technology). What we have here, ladies and gentlemen, is man vs machine. Ray Bradbury, George Orwell and Kurt Vonnegut (to name just a few) all wrote so-called science fiction stories set in a future wherein machines would steal our humanity and overtake mankind. In albeit an extreme sense and interpretation, this is what online dating has done.

Men and women have turned one another into inanimate commodities to be blithely swept and discarded. (Is it a coincidence that's the *actual* terminology used?) These are "profiles"—not people—therefore it's easy. No need or obligation to fuss with the common courtesies we practice person to person *in person*. And that—in the proverbial nutshell—is the problem with online dating: IT'S NOT IN PERSON. The practice of online dating is, in fact, so different from "in person" dating that the latter now has its own modern quantifier: "organic" dating. (This has nothing to do with pesticide-free, but rather with the dictionary definition of organic: of or related to living matter.) In other words, dating a real person in the real word as opposed to a virtual world.

In the real world action, reaction, behavior, words, humor, attitude, personality and just plain *chutzpah* all serve to *round* out the person who in a photo can't appear as anything but *flat*. I can give you a perfect example: the second guy I dated after moving to Philadelphia and our "meet" story:

It was early afternoon, a sunny crisp Sunday in November. (Picture fall foliage in gorgeous display.) I was sitting on a large rock, waiting for the bus. (The bus stop is actually located across the street, but there is no place to sit over there, and I had a good half hour to wait.) A pair of motorcycles roared up to the light and turned right. I paid no attention other than to be annoyed by the noise. A few minutes later a single motorcycle came thundering down the same street. But instead of turning at the intersection, as the first two had done, this one stopped. Its rider shouted to me over the engine: Did I need help?

Now granted, most people don't sit on a rock beside a busy highway. At least not wearing heels, hose and a tweed skirt. I'm sure I looked out of place. I had been to church, a good seven blocks away. (Hell, I had looked out of place *in* church! Question . . . When did people start wearing sweat pants and hoodies to Mass???!!! Answer . . . Obviously sometime after 1973 which was when I had stopped going.)

I told Easy Rider I was fine and waiting for the bus.

He gestured toward the back of his bike. "Hop on, I'll give you a lift."

*Not bloody damn likely,* was what I thought. What I said was a polite refusal, "No. Thank you. I'm fine."

"Come on," he goaded.

I stood up and indicated my pencil skirt and shouted over the noise. "I don't think so."

He turned off the engine and gestured me over.

I figured it was a busy intersection and a gas station was behind me. At least there'd be plenty of witnesses if he pulled a Hells Angels.

"Will you give me your number?" he asked, as I cautiously approached.

I laughed. "No."

"Why not?"

"Because I don't know you."

"Well, how about I take you out to lunch and you *can* get to know me?"

I had to give him credit for trying. Still, I shook my head. "I don't think so."

"Why not?"

"Again, I don't know you. You're a complete stranger."

"How are you supposed to get to know me if you won't go out with me?" He took off one of his gloves and extended his hand. "I'm Rob (nhrn)."

I shook his hand. "Judith."

"So where do you live, Judith?"

It isn't easy for me to be rude unless I'm pissed off. He was—or at least appeared to be—a nice enough guy. I didn't see harm in answering. He then told me where he lived, a town a couple towns over. (That's the way it is here. I swear, in two minutes you can go through five of them.) He told me he was headed home after participating in a fundraiser motorcycle ride for Mothers Against Drunk Driving. I figured that made him less an outlaw gang member and more a weekend road warrior. He then said they had done a ride the previous weekend for Toys for Tots. But as the weather would be getting cold, that would be it until spring. His bike would be going into his basement for the winter. I asked how in the world one could get a motorcycle down into a basement.

He laughed. "It's a pain in the ass. So . . . now I'm not a stranger. Let me buy you lunch. Do you know where CXXXXXXX is?" He named a sports bar walking distance from my house.

"Yes."

"So meet me there at 3."

I *really* had to give him credit for not giving up. Sunglasses, bandana, heavy Philly accent, blue collar to be sure. I knew he was younger. (And not all that great looking, if I'm being honest.) I shook my head and again said no.

"Why not? Just meet me there. We'll grab something to eat. You gotta eat."

"I'm too old for you."

"How do you know?"

"I know."

He looked me up and down. "How old are you?"

I wasn't going there. I deflected the question. "How old are *you*?"

"45."

"Yes. I'm too old."

"Age doesn't matter. You're sexy. Why do you think I turned around and came back? I told my buddy I was going back to ask you out. He said I was crazy."

I was flattered—and not. "So this actually is about you winning a bet or something?"

"Nah, this is about me asking you out."

As you know (because I earlier called him *the second guy I dated after moving to Philadelphia*), I did end up meeting him for lunch. We had a good time talking for a couple of hours. When he asked if I wanted to go do something, I felt comfortable enough to get in his truck. We went bowling. He then drove me home, didn't try anything and said he would really like to see me again. We dated for five months. Eventually it kind of just petered out. I was holding a line and had several flights scheduled and a couple of mini vacation getaways planned. I would be gone mid-March through April. The last time I saw him, he told me to call him when I got back to town. I said it wouldn't be until May. But when May came, I didn't call him.

Rob and I really didn't have much of anything in common. He was a truck driver. Not a problem per se. But the lack of any real substantive conversation between us was. Plus, we had stopped actually going out when we got together. He'd come over, and we'd walk to the pizza place down the street, order take-out and then go back and watch TV. It wasn't what I wanted. He wasn't what I wanted. It ran its course—for both of us—because he never called me either. I do have to admit though, he was a *great* kisser! And a pleasant couple/three times a month diversion. (Since it's now been well over two months since my last play date with Z, I do think once in a while about calling Rob. Anything is better than nothing. And better the devil you know, right?)

My point here in going down Memory Lane is this . . . had I only seen his photo or read his profile, I would have swiped "no." Hell, I saw him in person and still said "no." More than once, in fact. But he won me over. Yet without our initial "organic" interaction—me on a rock and him on a hog—there would have been no opportunity for him to change my opinion. That is the failing of online dating: It's not a person. It's a photo, a profile. A profile can't crack a joke or banter back or match wits. A photo can't refuse to take "no" for an answer. I say "no," and he's gone—a photo swiped left, not a human being swept aside.

Which brings me back to where this chapter started: ashamed of myself for my actions and now my thoughts, as well. I have been humbled by a bird house. So what do I do? What *can* I do? Really nothing—other than to remind myself always the photo or profile I'm looking at is someone's son, father, grandfather. Someone has loved him in the past and someone probably loves him now. All he wants is what I do . . . a someone who just might love him in the future, too.

# Chapter Nineteen
## Week 15—All Quiet on the Dating Front

If something doesn't happen soon, this is going to be the shortest chapter ever! You see, dear Reader, except for the informational/expository chapters (i.e. Chapters 8, 11 and 13—which require research and therefore take more time to compose, edit and fact-check) I am writing this in "real time." I am totally reliant on something occurring on my dating front in order to have material that can be turned into a chapter. But I have hit a wall. The concept basket is empty. The idea bulb has burned out. Week 15 will end in three days. I have next to nothing to write about. But here is what I *do* have ...

- The faces are *seriously* starting to all look alike. I swear I have not only seen these men before as repeat offenders and recycled matches on their respective sites—but now they seem to be cross-pollenating— appearing on the other site.
- Whether they are or not, they remain by far (and in large quantities) unattractive to me. It's rather amusing actually, to pull up the list of men who have either viewed, liked, smiled, winked, faved or written me—and then compare it to those I have in some way contacted. Beauty and the Beast . . . Care to go out on a limb and guess who is who?
- Speaking of my efforts at contacting those few, those very damn few (apologies to Mr. Shakespeare and his St Crispin's speech) who interest me . . . a few terms come to mind: An exercise in futility . . . much ado about nothing . . . there is no fool like an old fool. Except not every guy I've reached out

to *is* younger than I. They range in age from 45-61. I'm not sure what is worse:

1. To note that right after my message was read, my profile was viewed without subsequent response. Which means rejection any way you try to spin it.

2. To still have over half of the messages I have sent in the last two weeks remain unread. Which leads to suspicions of site seeding and/or photo plants. (I actually had a guy write me this week to inquire if I had, in fact, asked for his photo or was the site "drumming up business?" FYI . . . I *hadn't* asked. Hummmm . . .)

- Another annoyance besides unread emails are the profiles that wink, smile or even contact me, but when I try to respond, are suddenly "hidden" or disappeared entirely. I had one guy, actually good-looking, (salt and pepper hair—a Jeff Chandler type [LOVED him!]) send me a photo like *and* a wink. But when I attempted to respond literally minutes later, he was an "Oops! The profile you are seeking is unavailable at this time." WTF!
- Still under the annoyance heading . . . I tried to online chat with someone who had just viewed my profile. But I couldn't figure out

how. After I typed my message, I couldn't find a send button, so I gave up. (Yes. Techno idiot, I know.)

- Just as an observation . . . Site #2 is sending more and more photo-less "Partner Proposals." I guess they've run out of paying members to send me.

- Despite my *truly sincerely meant* intent to be kinder and less judgmental and superficial, I am having trouble dialing back my cringe-o-meter/opinion-ator—which apparently doesn't come with an on/off switch after all, much less a dimmer slide . . . Seriously, some of this sh*t just begs to be mocked!

  - ❖ a 5'7," high school educated, heavy-set, 64-year-old widower looking for chemistry?
  - ❖ a 67-year-old retiree looking for fun, but who is "not a paying member, so {I'm} going to have to be inventive to pass {him} some helpful info." The full-of-himself skinflint then has the stones to ask, "Just how resourceful are you?" *Oh, I'm plenty resourceful, cheap-ass. I'm just not one damned bit interested!*
  - ❖ a 58-year-old architect who says he wants

children at some point. Really? (I realize it's a personal choice, but I think about that kid with a 70-year-old father cheering at the Little League games. When his friends have grandfathers who are younger than that, it just seems like a selfish choice to me.)

❖ and finally (for now— because as sure as God made little green apples, there will be more) one guy's stated wish, were he to be granted just one: "Health and Wealth for my DNA offspring" (Seriously, is it me? Or is that *not* bizarre? And is there any other kind of offspring save DNA?)

❖ Speaking of bizarre . . . what would possess a guy to post his decades-old wedding photo as his profile pic on a dating site???

❖ And to conclude this list with a bang (pun absolutely intended!), I give you (drum roll, please) THE WORST BY FAR USERNAME YET: "pussyman4356." Now I ask you, where the eff were the site oversight police for that one!!!???

BTW . . . during this week of little new activity, I had plenty of time to vacillate over what to do about the old(er) guy who had contacted me a week or so ago. He initially wrote, explaining that he was new to the whole online dating thing, so he probably didn't know the correct protocol. But he had read my profile and wanted to respond. If you recall, he said he knew he was out of my stated age range preference, nevertheless, he felt that we matched extremely well—at least on paper. He had paid me a few nice compliments and reiterated how difficult it was to gauge a person's values and compatibility from a few paragraphs. He had invited me to read his profile and provided a contact number. To refresh your memory . . . he was 67 and a semi-retired widower.

Please know, I have seriously paraphrased his email here. In truth, it was several lengthy paragraphs long. All were well written and articulate. If either his age or looks had appealed, I could have easily overlooked the one that didn't. Still, I was entering my new-found kumbaya/kinder, gentler dater mode (See previous two chapters.) and so I wrote back. I thanked him for the compliments. I mentioned a couple of details from his profile and asked about a background detail in one of his photos. We exchanged a couple more emails, friendly and casual, in which he repeated that he hoped we might speak by phone and meet in person. I was scheduled to work three flights over the next week and a half which gave me an excuse to put his invitation off.

Now with those flights flown, the pretext has passed. I need to make a decision. On the one hand, I see no point in even starting anything. I cannot see myself with a man that old. Of course on the other, I have to ask myself what happened to my resolve to treat people like people? Just ignoring him isn't right. In the end, I decided to be honest. I wrote him and told him I really wasn't sure about the age difference. But perhaps we could see how it went after a phone call next week. (A part of me hoped he had moved on and he would now blow me off. I certainly wouldn't blame him if he did.)

The next day activity finally struck. While doing my usual morning email inbox delete-a-thon, I came across a message from Site #2. Apparently (because they now proceed to tell me so) they consider my "safety" while using their site one of their "primary concerns." In their email they go on to inform me that they *check each profile by hand at registration in order to protect {me} from users with dishonest or deceitful intention.* Oh, and they also *use some of the most sophisticated automated technologies* to catch these individuals. They further explain that *fake profiles created by scammers are an unfortunate reality of the online dating world, [and while] some of their less scrupulous competitors don't tell [their users] about them,* they are different (and better, no doubt). They *believe in full transparency.* Eventually, the email gets to its point. *"Regrettably such a user has been in contact with you. To counteract this, our fraud team has taken appropriate measures regarding this member, Axxxxxxxz, 54, from New York."* Next the email tells me *don't worry too much . . . provided you have not given them banking details or passwords, you should be fine.* They do however recommend I *cease all contact with this individual and do not disclose any personal or sensitive information.* (Duh!)

I know for a fact I didn't contact *Axxxxxxxz, 54, from New York.* He was blond and too short. I do remember him though. I went back to his profile a couple times, because he kept viewing mine. I'm also pretty sure he was the one who I thought seemed almost *too* interested—he had liked a couple of photos *and* sent a smile. But he wasn't my type. (Note to scammers . . . next time go darker and taller.)

Later in the morning after several cups of coffee, a peek at the news and watering my plants (Yes, my life is exciting.) I went back online to Site #1. I clicked on a couple of different links and soon realized I had found a new time-suck: a whole new means to trawl for viable matches. I call it the *Mohammed Method* (as in the Turkish proverb, if the mountain won't come to you . . . )

The method is simple to use. If you are on my site, go to the main menu and look for "search." Clicking will bring up three options. One is an additional link for a username search, which I have frequently used. One is a community search (if one wants to find someone who likes the same sports team, or such), which I have never used. Then there is a "Go Search" link. Click here and a variety of search options appear, including "age." (Since "good-looking," "smarter than a bread box" or "able to get it and keep it up without a little blue pill" were not available choices, I choose age.) After imputing my preference parameters, up popped a page full of profiles, about 2/3 with photos, all with ages and hometowns. Cool! Why wait for the site to send me matches? Or wait for someone to wink or write? I had the entire catalog available (within a 50 mile radius) right on my computer screen.

I went through 50 pages, 24 profiles a page. (Do the math if you're curious). It took a couple of hours. (There were still probably 30 more pages to click on, but I was over it by then.) Any one I was even vaguely attracted to, I looked at their profile. They ranged in age from 42-60, but most who caught my eye were mid to late 40's (surprise surprise). Most of these were looking for same age or younger. Some were willing to go a little older to 55. And some were going in the opposite direction. One 59-year-old was seeking 35. (Your choice, *hernyguy4u*. I'm not judging. Just saying . . . )

So out of the hundreds I looked at, I felt interested enough in them (or thought I was a viable enough option for them) to write to only eight. Within an hour, four of the eight had read my email. Three of that four had then proceeded to view me. (The fourth looked at my profile later that day.) Of the three who almost immediately looked at my profile, one actually responded. I hadn't been all the impressed with his looks, but had written to compliment his profile. It was short, but sincere. What truly had gotten to me though was the fact he trains dogs. In his email response it was also clear he had also bothered to read my profile—or at least the photo captions—as he cryptically indicated we shared a pretty serious commonality in regards to our children. He then said he had to ask . . . "the smoking is generally a stop do not go criteria but {I} seem very interesting." He signed off with his name. (The same first name as my late ex. Talk about a stop do not go criteria for me!)

Nonetheless, I wrote back and asked an equally cryptic question about what I thought we shared. I also told him I didn't think my smoking was an issue. (In an effort to be honest in my profile, I had chosen "trying to quit" over "no way" as a response to the smoking question.) I told Mr. No Smoking Allowed I had quit for 20 years before a personal tragedy a year ago had caused a relapse. I now go months and months without, and though I still occasionally relapse with a couple, I had been "clean" for over two weeks. (The absolute truth at the time I wrote him. But I've since weakened and have had two over wine and conversation with a similarly addicted girlfriend.) He promptly wrote back and said since I was "so cute," he would "make an exception." He provided his phone number, along with an invitation to talk further.

It might have been that thing about our children. I'm not sure . . . whatever it was, I did something I have never done before after just one or two emails. I called. I got a recording, some canned business spiel ala: "We are not here at the moment, but if you leave your number and a brief message, someone will return your call." I figured I'd been played and hung up. Almost instantly my cell rang. A male voice identified himself as the company I had just called. Could he help me? I said I was looking for Nick (nhrn), to which the speaker replied, "Jamada?"

We spoke for 30 minutes. I liked his voice. He was educated and sounded pretty normal. He asked how I was liking the site. I laughed. Loud. Long. We proceeded to share horror stories. At 59, he said he was getting a lot of contact from women who looked *much* older. (His emphasis, not mine.) He also told me that in his experience neither gender owns the market on mendacity. The lies women perpetuate about their ages are just as pervasive as those men tell. Not unsurprisingly, honesty is a big thing with him.

He is not alone. The lack thereof is probably the most frequently mentioned complaint about online daters. As far as online dating itself, as I have previously stated, superficiality is the biggest complaint. (Gee, could the two be somehow related?) A not too distant second is the time-suck factor.

Mr. No Smoking Allowed told me one woman he had been talking to claimed to get 15-20 emails a day. When he tried to ask her out for coffee or lunch, she said she had to get her calendar. She's booked out for the next 10 days! When he asked her if that wasn't a bit overwhelming, she told him she's having the time of her life. Because he had no desire to be yet another entry in her social calendar, he told her he wasn't interested to continue. (Or so he said he said.)

Curious as hell, I asked how old she is. I figured 40s. Nope, 54. (*Clearly* I am doing something *wrong!*) I asked him outright if she was drop-dead gorgeous. He said her face was pretty enough, but guys truly look at body type first. Most want slim, slender or average, he said. Since I do fit that mold—yet am lucky to get 3 emails a week—I felt compelled to ask what he thought I was doing wrong. (I really think it's my profile. It's too blunt.) He said my photo was good and that I have a "cute face." That being a word I have rarely—if ever—heard to describe me (and certainly one I've personally *never* used to describe myself), I challenged his choice of "cute." Alright "attractive," he corrected. He said he thought my stated age preference was the deal breaker. The 42-60 range was rather wide and might be interpreted by a man to indicate I was really interested in something else. (That should have helped me, I thought, not hurt me.)

His insight into the male online dater continued. He said most guys were not really looking for a relationship, despite what they write. "It's a video-game," he said. (Duh!)

I had reached (and written here) pretty much the same impression early on. The only difference in my opinion now is that I'm pretty certain they play it on Friday nights. This past week I had 2 profile views the entire week—but on Friday night my numbers soared to 17. Of course, Friday morning I had also been utilizing my new "Mohammed" search method. (Remember . . . when you look at them, you will appear in their "who has viewed me" list. Human nature is human nature—regardless of gender. Man or woman, we can't help the urge to go see who has looked at us.)

I told Mr. NSA I appreciated his honest opinion. As he claimed to have a business appointment, we said our good-byes with a tentative plan to maybe meet Monday for lunch. (See the next chapter for further details.)

BTW . . . I forgot to mention . . . At the beginning of the week (after a 4 day no-show/no-call absence), Mr. Baseball apparently found my phone number again. He not only called, he stepped back up to the plate. This time he actually swung (more like whiffed). He asked when we were going to get together for a glass of wine. I had a Cancun overnight with my "trying to quit too" girlfriend planned for the weekend. (She was working the flight. I was just tagging along for the free flight and hotel room.) If I then didn't get a flight Monday or Tuesday, I had planned to go back to Phoenix to see my grandson for his birthday. That visit might or might not have extended over the following weekend. So Mr. Baseball and I "penciled" in a Saturday in two weeks' time. (You must read further to learn whether he swung again. Spoiler alert . . . any fan of the game knows there are only three possible outcomes for a batter in the box:  1) to miss totally 2) solidly connect or 3) manage to get a piece—of *THE BALL*. ☺

## Chapter Twenty
## Week 16—Fishy, Fishy

With tens of millions of people online looking for love, the opportunity to make money off another person's loneliness is an irresistible temptation to con artists. And the money being stolen is not unsubstantial. In 2014 alone, according to an online article from *Huffington Post*, romance scammers swindled over $86 million from their victims. And that was only in the US—and only from the nearly 6000 poor suckers who actually reported being scammed! The numbers are surely higher.

Ladies, beware. Most experts agree *women in the 50-70 age range are the most susceptible* group to fall victim to an internet dating site scam or fraud. As a rule, we are financially more secure than our decades-younger sisters. (No point in shaking a bare money tree.) We can also be more emotionally vulnerable. Many women this age looking for love online are widows. Often that widowhood was preceded by a long illness, during which she may have been the sole caregiver. She wants—and deservedly feels—it should be her time now to enjoy life. Divorcees, who often may have sacrificed their career, identity and freedom for the sake of keeping the family together and raising children, can experience this same desire. The kids are grown, off living their own lives, the ex may have already upgraded to a newer model . . . so why not make it now about *me*?

Whether widow or divorcee, she is a sponge, laden with holes of hurt and dry in every meaning, eager—nay desperate—to soak up male kindness and attention. It therefore comes as no surprise the men scamming this age group nearly always present themselves as younger and extremely good-looking. (They use magazine photos or images lifted from the internet or other social media sources.) She hasn't "dated" or received attention from a man other than her husband for decades. This is new and exciting and intoxicating. And just like alcohol, the euphoria can dull good sense and elicit reckless behavior she would never ordinarily engage in. Again . . . this is *all part of the thrill* and it *can become addicting.* Heady stuff—feeling desired by a younger, handsome man—who seems to know how to say or write all the right things. (They know because they have made an art form of it.) In fact, emails and/or texting are their preferred *modus operandi* because (PAY ATTENTION now) the written word lends itself to a stronger connection than verbal interaction. There is no wondering what he said or forgetting the smallest detail. She can go back and read and reread their exchanges. Pull them apart, examine every word for every nuance. Again and again. Remember . . . sheer repetition implants it deeper—it's why rote memorization can last a lifetime.

BTW . . . men are no less vulnerable. Some would, in fact, say they are more so. (Not to be vulgar, but it's called POP [power of the pussy] for a reason.) Look at the number of famous and powerful men brought down by a pretty younger woman who demonstrated sexual interest. David Patraeus, anyone? In the world of online dating scams and frauds the most common players are 18-30 women targeting men 50-70 and 30-40 men targeting 50-70 women.

Asking for money from someone whom a con artist has befriended or purports to have fallen in love with is not a new scam. Women (and men) pen-paling with prisoners have fallen for this for as long as pen pals and prisons have been around, I would imagine. Online dating just opens up a broader sucker base. It's all about the numbers, after all. One of my sites actually provides a cover-their-ass disclaimer that pops up at the end of every email I send or receive. It warns not to provide credit card info or to send money to anyone I have met on the site. (Ya think?) Two of the biggest and most well-known of the romance scams are the so-called **Sweetheart Swindle** and the **Catfish Fraud.** Ironically, the latter isn't always about money, however. Nor do *Catfish Frauds* only reel in the over 50 Depends and denture crowd.

The term *catfish* or the action of *catfishing* are popularly thought to have been coined in 2010, when a New York City man went to Michigan to meet the 19-year-old woman he had been having an internet relationship with—only to discover she was in reality a married (and I shall assume bored and lonely) 40-year-old housewife. A popular MTV television series soon followed, wherein a couple of guys traveled around the country exposing similar deceptions. The most famous incident of catfishing occurred in 2012, when a Notre Dame football player spent his entire season openly mourning the death of his girlfriend—who never existed. Talk about a humiliation played out in the public eye!

In truth, no one really knows how the terms were coined. (There are a couple of stories and theories, including a Christian parable and an urban myth about shipping catfish with cod in order to keep the cod active in transport thereby preventing mushy and tasteless fish flesh.) The point remains however, that today the words are less likely to refer to a bottom feeder fish with whiskers, as to someone, not only pretending to be someone else more attractive and exciting, but actually deceiving another into believing the make-believe.

In a January 2016 article, *Washington Post* writer Ellen McCarthy called catfishing "a uniquely modern phenomenon . . . a lie enabled by the cloak of technology." (Good phrasing, Ellen!) Experts think there are two answers as to why someone would "catfish" another. In some instances, the hoax is a sick joke, a power trip, a "can I do this?" challenge. But in other cases, it's thought that the perpetrators are not actually acting with malicious intent. They simply believe that as they really are, they are not good enough to find love. Ergo the made-up personas, names and identities, whereby they become more attractive, exciting and desirable to someone who might not otherwise be interested. It's rather sad, actually. For both parties: the person who can't find real love as is and the one who falls in love with what is not real.

One of my sons was catfished a couple of years ago. He met a girl through one of the biggest and most well-known of the online dating sites. She lived in another city, a few hours away. She was his type to a T—dark-haired, fit, smart and exotic. They seemed to have a lot in common as well, and their relationship quickly progressed to offsite texting and phone conversations. They planned to meet face to face when both were coincidentally arriving at the same airport on the same date. He waited hours for someone who never showed, meeting every flight that came in that day from the city she said she was coming in from. Calls to her went to voicemail. Texts went unanswered. He was actually worried something had happened to her—until he tried to contact her through the site. Her profile had disappeared. He began to get a clue. Then he got a phone call from someone claiming to be her sister. According to the "sister", Ms. T had been in a car accident on the way to the airport and the police had taken her cell phone, preventing her from calling him. (No one memorizes a phone number anymore!) He wanted to believe the story, but was suspicious. (Mama didn't raise no fool!) I happened to be flying into the city in which she was supposedly hospitalized. I told him to ask the sister which hospital and I would happily go visit her on his behalf. Funny thing. The "sister" hung up. Weeks later Ms. T's photo reappeared on the same dating site, but under a different username.

Ms. T never asked my son for money—but that's not to say it might not have evolved from a catfish fraud to a romance scam. Which brings us to the cons and swindles that *are* all about the Benjamins. *The Sweetheart Swindle* is pretty much as it sounds. A lonely, usually older, individual meets a younger, usually very attractive, person on line. Things progress quickly, and they fall in love. (Ahhhhhh. Cue the cupids, hearts and flowers.) It all seems like a fairy tale. The only fly in the proverbial ointment is that plans to *actually meet face to face* just never seem to work out. (Oh darn!) Hospitalizations, deployments, overseas travel, business meetings, last minute hiccups of some type or other *always* seem to suddenly crop up. Then TRAGEDY strikes. Car accidents, deaths and cancer are all frequent occurrences in the *Sweetheart Swindle*. Now Lover Boy or Sexy Susie strikes. They ask for financial help—a loan of course! And of course In Love Larry and Stars in Eyes Stella happily comply. These scams have swindled some individuals out of tens of thousands of dollars! Yes, love is blind. It's also deaf, dumb and STUPID.

Speaking of stupid, here's my favorite romance scam . . . It is far less publicized than the *Sweetheart Swindle* or the *Catfish Fraud*, therefore it is rather obscure. (It's my favorite because it's the one I would have fallen victim to, *if* the "U-C-K" Z had been after had started with a "B" instead of an "F.") I call it the **Intimate Extortion**. This money scam occurs when one half of a "dating" couple saves and uploads their supposed private texts and sexting conversations to a website that posts them for public viewing. The extortionist then threatens to also post his/her partner's photo, phone number and even their name unless they pay up. Now depending upon the level of kink contained in the texts, the victim's standing in society, church, the work force, etc. and whether they are married, this "outing" could be merely extremely embarrassing—or a real professional and/or public/private life disaster! The usual take from this scam is relatively small compared to other scams—a few hundred or maybe a thousand dollars. (On second thought . . . Considering what I have written in the previous nineteen chapters, my bar for embarrassment is pretty high. Z wouldn't have gotten a dime. And the exposure might have done my non-existent dating life some good!)

All joking now aside, romance scams, frauds and swindles net tens of millions of dollars a year. They have become so prevalent that the articles about them no longer appear only in the Life and Leisure pages or under an Arts and Entertainment heading. The "fluff" piece has become a "real" news story, landing in prominent business publications and mainstream magazines and newspapers. Even national law enforcement agencies have climbed on the bandwagon. *Money Watch* published an article in 2014, listing the most common warning signs of an online dating money scam. San Diego FBI agent Darrell Foxworth wrote a similar article a year earlier, in 2013. According to *Money Watch*'s Kathy Kristof and Agent Foxworth, these red flags are some of the *same red flags* I have warned against in previous chapters. (Who knew I was on to something?)

Not every red flag equates to a scam. But more than one from any of the eight listed below would certainly give me cause to question just who the hell I'm involving myself with.

1. Beware when the person you are corresponding with suddenly wants to begin communication off site via personal email or instant messaging, because they are leaving the site. The most common lines given are the hackneyed: "I'm leaving the site soon" or "My membership is about to expire."

2. Beware the instant "too good to be true" attraction. Effusive declarations and over-the-top statements of affection and soul-

based connection rarely occur in the real world. When they happen too quickly and in an over–the-top too much/too soon manner, it's not fate—it's fraud.

3. Beware even more the gross differences between you and Prince or Princess Charming, i.e. May/December age differences or the exceptionally attractive person going gaga over Mr. or Ms. Average on a Good Day. Cases in point: the 23-year-old woman and the 66-year-old man or the 59-year-old woman and the 31-year-old guy? Seriously, people? Be realistic.

4. Speaking of . . . watch out for slick, professional head shots, glamorous photos and/or pictures taken in exotic locales. Many are lifted from the internet without the real person's knowledge.

5. Traveling constantly is a cause for concern. Money fraud scammers often claim to have to travel for work, usually outside the U.S. Living abroad or claiming to be a foreign national are also common traits for this brand of con artist.

6. Look out for linguistic anomalies, vocabulary that is "off" or grammar that doesn't seem right given the person's supposed education, profession or background. Many of these scams originate overseas. (Hey, silver lining—at least the "foreign national" part is true.) Nigeria is known for them, in particular.

7. Excuses abound. He or she always has an explanation, a reason why you can't meet or why plans to visit don't work out. Even when it's been all arranged, some emergency or last minute work-related issue will arise and your long anticipated face to face will be yet again postponed.

8. Tragedy always strikes! Frantic requests for money ensue, following some kind of emergency or calamity. A stolen passport, automobile accident or ill family member are common misfortunes used. The person always has a reason why they are in need of funds *now*—frozen account, stolen wallet, a check that will clear any day. Usually the request for money is accompanied by the promise to pay it back in spades. (They may have actually even borrowed from you previously and paid you back, just so you will believe them when it comes time for the big score.)

Remember, flattery and attention lavished on vulnerable people is the scammer's *modus operandi.* One woman received flowers constantly from her online admirer. These bastards know what they are doing. They tap into loss and sorrow, longing and desire, and offer a too good to be true fairy tale.

FBI data confirms that the most *financially vulnerable*—and ergo the favorite target of money scammers—are women over 40, divorced or widowed. The most *emotionally vulnerable* are the overweight (or anyone who has had trouble dating in the off line world) and those recently single after a long relationship, especially if it ended with their partner dying after a protracted illness. Such marks are lonely and want desperately to believe someone has fallen for them for them—and not for how they look. Or they think fate has finally smiled. After having survived such a tragic loss, they are entitled to happiness, right? Wrong. Not from a person you know only from a photo.

The FBI has a website to report such scams. Ladies and gentlemen, use it: The FBI Internet Crime Complaint Center, https://www.ic3.gov. For the latest e-scams and warnings, you can also visit www.fbi.gov/scams-and-safety/on-the-internet.

# Chapter Twenty-one
## Month 4—My SMV Goes Up

Nearly two thirds now through this experience/experiment, my expectations—and even my purpose—have shifted once again. The idea of finding my soulmate was never a goal. One has to believe in such a thing. Ironically—or so I read somewhere—men believe in the concept of a soulmate more than women! (It's probably the same ingrained fantasy mentality that prompts a beer-bellied, snaggle-toothed redneck to wolf whistle at a cute college coed.) Self-professed romantic that I was at the onset of this journey down the dot com dating rabbit-hole, I never believed in *that* fairy tale. At least not for me.

I think I must have always been a cynic—even in my pre-birth, pre-body, only soul floating in the cosmos days. I'm not sure which line I was standing in (metaphysically speaking, of course) when they were handing out soulmates for the physical life to come, but I'm pretty sure I scoffed at the idea and went and stood in the Stubborn and Strength Queue instead. (I *do* know I somehow managed to miss the line for boobs and ended up going through the line for noses twice by mistake!)

So . . . four months ago when I signed up, I wasn't seeking a soulmate. I was seeking a companion and a lover. I've since realized, however, I may not actually need or even want a companion. And while I'm still very much in the market for a lover, I've begun to think I'm either shopping in the wrong store or it's an item that has unfortunately been discontinued. Whether or not it's a product that might come back on the market is a matter out of my control entirely. But since I really liked what I previously had, I filled out the request form to notify me if it ever comes back in stock. For now I'll continue to do without and wait, while hoping to find a different product that won't replace, but will suffice.

Which is what I'm doing now. Spurred by the need for material for this book, I've decided to suspend the search for tall, dark, young and handsome to fill the occasional night—and start looking for half-way decent, with a brain, who can pay and help fill nine remaining weeks of chapters. Funny. Once I had agreed to the substitution, the dot com dating store suddenly had available stock.

Week 16 started out with a bang. It might have still been the fallout from the Mohammed search, or my afore-mentioned agreement with the universe. But whatever the reason, material for this chapter was abundant. I had not only three ongoing relationships (and I use that word LOOSELY) to recount, but two brand-new ones.

Let me begin first by tying up several loose ends, starting with the 67-year-old widower. To recap . . . Mr. Nice Guy Too Old had really believed we matched on paper, but I had been put off by his age. Guilt and the desire to be a kinder online dater had compelled me to write after having pulled a week and a half Casper act. I apologized, reiterated my busy flying schedule as my excuse and finally fessed up to my real reluctance. I was not sure about the age thing. But if he wanted to still continue, I was game to try. I didn't hear back from him for several days. Relieved, I figured he had moved on. Then I received his reply.

He had "agonized" over whether to write me back. It seems in the interim, while I was trying to decide what to do, he had begun talking to another woman. Things had progressed to his "accepting a date" from her. And while he still believed he and I would be a good match and get along well together, he did not believe it was fair to any of us for him to date two women at the same time. And while he really did "wish we had been able to date earlier on," he felt he needed to see it through. He repeated I was a classy, down to earth, attractive woman, and he wished me and himself "the best of success in our journey for a mate/soulmate."

I was happy for him. He had seemed like a genuinely good guy, not right for me, but surely perfect for some other woman out there on our superficial, soulless site. I wrote back and sincerely wished him success with his new relationship.

Loose end #2 . . . Mr. Baseball disappeared again. I have heard nothing from him since the beginning of last week—despite a bikini pic sent from Cancun over the weekend. (Believe me, less racy than it sounds. I was on the beach with two other female flight attendants. One was wearing shorts, the other a mid-thigh cover-up and I had an ankle-length sarong tied around my hips. BTW and totally off topic . . . Cancun has some gorgeous powdery white sand beaches!) He knew I was going to be out of town till the beginning of next week—ergo our "penciled in" wine date two weekends hence, so I guess I have to give him a pass. Besides, I'm not invested. Although I have enjoyed our phone conversations, if I don't hear from him, I don't obsess. In fact, I don't much care either way. Which is a refreshing change. He remains an end still loose. For now.

As for my other so-called "penciled in" date with Mr. No Smoking Allowed . . . it didn't happen. We had left it rather open-ended. We'd be in touch Sunday evening or Monday morning to set a definite time and place (assuming I wasn't given a flight). I texted around 9am and asked if we were erasing or jotting down in ink. I didn't hear back until late afternoon. Mr. NSA claimed to have gotten caught up at work. He also claimed to have sent a text earlier that happened not to send for whatever reason. Whatever. As with Mr. Baseball, I didn't much care either way. Besides, I had woken up to ants all over my kitchen counter, and a trip for ant-killer spray had been far more pressing than a blind date/lunch date. He texted later that evening, apologizing again. He asked if I was still headed out of town for the rest of the week. As I was, we agreed to remain in touch and reschedule for some time next week. Another end still loose, I guess . . .

Sometime between texting Mr. NSA, running to Home Depot and staving off another ant invasion, I checked my inbox and found a message from Site # 2 informing me of yet another security breach. Word for word as their last email, this one differed only in the name of the scammer: PXXX, 50, from Yakima had been uncovered by their fraud team and their "sophisticated automated technologies" to be a fake profile—i.e. one of those "unfortunate realit[ies] of the online dating world." Once again, I had nothing to worry about though, unless I had given him sensitive information. Truthfully, I didn't remember this guy in the least. But really? Two in two weeks?

Speaking of two . . . two men found via the Mohammed Method have begun writing in earnest. The first to write—and ergo the first to be discussed now—was a 49-year-old professional musician seeking women 45-55. I initially wrote him because of the content and sarcasm in his profile paragraph. He decried the fact that women don't seem to want an old-fashioned man of strength and flaws. He called himself "a knight not white." Since I was beyond his desired age range, I wasn't really wanting or hoping to start anything. I just felt compelled to comment. I wrote and told him that as a former author of medieval romance novels, he could trust my opinion: The dark knight is always a more interesting character. He thanked me for the kind words, writing "these days most western women are confused or indifferent towards men that behave sincerely or manly." I wrote back that his reply was quite unexpected. "These days most western men seem not to possess either manners or common courtesy." I thanked him for having both. Rather a finite closing, I thought.

191

He wrote the next day. He told me he could be nice until he wasn't. He then proceeded to opine that some fault must lie perhaps with the frustrating dating scene:

> *Most men (me in particular), have learned that online dating is one sided; in other words, women that are a 5 or 6, on a scale of 1-10, receive as many suitors as women that are a 7 or above. This gives the average looking woman the impression that she has a higher sexual market value (SMV). The effects of this illusion becomes [sic] an addiction to attention, rendering the average woman into a vicious cycle of perpetually trading up. As far as the women that are seven and above...well, that's a whole other issue*

I wrote back, intrigued as hell by his perspective—which echoed nearly word for word the standpoint I had previously encountered (and recounted in Chapter 13). I told him he had my attention. Able to view this nonsense only from the female side, I had no idea as to the reverse (male) side of things. Of course I was also wondering where *I* fell on his scale. To which he replied:

> *I think it is obvious where you fall into the scale, darling. Of course, that could be my libido talking, but after all, the male libido is the crux of our perception of women.*

He asked how I'd like to "indulge my attention." I answered "with a name to start." He had me at a disadvantage. He knew mine. I also told him that as much as I'd love to continue our conversation, I was fading fast. I explained I had just flown in from Cancun. (I was also not in a mood to play sexual innuendo.) I said good night and signed off. I didn't hear from him the next day. The following I wrote a simple good morning message. I received no answer until that afternoon. He wrote he'd had a stressful day at work, apologized for his absence and said he would catch up with me sometime later that day. He didn't. Another end still loose?

As with my other loose ends, I don't much care. I think Sir Not White Knight is probably an arrogant ass, but he amuses me. He is articulate and free with his opinions, and I appreciate the look at the other side he provides. Besides, he gave me the title for this chapter.

Speaking of my SMV, the next guy to reinforce by action this week's inexplicable uptick I have named Traveler—for the abundance of travel and time spent overseas mentioned in his profile. I initially wrote referencing our shared common ground. My travel and overseas time was owing to an ex-military brat background. I asked him the cause for his. Bald, blue eyes, 52, with a demeanor I should have recognized immediately—but didn't, Traveler didn't reply for several days. I had written him off actually. Then out of the blue he wrote and asked how I was "an ex-military brat. Wouldn't [I] still be a military brat . . . ;)"

I was impressed as hell at his catch. I told him I stood corrected. And asked again the reason for his extensive travel background. He explained he had been in the military, but had grown up in the Philly area. I thanked him for his service and introduced myself. He asked if I had ever been to New Hope. I didn't know if it was a church or a town (and given the preponderance of men online touting their special relationship with God), I asked, explaining I was new to driving in the area and still very GPS dependent. I also asked again for his name. He laughed at his omission, gave it and then inquired what I had done before GPS. I answered:   Mapquest. Or I got lost and unlike most men asked for directions. But as I had been in the same area for 30 years, it hadn't been an issue. He wanted to know where it was I had been for 30 years. I explained I had transferred bases and moved from Phoenix. He wrote back, inquiring what I did, but then instantly sent a second follow-up email when he realized the answer for himself from one of my posted photos. It was past 10 pm, so I didn't write back. I waited instead until the next morning. I told him I had googled New Hope. It was definitely a place I'd like to explore.

At this point we were 16 or 17 emails into our correspondence. He asked if I would like to exchange numbers or was I wanting to communicate on site forever. I liked his style. A lot. I answered that I had just been waiting for him to ask. I was old school and believed the man should make the first move. I included my number. He texted almost immediately, saying that he was "old school too, but [had] learned to pace the request." I liked the answer. A lot. He asked if I was off all week. I explained the concept of being on call and said I was headed to Phoenix in the next couple days for my grandson's birthday. He said it was "a shame" we couldn't meet for a drink before I went. It was indeed, I wrote back, asking for a raincheck. He then wrote, informing me he was going to be "old school" and give me a call.

And he did. We spoke for quite a while. I liked him. A lot. Now in law enforcement, he was intelligent, well-spoken and well-read, with an interest in history— particularly biographies. Damn! He was suddenly hitting on a lot of cylinders! But I've learned nothing if not to not get my hopes up. Traveler explained he was working the night shift. My father had been a cop as well as my oldest son. I was—and am—very familiar with their shifts and schedules. He wished me a good trip and reiterated we would have to get together when I returned.

The next morning back on site in my email list for the purpose of transcribing correctly the emails from Sir Not White Knight, I noticed Traveler had changed his profile picture. He looked good in it. I tamped down my budding interest. He was shaping up to be too good to be true—and that NEVER works out for me. I made a photo comment on site. A little while later he texted and teased me about leaving the Philly humidity for the dry heat of Phoenix. We sent a few texts back and forth, and he thanked me for the compliment on his photo. I told him I had meant it. And left it at that. I needed to shower, pack and get ready to leave town for a few days. Traveler would—or wouldn't—be there when I got back.

Just as the week ended, I received an email contact from another guy located via the Mohammed Method. Truth be told, I was rather surprised to hear from this one. He was 49 and seeking 35-45. I'm not really sure why I even contacted him initially. Given his age preference, he was more than a dark horse and long shot. New to the whole thing, or so he claimed, he thanked me for writing. Tall, Hispanic, still in his 40s (and looking so), he definitely fit my physical type better than No Smoking Allowed (NSA), Not White Knight (NWK) and Traveler. Not one to look a gift horse (dark or otherwise) in the mouth, I wrote back and thanked him for replying, wishing him well. We exchanged a couple more emails, and then he asked if I would like to meet. I would. But as I was headed out of town, I wondered if we might plan something when I returned? Dark Horse agreed. He wished me a safe flight . . . with nary an inkling that he had just been put on the Loose Ends list.

# Chapter Twenty-two
## Week 17—Loose Ends & Safety Tips

This week began on a far higher note than usual. Shockingly, I was still in regular contact with four men located via the Mohammed Method, plus Mr. Baseball—an as yet unresolved holdout from Week 12. With five men on the proverbial dating hook, I was feeling optimistic. In fact, this was the most hopeful I'd been since Week 1 when I was a naïve online dating newbie. I figured the odds had to be in my favor. Five men . . . four of whom had actually asked me out and one who had expressed the interest to do so . . . how could it (I) go wrong? Despite a still deeply ingrained cynicism regarding this whole online dating process, I had turned a slight corner. I was starting to think it might actually be possible I could find a man I'd be interested in seeing more than once.

Pause here for an important side note:  Soulmate, fireworks, love at first sight—whatever the designation— I'm afraid I really do believe its occurrence—at least for me—is as improbable as an encounter with the Loch Ness Monster or Bigfoot. In fact, if there exists an actual list of urban legends and pop culture myths, I'm pretty sure my future mate is located alphabetically between The Jersey Devil and Nessie:

## <u>Characters of Myth, Urban Legend and Pop Culture</u>

- ❖ Adomidable Snowman
- ❖ Bigfoot
- ❖ Chupacabra
- ❖ Jersey Devil
- ❖ Judith's Boyfriend
- ❖ Loch Ness Monster
- ❖ Yeti

I realize this pessimism flies in the face of Oprah's "Visualize it, say it out loud, believe it will happen—and it will!" philosophy. But that's me. In 44 days from the day of this writing, I'll be turning 60. Paraphrasing the saying about elderly dogs . . . this is one old bitch not likely to change. But let's continue and start tying up those ends still loose from the last chapter.

Mid-way through the week, I conceded it was probably time to make the call on Mr. Baseball. Although we had penciled in a date for wine on the coming Saturday, he had been a no-show for over a week and a half. Still, I sent him a text, asking if he was still around. Given the hours we had spent on the phone, I felt invested enough to reach out one last time before issuing the final thumb's out. Not so the case with either No Smoking Allowed (NSA) or Not White Knight (NWK). With both it was definitely time to cut bait.

I had spoken only once by phone with NSA. As pleasant as the conversation had been—and despite an agreed upon a lunch date—he had bailed with a "caught up at work excuse." If true, I should have heard from him again. I hadn't. On day 7 of his disappearance I went outside and had a cigarette to fittingly mark NSA's exit. There is one hard and fast rule about men, ladies: If a guy is truly interested, *he will make the time.*

It had also been a week since I'd last heard from NWK. Following his apology text for disappearing, he'd vowed to be back in touch by the end of the day. He wasn't. Barring death, plague or war, my standard allowed grace period is 7-8 days. Fare thee well, Sir Knight. Your self-professed cloak of old-fashioned chivalry is a figment of your imagination. Like the Emperor with no clothes, you are bare-ass naked. And at a balding 49 years of age—trust me—it ain't much to look at. A second hard and fast rule, ladies: Only extremely good-looking men can typically and successfully pull off the arrogant asshole shtick.

In contrast to NSA and NWK and their Casper acts, Traveler maintained steady contact and we eventually we set up a definitive time and place to meet the next evening. The last of the loose ends, Dark Horse, was also still in the picture. As the saying goes, stay tuned here for further details . . .

But first a recap of my date with Traveler. Where do I start? Blow by blow—or should I just cut to the chase and issue now a proclamation summarizing my second online-generated outing with an utter stranger? Oh, hell! Why prolong the suspense?

It was a 100% improvement over the date with Al Gomer.

And yet still a waste of a pedicure and manicure and make-up.

But let's rewind . . . T earned major points remaining in contact throughout the day and informing me of when exactly he was leaving work. (Law enforcement does not typically lend itself to time-clock hours.) With further circumstances beyond his control (rush hour on one of Philadelphia's major traffic arteries) dictating his actual arrival time at our rendezvous site, he made a truly admirable effort to keep me apprised. He called me 20 minutes out, and I headed down the 10 minute straight stretch of highway that would take me to the casino where we would meet and have a drink. I was early and sat outside the main entrance to wait. He texted he was there and asked where was I? Under the red neon lights, I answered.

And so under that garish illumination it occurred— that all-important, all-determining (usually) moment of first sight . . . Of course, I have no idea what his initial impression of me was. I had dressed more casually than I had for my dinner date with Al Gomer. A drink at a casino didn't merit a full-out effort, in my opinion. Plus, I had just read a book on dating advice written by a professional matchmaker. She advises women to tone it down on the first date. (Her thinking is that a woman should leave room to kick it up a notch. Otherwise there's no "Wow! You look amazing!" moment for the future. It made perfect sense to me.) Given the heat and humidity I left my hair "natural." (Why bother with a curling iron when it would frizz and curl anyway?) I also broke one on my cardinal wardrobe rules: I wore a sleeveless black top. A go-to black skirt completed the look, along with black patent and cream wedge sandals. (Why let a brand-new pedi go to waste?)

I didn't see him approach. So I was caught a little off guard. He was more slender than I expected and looked much younger than his purported 52 years. (Normally this should have been a positive, but he was almost baby-faced. Coupled with his slight size—at least he was tall enough—I wasn't feeling any instant attraction.) Nice blue eyes though, a long-sleeved blue dress shirt and dress slacks with dress shoes. Again, while no instant fireworks went off, he was a damn sight better than Al Gomer and his Dockers and running shoes. But unlike Al, Traveler made no comment or compliment about my own appearance. I had a feeling T wasn't much impressed. Ditto. My previous nervousness disappeared. I knew somehow this was going to be just a pleasant conversation over a drink. And into the casino we went.

Even toned down, I was better dressed than any other woman there. Who, BTW, averaged about 70. Mid-week it was not a hot spot, by any stretch of the imagination. I think he realized his error in having suggesting it, as he made a comment of surprise about the emptiness of the place. We wandered around awkwardly looking for a bar. (In hindsight, the uncomfortableness I was picking up on probably had more to do with his disappointment with me than the vacantness of the venue.) Eventually we took up seats on a couple tall stools at the bar of a centrally located watering hole. Save a bartender clearly supplementing his Social Security checks, there was not another soul in sight. (Did I mention how empty the place was?) At least it was quiet, the ubiquitous cacophony of slot machines well in the background. I ordered a wine, he a beer.

Despite the bartender informing us there was a second bar that served food located on another floor with view of the horse track and the evening's races, my "date" made no suggestion we move. (That should have been my second clue.) And so we sat and talked. We covered basic background stuff again. We each spoke of our kids, touched on dogs (he's a lover thereof, too) and shared military experiences—his and my son's. We then launched pretty heavily into history. It was an interesting discussion. A good give and take flow, absent awkward pauses and dead air. He ordered a second beer. (The $3 special on tap, BTW.) I abstained. I was driving and on an empty stomach I wasn't taking the risk. Before I knew it, he announced it was 8:35. A couple of hours had passed. (Whether he had been watching the clock because he had to pick up his daughter, or had been biding his time before he could make a gracious escape, I'll never know.)

In the lobby on the way out, we paused to say our goodbyes. I told him I had had a nice time. Which I did. Though he had said nothing about getting together again, he suddenly kissed my cheek and then went for my lips. The dry clumsy peck reminded me so much of the boring 62-year-old I had dated and dumped months ago, I was momentarily dumbstruck. Then I was annoyed. He had said not one word about enjoying my company, liking the conversation, appreciating my intellect or complimenting my looks. I realize I won't always appeal or be someone's type, but I don't look bad for my age. He might have thrown me a bone! The only remark even remotely touching on appearance had come when I said I was older enough to remember something he didn't. He asked how old I was. "Sixty in September, which makes me eight years older," I answered. "Actually only seven and a half," he replied. I had laughed and sarcastically said, "Oh, well that's sooo much better."

It is imperative for me now to make note that not one person, male or female, in a similar situation and/or point in a conversation as that, has *ever* failed to make some comment that age is a number and doesn't matter. Apparently to him, it does however. And that's fine. Really, it is. It's also fine he felt no compulsion to pay me an insincere compliment or buy me a meal. I appreciate honesty and abhor fake sentiment and flattery. But a lack of common courtesy is another matter. Still, the point of the meet was to see if we clicked. We didn't. No harm, no foul. We part with no hard feelings. Which brings me back to the kiss. WTF??!! Seriously?

Was is it with men? Do they think it's expected protocol—like picking up the check? Or do they feel entitled *because* they shelled out for said drink and/or dinner? Maybe they're just on primordial auto pilot? Helpless to buck 1.8 million years of evolutionary programming—and regardless of clearly contrary knowledge—they will *still* make that last ditch effort to see if they've got a hope in hell shot at sex? I don't get it. Someone, please explain it to me. Al Gomer had to know *I* was never going to see him again—and yet he tried. Traveler was even worse. He knew *he* was never going to see me again—and still he tried. (I later asked one of my sons for his male view point. He thinks it's either a solid sign of attraction and confidence or a "what the hell, go for it in case something sparks" action.)

After the kiss, Traveler made an insincere offer to walk me to my car. I knew he was late to pick up his kid and told him it wasn't necessary. The next day I texted to thank him for a referral he had given me for a physical therapist. (I had gone and really liked her.) I thanked him also for the wine and reiterated I had enjoyed talking to him. He responded in a timely and quite courteous fashion, asking a few questions about the verdict on my shoulder (Maybe not a torn rotator cuff after all—another story and irrelevant here.) When I said stretching exercises had been recommended as I hadn't lost strength, just flexibility, he responded that the very topic had just been discussed at work. "As we get older we need to do more of that type exercise," he texted. "I know. lol Lots of stuff doesn't work as well," I wrote in response. "Well I haven't had that problem yet," he declared. I wasn't sure if he was flirting or not. "Good to know," I replied with a wink.

At this point I must admit I wasn't absolutely certain where—or if—this was going to progress. According to the matchmaking/dating expert and her book, one should go out on three dates before deciding someone is a no-go. I figured I would go out with him again—if he asked. However, since that text conversation was yesterday morning and I've not heard a word since, I'm pretty sure I can tie up T's loose end in a nice bow.

And so to summarize . . . and then there was one. Of the five loose ends with which the week had commenced, by its conclusion, only Dark Horse was still an end loose. While I hadn't heard from him, he still had a couple of days remaining in his grace period. Then, ironically the day after my failed date with Traveler, I suddenly heard from him. Dark Horse had been out of the country—or so he said, taking care of family obligations. He apologized for his absence. Having worked flights to the Caribbean island I suspected was his homeland, I teased him that at least I knew now how he drank his coffee. (Without mentioning any particulars, let's just say we typically run out of sugar on those flights!) He laughed and affirmed my assessment. Figuring I had nothing to lose since he was the Last of My Mohammed Mohicans, I put it all out there. I expressed my interest still to meet and asked about his weekend plans. Surprisingly, he replied and stated the same. He wanted to meet me as well. Although he had to work Saturday, he would be open Sunday. I wrote back, concurring that Sunday would also work for me. I included my number. He answered back immediately: "Great!!! I'll be calling you soon."

As Dark Horse lives a half hour drive from me, my thoughts turned to logistics: the when, where and how. Which got me thinking about a topic I have meant to discuss, but as yet have not covered.

Ladies, let's talk now about SECURITY. No matter how often you have emailed, texted—or even spoken to him on the phone—until you actually meet him, this online match/partner proposal/internet connection *is a stranger*. And even meeting him in person doesn't suddenly make him less so! I made a HUGE MISTAKE with Z that luckily did not turn into a headline news item: *Local woman raped and killed by stranger she met through online dating site.* Please, please, please. Don't do as I did, but do as I now say. Be smart. Be careful. Be safe. And behold the following common sense rules and safety tips:

**Online:**

- DO NOT give out personal information—home phone number, address, personal email address, place of employment, etc.
- Go slow. Don't leave the site and immediately jump to texting or phone calls. Especially if he's pressuring you to do so.
- Ask yourself if his emails are generic and general—or are they personal, containing details and appropriate responses to your correspondence with him?

- Verify online and via those emails not only what he is telling you, but what his profile claims:
  - ✓ Do his grammar and spelling match his purported education level?
  - ✓ Does the content of his photos coincide with his supposed income level, profession, hobbies, lifestyle, etc.?
  - ✓ Remember the site may be able to tell you when he was last logged on. Does this confirm or deny his "I'm hardly ever on the site" statement?
  - ✓ Realize one lie or untruth is very likely not the only one.
- Question inordinately long lapses between emails—or emails that are sent only on particular days or at certain times of day, especially late at night. Example: What is a nine to fiver lawyer doing online at 3 am? Yes, it could be his work schedule or insomnia—or it might be that he's no more a lawyer than I am. Or maybe it's the only time his wife isn't looking over his shoulder?

**Texting:**

- Realize that giving out your cell number can be opening a Pandora's Box, exposing you to a variety of ills, not the least of which are obscene phone calls, telemarketers and identity theft. Seriously consider getting a second number (or even a cheap cell phone with a separate number) that you can reserve for online dating purposes.
- Go slow. Too much too fast or too good-to-be-true rarely—if ever—work out.
- Know that whatever you are texting has the capability of being made public. Maybe I've seen one too many episodes of *Blue Bloods* involving phone logs and recovered emails, but no communication is truly private or secure anymore. Especially in the early stages, don't text anything you wouldn't want your kids to read. (Yes. I know. Don't do as I did . . .)
- Again question the lag time between responses or restrictions he places upon your communication. Does he seem never to respond to a text during business hours and only texts you late at night?
- Watch out for the same language anomalies in his texts as you did in his emails. Do they seem to be coming from the same person? (A friend of mine left a site when she suspected she was, in fact,

corresponding with at least two different men who were using the same user ID.)

## On the Phone:

- Listen to your gut. Something that doesn't sound right, probably isn't.
- Don't kid yourself. Voice matters. If you hate it now—you will *really* hate it later.
- If the "relationship" continues past one or two phones calls, ask for his last name. (One of Al Gomer's few attributes was that he provided his full name up front—along with the invitation to check him out on LinkedIn.)
- Talk first—enough to know you really *do* want to go out with him.
- Long and/or uncomfortable lapses in conversation may be indications that an in-person interaction is not going to fare any better.
- Be careful with the personal details you divulge. He is still just a voice on the phone.
- Be smart. It's not a good sign if he never answers and your calls to him always go to voice mail.
- A sudden hang-up or any type of secretive behavior or irregular phone communication can speak volumes. So too an insistence upon certain times for contact.
- Be honest. If you have progressed to talking somewhat regularly, one or

both of you is invested and/or interested enough that a face to face should be on the near horizon. If you seriously think he's not going to care that you are really 65 and not 45, or that your body type is more plus than slender, you are sadly mistaken.

- Unless you are satisfied with the status quo (and content with just a voice on the phone), push for an actual date. But beware and ready for disappointment. This is the point when a vast majority of the liars Casper out.

In summary, whether in regard to written or verbal communication, never forget the flowing statistic: Estimates range that from *25 – 34%\** of the people on dating sites are ***married!*** Whether they are cheating or just playing in the candy store, there will always be signs. You need to look for them.

Assuming you are in the 67% of online daters who do progress to that all important first date/first meet (Remember too, *33%\** of online daters have ***never actually gone out*** on a date with someone they met online dating!), here is a vital list of "Dos and Don'ts" gleaned from experience and/or research:

### When meeting for the first time:

- Meet at a neutral location, preferable during daytime hours.
- If at all possible, drive your own car.
- Always have your cell phone, ID, credit card and money on you. If you want to get up and walk out for

whatever reason, you need to have the means to do so—money for cab etc. (I strongly believe this rule should apply to all dates—first or otherwise. A girlfriend sat through a humiliating dinner with a belligerent now ex-boyfriend because she had forgotten her phone and money and had no way to get home.)

- If you are going to be picked up, arrange it at a public place, not your home. (If you are seriously considering having a friend be there at the agreed upon location so she can jot down his car's color, make, model and license number, I think you should seriously reconsider the date.)
- Have someone call you at an agreed upon time in case you need to bail.
- Make sure someone knows where and with whom you are out.
- Never leave food or drink unattended.
- Don't drink too much or don't drink at all.
- If you drove, leave on your own. Don't go straight home. Stop at a store or a gas station.
- Let someone know when you are expected back and have them call to check that you are.

*Gee, do ya think these two statistics could possibly be related!?

Much of this is common sense. But one of the biggest problems is good sense is often at odds with good

208

manners. A colleague and friend of mine went out with a guy she really felt no attraction toward because she was too nice to say no. They had arranged to meet at a hotel he was staying at for business that was known for its seafood restaurant. During dinner he not only raved about the penthouse suite he had been given, he touted its amazing view and asked her to come up after dessert to see it. She didn't want to be rude, especially because he had just bought her a *really* expensive 4 course dinner. Besides, she didn't see the harm. He had been a perfect gentleman the entire evening. (You probably think you know where this is going. You don't.)

He remained a gentleman the entire 10 minutes she was in the suite's living room. She admired the view, sat on the sofa for a few moments, and then said she had an early day and needed to go. He walked her to the door where he asked if he could give her a kiss. She offered her cheek, and he gave her a quick peck, telling her how much he had enjoyed their date. The next day he called and asked her out again. At this point my tender-hearted colleague knew it was better to let him down than to encourage him further. As gently as possible she told him that while he was a great guy, she just didn't feel that that they had much of a connection. *Now* is when Dr. Jekyll became Mr. Hyde. He called her every name in the book starting with B and C, before moving on to S—as in slut—who had led him on by going up to his hotel room and kissing him. Men may well be from Mars and women from Venus. But I don't know what planet that idiot was from! He continued to stalk my friend with nasty voice mail messages for several weeks thereafter.

Ladies, I don't care how much a man paid for your dinner. You don't owe him anything. I know I've previously said to be polite, be nice, be kind. But that advice applies to written or phone contact. One on one, face to face there is only one "be." Be smart—which means be careful and be rude if you have to.

A final note. You are paying for a service. If anything hinky happens whether online, in a text or email or in person with someone you've met on a dating site, report it to the site! In a related, but different, issue . . . if you are not satisfied, complain! A woman I know through mutual friends was briefly on a different site from my two. She told me this story: She had requested tall for her preference, over 5'10". Yet she was getting men who were 5'5", 5'6", 5'7". Worse, they were all overweight and unattractive. (FYI, she likes big men with meat—so when she says "overweight," obese is probably closer to the mark.) When she called to express her dissatisfaction with the matches the site was providing, the young man on the phone condescendingly told her she could just delete the ones she was not interested in. This lady is from Pittsburgh. They don't do condescending. She told him she couldn't do that *because they were all fat and ugly!* "You put me on hold right now and go look at what you've given me," she demanded. "Go ahead. Do it. I'll wait." He came back on the line and told her they would be issuing her a refund. (God, I love people from Pitt!)

So back now to Dark Horse who had texted he would be calling me soon . . . He didn't. So what went wrong? I don't know. I do know that when I logged on Sunday morning (to see if he had maybe viewed me again and no doubt then decided "no"), his profile came up "unavailable." At first I thought he had blocked me, but in reading the site's explanations, I discovered that particular action does not stop a profile from appearing. So what does prompt an "unavailable" message? According to my site: "It is usually because they have chosen to take a break to pursue a relationship, or for some other reasons have chosen to hide their profile. Occasionally [however] members are removed suddenly due to security violations that result in their removal from the site." Wonderful. Best case scenario, that "other reason" was because he is a coward who gets off on the game—or a liar about to be outed. Worst case, he's a thief or scam artist who now has my phone number.

Christ! I need to follow my own advice! Once again, please do as I say—not as I do!

And so the week ended on a low note as low as the high note it began with was high. Wow! Freakin' amazing, if you think about it! There were five. Now there are none. In less than a week's time, no less! It has got to be some kind of record!


Postscript: Monday morning Dark Horse's profile magically reappeared. I guess I should be happy. The only harm of his con was to my ego and an ever weakening self-esteem.

## Chapter Twenty-three
## Week 18—Brass Balls

**Self esteem** (mine rather weak and wilted at the current moment) is the subject of this next chapter. Given the prior week's turn of events and my now obviously falling SMV—concomitant with a flagging sense of feminine worth—it is not surprising I've begun to contemplate its polar opposite: the male's seemingly over-inflated sense of his masculine self-worth. Whether primordial, innate or learned, however it is acquired, it exists. And it is strong. A swollen, enlarged and extended perception of his import and allure to the female gender that governs a man's attitude and behavior. In the online dating arena, this phenomenon is particularly prevalent and easy to spot

Studies have shown that men will typically rate their own looks higher, while women will underrate theirs. This is not to say there is not the occasional anomaly—the good-looking guy who doesn't think he's all that. Often, members of this minority have been previously and grievously hurt, beaten down by life or a lover. Yet there is also among this small number, the rarest of the rare. He is the man who truly doesn't care about such shallow silliness as his outward appearance. He is the antonym of vainglorious, possessive of a personal standard of worth, duty, and morality impenetrable by society's expectations or measurements. (If you are curious to see an example of this extraordinary human being, goggle "Pat Tillman.") But I digress . . .

Online, cloaked in anonymity and absent evidence to the contrary, men are able to fully indulge, exhibit and practice their skewed opinions of their own attractiveness and appeal to the opposite sex. Served up on a computer screen, it's a veritable alphabet soup of masculine narcissism, beginning with the ABCDs (audacity, bravado, confidence, and daring), the FGHs (freedom from doubt, guts, hutzpah), and most of all, what falls between: the two Es (ego and entitlement). Regardless of age, appearance or circumstance, men truly believe they have something women just can't do without. (It's not a coincidence the word "cocksureness" contains the first syllable it does!) This conviction triggers the most astounding behavior.

Case in point, I am constantly amazed at the number of average looking men (at best!) in their 50s who are online looking for women in their 30s and younger. The winner's crown in this category has to belong to the 55-year-old in Philly, PA seeking a mate 18-19 years old within 50 miles of Mesa, AZ. (As this is a Mormon-predominant suburb of Phoenix, I can't help but wonder if he's not shopping for celestial bride #6?)

Granted, money, position and power have always had a great deal to do with the whole trophy girlfriend/wife penchant. But think about it. If multi-millionaire Hugh Hefner in his Playboy mansion were broke-ass Hugo Huff living in a double-wide, do you think he'd have a single bunny? Yet it's not just middle-aged men with significant money and/or power who think they can get any woman they want. I have seen more than my share of short, bald, (and cheap!), 50-plus-year-old pilots who think the cute 23-year-old flight attendant who lets him buy her a drink on a Fort Lauderdale layover is interested in doing him. Trust me. Unless she has major daddy-issues or is looking for a sugar one, she isn't. And if she *is* looking for a Sugar Daddy, a pilot will probably not cut it. They are a notoriously tight-wadded bunch. My favorite joke about these airline sky jockeys? Question: Why does the pilot like to run the porno flick backwards? Answer: He likes watching the hooker give the money back. (Oh, come on . . . that's funny! And it's funny because it rings so true. Speaking of funny 'cause it's true . . . Here's one that slams flight attendants: How do you keep a flight attendant from orgasming? Push the call button. She'll never come.)

But I'm looking for younger too, so let's drop the age gap preference thing and discuss other aspects of the male's ego-laden online dating search *modus*. I know I have mentioned usernames before. But the sheer number of men who choose macho monikers bears repeating. For a simple and single example: I did a username search for "Stud." And found 99 men, ranging in age from 18-67! (BTW, there were lots and lots and lots of related designations [i.e. *Stud4u*] that I didn't even bother to try counting.) Curiously—or not—the vast majority of these self-professed studs didn't provide a photo. Of those that did, only a handful looked to be able to deliver. The remainder? Closer to "Dud" than "Stud." But seriously? How confident does a nothing-to-look at 59-year-old guy have to be to dub himself *Italianstal*? Talk about flattering yourself! It would be like me calling myself *Hotmama*. (On second thought—maybe I should?)

Curious, I did a username search and found seven women using *Hotmama*, one using *Hotmama4u*, one calling herself *Hotmama69* (eeww!) and one boldly going with *redhotmama*. Most didn't have a photo either. And *none* who did, lived up to the description, including an overweight woman looking for "tall, dark and handsome" to spoil her. Good luck, honey. Conclusion: I guess some women *do* possess the same inflated sense of self-worth as men do—but in far fewer numbers would be my guess.

Returning to the subject at hand . . . The award for the most overconfidently (and offensive) username goes to *Bigdickhurts*. (I called and complained to the site about that one! They told me it was "not allowed." Ya think? Then they asked if I had corresponded with him. *Seriously*???)

Another tact evident in many online profiles is the propensity to revisit the past in order to milk long-gone glories. (Think *Married With Children's* Al Bundy and his quarterback days.) Months ago I came across the profile of a guy in his 50s whose only photo was a high school yearbook picture of himself playing ice hockey. I get that a claim to fame is a claim to fame. But after some passage of time—let's say a couple of decades—does it really still belong in a semi-retiree's online dating profile?

Worse than the guy who touts his past as predicate for the future is the one who doesn't bother touting anything. In fact, this ilk of online fisherman doesn't bother with anything *at all!* He doesn't select preferences or write responses—and if he does, they are monosyllabic. I have seen profiles with less than a half dozen words. Total. As if the mere act of listing himself as looking is lure enough? I haven't figured out if this is clueless or confidence. Either way, I can't imagine an empty hook gets many nibbles, much less a bite . . . unless the fishing is for a different kind of hook-er?

The opposite of the blank profile is the blind one, as in regard to its author's handling of factors one would think to be deal-breakers. Examples of either blinders or blindness that illustrate the male's inexorable ability to *still* see himself as able to attract a woman are not exactly few and far between online. I just don't think (but I could be wrong) that most women would have the guts/nerve/desperation/drive or self-confidence to put themselves out there under similar circumstances. (Remember the guy who had had a stroke I met at speed dating? I *know* I would not have the courage to do the same!) But you be the judge: A 68-year-old standing with the aid of two canes, who admits to a recent gastric bypass and the inability to get around at all; another who immediately reveals he has an Ileostomy, but hopes to find a woman who won't care; and a guy in a power chair because of a car accident whose favorite form of entertainment is cruising the malls. These are three very real online profiles provoking profoundly mixed feelings in me. On the one hand, while I feel sadness at a loneliness that is palpable, I still think REALLY??? But on the other . . . Man, I gotta admire their pluck! I don't understand it. But I sure as f\*\*k have to admire it.

As amusing—or baffling—as the male online dater's "macho man" usernames, dated photos and empty or "hanging it all out there" profiles are, they are relatively harmless and affect no one. Behavior is another matter. The offense engendered can be as slight as suddenly contacting again a woman he has ignored for weeks—just sure she's going to be delighted to be back on his radar (and sadly many times she is)—or as disgusting as posting the following profile (THE most offensive profile I've EVER come across!):

> *"I'm a player. I've spent hours on line looking for something on line with big breasts while involved with a woman for a year and a half. It's a hobby."*

(Just so you know . . . Boobman is a 49-year-old divorced, heavyset, 5' atheist. The only pictures he posted were of said girlfriend and her huge ta-tas. Again, the site police must have been on a donut break.)

As a rule, men have the unmitigated gall to act as they will to get what they want, oblivious to fallout. Women, as a rule, don't. We are hard-wired to maintain the community well-being over our individual wants, and so will usually stop and consider someone else's feelings.

Maybe it is just me though. Maybe I am too sensitive. But I consider the wink I just received yesterday from a guy I had been in regular contact with *two months ago*, who then ghosted me, to be ballsy. Either he doesn't remember me (which indicates he's been so active online that the women have become indistinguishably unmemorable) or he is arrogant enough to think I might overlook the Casper act. Or maybe I should just chill—and give the benefit of the doubt? Maybe he faded in order to pursue someone that didn't work out, so he's back to trolling?

Speaking of being "back" . . . After a 5-day absence, Traveler emailed me this morning. His out-of-the-blue text was either bold or oblivious—and a further impetus to continue writing this chapter about men's collective nerve. And while we are on this subject of male nerve—hutzpah—guts—audacity—confidence—healthy/bordering on inflated self-esteem . . . I have a counterpart for that woman with her 10-day-out-full social calendar. Last night a girlfriend (who knows I'm writing this) wanted to be sure I knew about one of her co-workers: a middle-aged guy who brags practically daily that he is going broke dating women he has met online. According to her, he claims to go out with 4-6 different women a week. Wow. I'm impressed. And I'm not. What I am is *in awe*. In awe of the stones a guy has to have to pull that off. (Literally and figuratively!)

And so it is to those nickel nuts, copper *cajones*, brass balls, titanium testicles—or whatever else metal medal to male mettle you can conjure—that I dedicate and devote this chapter.

Especially because I have found their crowned head (pun intended).

Ladies, I present you now with The King of Brazen and The Tsar of Brass Balls: *Realman*, a true master of the inflated male ego. (BTW, I counted 103 users on my site with the name *Realman*. They range in age from 18-73. They are of every race and ethnicity and reside all over the country. A fact that should now be a source of some comfort to women everywhere fearful that real men don't exist anymore. Sisters, you can rest easy. They may be a dying breed, but on one dot com dating site alone there are over 100 self-professed ones.)

So let's return to *Realman* who shall now be known as Brass Balls (BB). I encountered him at the beginning of the week. Or rather I encountered his profile. Divorced with no kids and semi-retired, claiming an income of 150k+, Brass Balls described himself as average in body type and 5'9". While he posted no picture (Yes. I know . . . a *big* no-no!), the rest of his profile was boldly intriguing. He wrote that he was looking for a woman "who knows how to carry herself in a social setting, has personality, that has that something about her quality, more than just beauty (which doesn't last anyway)." He went to describe his ideal match as a woman "that knows how to dress, that can vogue it up or throw on a pair of jeans and tee shirt when need{sic} to."

I figured, so far so good. So I read on.

*I want a woman who is affectionate, that LOVES to kiss and make love, that will communicate with me emotionally and sexually, that is not only a confidant and lover, but loves that art of sex and seduction, intimacy, that loves being sexually open, having uninhibited, passionate, hot, erotic, mind-blowing sex.*

At this point he had crossed a couple lines, to be sure. But I had to appreciate his explicit candor. It was what the guy wanted, so why not say so? Moreover, I ready for different. After four months, I've truly read my fill of "cuddle on the couch and walk on the beach with my best friend and partner for the last chapter of our lives" profiles. BB clearly had a healthy sexual appetite. There could be worse things. And so I read on.

218

*If you are interested, like mysterious, a man that's young in heart and energy and don't want the same old, same old, and want to express your inner desires and have them met in all ways, I would love to hear from you, and not just do you have a pic, tell me something.*

Again, he had crossed the line, but he had also gotten my attention. I was fascinated by his brazenness and lured by his confidence. I decided to ignore one of my most hard fast rules (that "no photo" one) and contact him.

Too, I had already started this chapter on male self-esteem. He fit into its theme beautifully. I saw possible paragraphs, if not pages, on the horizon. I wrote BB. I told him I was intrigued and that he talked a good talk. He wrote back. Proclaiming he could back it up, he suggested we chat. I sent a second email, this one bolder. I told him I had reread his profile and that he had "balls to be sure" to put it all out there as he had. Then I said it was my turn to do the same. I wrote that I didn't need a man emotionally or financially. I wanted one. Paraphrased, I told him I wanted what was missing in my life. I wanted intimacy, passion, adventure and excitement. In other words, "all the colors in the crayon box." But I also needed "intellect and a challenge." I did ask why he posted no photo and concluded with my name and number. (I believe I have previously mentioned that I have an excellent phone number blocker app.)

I figured I'd take one for the team. After all, how bad could he be? I was in full research mode. I wanted to discover what made this guy tick and see where it went. I do have to admit, however, my "clinical" curiosity aside, he did interest me. That amount of self-assurance had to come from somewhere. Besides, after 17+ weeks in this dating hell-hole, chances were fading I'd be finding love. Why not settle for good sex if I stumbled upon it?

BB called me almost immediately. He actually had the best voice I'd heard to date (pun intended). He stressed he wasn't looking to serial date. We chatted pleasantly and over a variety of subjects. Ever so slowly and subtly, the tone began to turn sensual and the content sexual. Honestly, he reminded me a lot of Z. (That should have been a warning siren. It wasn't.) Eventually and inevitably, we ended up in "talk dirty to me" territory. (Yes. I know. STUPID. You can't tell me anything here I haven't already told myself!) But he truly talked a great game and said all the right things—even if they were beyond proprieties' boundary. He definitely thought he was—as my oldest son is so fond of saying—all that and a bag of chips.

My problem—I know *now*—is that I couldn't see how a guy could act that way and *not* be able to back it up. Brass balls is one thing. Downright delusional is another. He suggested we meet. I told him I was going be sorely disappointed if he turned out to short and bald. He laughed. Assuring me he was as advertised, with light brown hair, he declared, "You won't be disappointed." During our conversation he had told me he had been married once to a truly beautiful woman whose beauty was regrettable only external. I figured that was a further positive sign, as people typically seek their own levels when it comes to looks. We arranged to meet in a couple hours' time in the parking lot of the bar and grill down the street from me. He told me what he would be driving (a definitely higher-end make and model automobile).

Once again I made that all important wardrobe choice. It was humid as hell and hotter than it had been all week. Hair "natural," mid-calf length black skirt and matching halter top (that has a tendency to ride up a little. My stomach is still pretty flat and therefore one of my better features. So why not?) Flat sandals. As I was getting dressed, he sent a text telling me how excited he was. Was I? he asked.

Not really. Walking to the bar, I was nervous. I felt like I was about to interview for a job I wasn't sure I even wanted. I am a firm believer in fireworks, aka instant physical attraction. Regardless of anything that had been said on the phone, in my mind—absent that spark—there would be nothing but a drink and conversation happening. I assumed he would be of a like mindset. No spark, no sizzle. It's the way it works. Isn't it?

I was a block from the bar when he texted he was there. I typed back that I was "almost." Then I saw a vehicle, the color he had given, exit the parking lot and make its way down the street toward me. It turned and stopped in front of me. The door opened. And I got my first sight of BB.

I reeled. I saw a blob behind the steering wheel covered in blue plaid. He was dough-bodied and dough-faced. WASP all the way with a pretty good receding hairline. Small wonder he doesn't include a photo! His profile had said "average" body type. "A few extra ponds" would have been kind. "Overweight" was far closer to the mark. My mind shouted, "Oh, no! Oh hell, no!" But my mouth smiled and said. "Hi."

"Hey, Babe. Get in."

I thought he'd turn the car back toward the bar. I thought we'd sit and talk and have a drink. I thought I'd be polite and pleasant, ala speed dating, and bail as soon as humanly possible. Indeed, I thought a lot of things in that split second—like what a mistake I had made. He threw his arm around my shoulder, pulled me close and started to kiss me. Not a peck, mind you. But a full tongue in, full-out sloppy, wet assault that caught me utterly off-guard.

*Fine. Get it over with,* I thought. He wasn't the first toad I'd somehow ended up lip-locked with. The problem was he wasn't stopping. I tried a subtle pull-back gesture that normally signals "Stop." He just tightened his grip. I thought I was going to gag. Besides doing nothing for me, he had bad breath. Not the kind from when someone hasn't brushed their teeth—the kind from when someone hasn't been to the dentist for a while. I pushed back, hard. As I gasped for air, I grasped for a lie.

"I'm sorry," I think I said. "This isn't going to happen after all. I've been called out to work."

"Really?" He sat back and looked at me. "Or do you just not like me?" His eyes narrowed.

"Both actually," I said.

"What's wrong with me?"

At this point I still wanted to end this amicably. "You're just not really my type."

"And what is your type?"

"Dark. Exotic."

"I told you I had brown hair."

*But you didn't tell me you were fat and repulsive*, was what I wanted to say. What I did say, "I'm sorry. There's just no attraction. I really need to go. I have to work a flight in a couple of hours."

"Why didn't you call and tell me that?" There was an edge to his voice I didn't like.

I really wish I had just gotten out of the car then and there. But I really did feel bad, guilty and responsible for this mess I was in. "Because I just found out 15 minutes ago," I lied. "The deadline for being called out for an international had passed, so I figured I was safe. (Lie, lie, lie) But they are short-staffed and out of reserves. Since I'm on call, they called me. I have to work a domestic to Minneapolis." (It was the first city that popped into my mind—probably because I *do* have a flight there next month.)

He just stared at me. I knew he didn't believe me.

"I'm sorry," I repeated. I reached for the door handle.

"Let me drive you," he said, putting the car into gear.

"It's just down there." I gestured. I felt bad. I really did. But I couldn't help how I felt.

A block away I told him to stop. "Right here is fine." My house was straight ahead, but I wasn't about to let him know that.

He stopped the car and looked at me. "Let me come in and (bleep) your (bleep). It will be good."

Finally I felt anger. It reared up and buried my guilt. Hard and resolute, my answer issued from my very core. "NO." Without another word, I got out. I walked to the rear of his car, turned right and kept going—away from my house.

I couldn't get rid of the smell of his cologne on me. The taste of him in my mouth. I literally wanted to throw up. That faint bad breath tang wouldn't go away. I kept swallowing the taste of bile. I needed a cigarette and wanted a drink. I turned the next corner to head back toward the bar, but when I saw a car the same color of his drive past, I panicked. I turned around and headed for the little Asian market a few blocks away. I'd buy a pack of cigarettes and then head home. I needed to brush my teeth.

I walked in and asked for my preferred brand. They don't carry it, Mrs. Park (nhrn) said, but the gas station does. I turned to leave. As I was about to exit, the door opened and some yahoo stood there, staring. He didn't have the manners or wherewithal to hold the door for me or to just get out of my way. I pushed past him. I headed home, having decided after I brushed my teeth, I'd grab my car keys. I doubted BB was still around. But if he was and cruising the neighborhood, he didn't know what I drive. Two blocks from my house, the idiot from the grocery pulled up in his truck and asked if I needed a ride somewhere. I wanted to scream "Eff off, idiot." But I didn't. I just waved him off.

When I walked in, the grandfather clock in the living room showed straight up one o'clock. I couldn't believe the entire disgusting experience had transpired in only 15 minutes. (Please know, I am *not* exaggerating.) I was still nauseated. It was beyond a doubt the single worst encounter with a man I have ever had in my entire life. And that's saying something—considering when I was 20, I was almost raped by an Italian taxi driver on a bridge outside Bolzano. This was worse. Worse because it was a situation totally of my own making.

I brushed my teeth, desperate to make my screw-up a distant memory. (I had no idea it was about to get even worse.) I grabbed a spiral notebook and keys and left. I drove to the convenience store near the bar for cigarettes. Before parking, I scoped out the lot for any car his car's color. (It was easy. There were only two.) In relief I walked into that cool and welcoming dark bar—where no one knew my name. I ordered a wine, then headed straight to the patio for a cigarette. One quickly turned into six, as details and comments I had forgotten started to return. He had groped me. While I was sitting, stunned and searching for words, he had told me he "loved it" that I wasn't wearing a bra. I started writing down everything that came to mind. It was why I had brought the notebook in the first place. (Over the last couple of difficult years I've learned that writing helps to sort out my thoughts and emotions.)

Then I made the mistake of looking at my phone. Damn! If ever there was a time for a Casper act! (Dude! Just disappear and be gone!) But no . . . not this guy. Going against type in a big way, he wanted his feelings known!

*I'm somewhat baffled. We kiss good {sic}*
*together. The sex would have been really*

*good AND I'm not your type WHAT? If you didn't think my looks lived up to your standard . . . I'd really like to know WHO? You are dating. Because I can't believe your {sic} meeting better out there. Totally baffled!!! You should have had sex with me and got to know me . . . It's why you'll still be single years from now, I'd bet on that! Good luck to you. That was bizarre and I think you made the work thing up.*

I really wanted to take the high road. I really truly did. I didn't want to engage in some stupid text battle. It was over. I never ever wanted to even think about him again. And yet I felt I owed him the truth. I don't know why. Guilt for having led him on over the phone? I silenced the inner voice that wanted to point out to him that most normal people get to know one another *first*—before they have *sex*. Not the other way around. Whatever verbal games we'd played . . . there had been no promise or guarantee given that they would be acted upon the instant we were in each other's presence! (For that, I'm pretty sure you have to order a hooker.) To my thinking, the sex talk we'd exchanged on the phone fell under the same "get to know you" column as comparing other preferences—like restaurants, movies and TV shows. It's flirting not foreplay. (WHICH WILL NOT OCCUR AGAIN.)

I wrote back:
*I did. There was absolutely no attraction and I wanted to spare your feelings.*

He immediately responded, this time with two texts:
*Babe let me be honest with you. Your {sic} not the most attractive woman either, but I*

*would have been open to get {sic} to know you. I've dated far more attractive. Your {sic} not exactly thin from the waist down and your calfs {sic}. But I didn't have an immediate attraction but was open to letting you "grow on me." I think in the long run and for being 59 you fucked up there. Especially knowing we could kiss!!!*

*And we probably would have been more attracted to each other after all the cock and sex we had! So for you to think I'm not in your league is head shaking. Never had that happen. Good luck babe . . . And if you come to your senses before you get any older . . . Text me something good!!!*

I was in shock. First of all, I hadn't said he was not in my league. (Though I believed he wasn't.) I had tried to be as kind as I could be, by simply saying I wasn't attracted to him. I certainly had not expected an attack in return, targeting my appearance and age. He had dated "far more attractive?" *In what decade?* I was "not exactly thin?" *Had he looked in a mirror recently?* I could not believe this guy's gall! He'd not had an immediate attraction either, but was "open" to letting me "grow" on him? Wow! That was supposed to make him the better person? *The more desperate one is more like it!* And then to state that *after* (insert vulgar description) I'd be "more attracted"??? Talk about delusions of grandeur! I don't know a single woman anywhere, other than one getting paid for it, who would have sex with a man she was not attracted to in the off chance that doing so might miraculously make it happen. Cart before the horse! *Does this ass-backward technique really work for him?* Besides, there's a profound difference between skin-tingling and skin-crawling. (If you have to keep your eyes closed in order not to puke, no orgasm is worth it. Get a toy!) His final "if I came to my senses" dig before I got "any older" was the last straw.

The high road I'd wanted to take turned into a down and dirty mud bog. He might have written he "really wanted to know WHO" I was dating and meeting that was better than him, but it wasn't "dating and meeting" that he'd been interested in half an hour ago. As he was clearly all about the fuck, I would show him! I pulled up Z's picture and added the message "FYI this is the last guy I fucked." I then scrolled down my contact list looking for his name and hit send.

I ordered a second wine, feeling vindicated.

And then my text message alert sounded. I clicked on the appropriate icon and read: "Was this a mistext?" For a moment I was confused. Then I was horrified. I had sent Z's picture and the added message to Traveler by mistake! Beyond mortified, I typed an intense apology, explaining that I had meant the text for an asshole I'd met online who'd told me I was too old and unattractive to attract better than him. Traveler wrote back: "I figured." While I had pretty much written him off days ago given our lack of contact, I was still embarrassed. I apologized again. He was gracious enough to text back: "No worries." "Are you sure?" I wrote, "I am extremely humiliated." "It happens," he said with a smiley face, "It's why we are humans and not gods."

Still humiliated, but knowing what was done was done and could not be undone, I returned to doing what I hadn't done—hitting BB where I knew it would hurt. I pulled up Z's photo again. To the original message I added: "Lose my number." I hit send again, this time to the intended recipient asshole. I should have known better than to attack the male ego, however.

He fired back viciously:

*Yeah . . . And blew you off!! Where is he now? All you were was a f\*%k!!! Even that didn't keep him around.*

By the tone and tenor of his response I knew I had scored a pretty good hit. It mattered to me Z wasn't still around. But it mattered more to BB that he'd failed to nail what a younger and better looking guy had. In the realm of men, trust me, it's all about competition and hierarchy. He had lost. The top cock slot belonged to another. Besides, I had cooled down enough to think more clearly. BB was lying through his teeth. If he really wasn't all that attracted, then why the anger and the need to strike? Wouldn't he have counted his blessings? Or shrugged it all off as an online dating experience to be filed away under "bizarre," with a footnote of "cray-cray?" And why the invitation to me to text him "something good" if I came to my senses? I'll tell you why. He was trying to save face. He knew his last words had been a pathetic last ditch effort to salvage what he still wanted. As old, thick below the waist and unattractive as it was, he'd still wanted it. He knew it. And I knew it. I had ended up on top, and he was desperate to take me down.

But I didn't care anymore. I was done. BB wasn't. At least not yet:

*Also here is a piece of advice... Get rid of those curls, they don't work on you. Get a blow out... Your hair looks much better straighter!*

I actually laughed. *Like I give a fuck what his opinion of my hair is?* Seriously? How immature and petty was this insult? *He should have attacked my saggy tits!* I thought. I finished transcribing his texts verbatim into my notebook (for later inclusion here), joyfully hit DELETE

ALL and turned off my phone. Emotions still raging, I turned to a new page in the notebook. As much as I was determined not to let his texts get to me, they did. I sat there in the heat and humidity, literally chain-smoking and writing down random thoughts as feverishly as they came. When I looked at my notebook the next day I saw pain. But I also read resolve:

> *I want to go home and cry. But I won't. I won't give the asshole that satisfaction. But I have to take something valuable away from this. If I had insisted upon a photo from the very beginning, it would have never started. But that's not the best lesson to be learned from this. My frustration and dissatisfaction with how my so-called love life is going, has made me stupid and reckless and desperate. It stops now!!!*
>
> *It's ironic. He said I was old, fat and unattractive. And probably so. He certainly hit all the insecurities. And yet I still thought I was too good for him? Wow! it's hard to believe a woman with such low self-esteem could still be so arrogant as to think she is too good for the ugly old losers who are interested in her. But I do. And I am. And if I'm not, fuck it! I'm not relenting. I'll be celibate. Gladly. For the rest of my days . . . .*

I don't know if another woman can relate to any of this. I do know this was the most difficult chapter I've written so far. If it contains too much unnecessary detail and vulgarity, I apologize. But only in the raw emotional ramblings and crude language can the experience be accurately relayed. I had been lucky. I had played with fire with Z and not gotten burned. But this time I screwed up big time. And was even luckier. There will not be a third time.

Online dating is a world of its own. A cyber world where boundaries recede until abnormal somehow becomes normal. I deplore what I allowed to happen. What I willingly engaged in. But berating myself won't help. All I can do is learn the lessons to be learned. And move forward, a wiser and far more cautious woman than I was a week ago.

The purpose of this book was originally twofold: to chronicle my experience as entertainment and to provide useful information as a "do/do not do" guide to others. I certainly didn't expect this trip down the rabbit-hole of dot com dating to turn into a story of personal discovery. But it has. And every good story has a climax—that turning point in the narrative when the highest tension is reached. This was mine.

Of course, as any English teacher knows, climax drives what comes next—the *dénouement*, when the chain of events in a complicated plot finally concludes and provides resolution. I am as curious as you to see what that might be. Because in four months four things have become clear to me.

1. No matter how dry my idea riverbed is getting, someone—or something—always surfaces to float up a new chapter.
2. Fact is infinitely stranger—and way more interesting—than fiction.
3. Even if I tried, I could not make this sh*t up!
4. This book is writing itself.

After four days of blessed silence, BB sent another text. I have neither desire nor interest any longer to look for answers, assign fault, interpret, react or draw conclusions. But please, do feel free to so . . .

*Just for the record. I wasn't upset. It was more baffling and I laugh over how women over estimate themselves. I'm a realist guy and was just letting you know how your {sic} not. That guy pic you sent was nothing to write home about. I was thinking this weekend when I was away. For two people who didn't have that immediately attraction for each other ... We sure could kiss! We had that chemistry down. We should have just had sex, because we probably would have had real good chemistry there too and hung out after and talked and laugh {sic} together and grew on each other. I just don't get what your {sic} thinking for a 59 year old woman. But you were a good kisser! That I will say. You should have had sex with me and you would have found out what a good guy I was too. Instead of pre judge?*

Having forgotten to so, I blocked his number. Like I said . . . stranger than fiction and it writes itself!

231

## Chapter Twenty-four
## Week 19—Let's Dance

Hope springs eternal, or so they say. Monday morning I took my 59-year-old, not exactly thin below the waist, frizzy-haired self back to the drawing board. Over four months in, and I was back to trawling. (Yippee.)

Believe me . . . at this point I know the process. It is humbling, depressing, embarrassing. I don't have enough adjectives. It is constant rejection. Interspersed with tiny flickers of hope. You are making yours elf deliberately vulnerable and opening yourself up to insult, hurt and depression. (Yippee skippy.)

Like any process, online dating has a beginning, a middle and an end with an established goal. The progression through all phases and stages is pre-determined and set with a specific sequence of steps, like a well-laid out flow chart—actually more like a well-choreographed dance.

However, I am not in the mood to dance. The mere thought of going back online makes my stomach turn. It's not happening. Not this week . . . maybe the next. But I need a chapter.

So like the adage goes . . . those that do, do. Those that can't, teach.

### A 12-Step Tango to Online Dating Success

**Step 1**. Find a photo of a man whose look (for whatever reason) appeals. This discovery can occur in one of four ways. He was/is

    a.  provided by the site as a match
    b.  located via my Mohammed Search Method
    c.  found thru the "If you like X . . ." route
    d.  on your radar because he contacted you in some manner (wink, fav, like, email, etc.)

**Step 2**. Look at his profile and read his paragraph(s). If he still appeals—and if you fall within his stated preferences or think you might—proceed.

**Step 3**. Reach out. Depending upon level of interest, least to greatest, my preferred order is

    a.  send a photo like
    b.  a wink
    c.  an actual email.

Be aware: This step is an extremely humbling act. You are putting yourself out there and opening yourself up to almost immediate rejection. Because the next step *is* immediate. And defining. And it happens almost every time.

**Step 4**. He looks at your profile. Regards of what you write, the curiosity to see who is interested in him is pretty much irresistible. He looks. Maybe he reads. And then he judges you worthy of his pursuit—or not.

Note: This is the stage at which most of my online "dating" ends. For reasons I probably don't want to know anyway, the dance is over before the music really starts. Nine times out of ten they never respond back. It's a song as old as time—and it aint' sung by a frickin' teapot: You don't appeal. You are either "too" (old, thick below the waist or something) or "not enough" (attractive, slender, etc.). Fa la la la. For whatever reason you are somehow not a person they are interested in. Don't fool yourself. It stings. Every time. No matter how many times it happens. It's even worse when they really don't interest you that much, but you are still trying, playing the numbers game. But, on the (for me) rare occasion where "too" or "not enough" don't happen, the next step does.

**Step 5**. He sends an email back. Usually it is short and usually he includes his first name. In some manner he indicates he is interested and wants to continue the "conversation." Sometimes he will jump to step 8 and send his phone number with an invitation to "chat."

**Step 6**. It is your turn now. Write back—or not. Depending on my attraction and level of interest, I have been known to bypass this step and skip to steps 8 or even 9.

**Step** 7. Email communication continues. Back and forth. Back and forth. The number of times you repeat this will vary and depend upon your partner and your level of interest.

Alert! Know you can exchange multiple messages over the next few days and think everything is going great. Then suddenly the music stops, signaling an end to the dance. The number of times this "to and fro" shuffle is repeated before this can happen has no set frequency. For me it has been as few as 2-3 or as many as 20. The higher the number, however, the less likely I will be the one to call it quits.

**Step 8**. Emails turn into texts. This is a slight step forward, but still a "to and fro" shuffle. Again, the number of exchanged texts is not a set one. Again, this can be the final step. (And again, I am not likely the one to bail at this point of the dance.) Depending on my continued interest and/or his continued attraction, the next step is a big one. I tend to let him make it first. But again, depending upon my interest or desire to control the situation, I may take the lead.

**Step 9**. You talk by phone. This is not only a huge step forward, it can be the one that leads to a bow-out. Once again, the number of phone conversations that occur—and even the length of their duration—can have no bearing on the next step occurring. (I have been asked out during the first conversation, and at other times it took hours on the phone to elicit that all-important next move.)

**Step 10**. Think of this as a twirl that leads into a definite change of direction and tempo. He asks you out or you arrange a face to face meet. These are not exactly the same thing. Whether I was tired of carrying on with someone I'd never met or he wanted to see me in the flesh, at some point it has to be time to "sh*t or get off the pot" as my dad loved to say. (Military are punctual—and also crude.) Upon multiple occasions a date and/or time was "penciled in," rather than set firmly. At the time I thought it was because of my erratic work schedule, I now think it's a means of giving them wiggle-out room.

**Step 11**. The Meet, i.e. first date. My site loves to tout the fact they result in more second dates that any other site, I wouldn't know. All three times the dance has ended here for me. But assuming you are luckier than I . . .

**Step 12**. The second date. This is a twirl and dip flourish, the dramatic ending as the last note fades. At this step, The Online Tango number has been danced to its end. Should you decide to take the floor again with this same partner, you will be dancing to a new tune—the so-called "normal" Dating Cha-Cha. The music for this dance is unique in that it can remain the same and never change—or it can end at any point. It can also evolve into the song needed for the dance many dancers are hoping to dance—The Relationship Rumba. Good luck. I truly hope you find the love and happiness you seek!

Ladies, be aware that at any point in any dance a third party can step onto the dance floor, tap your partner on the shoulder and cut in. Sometimes you won't know this is happening until you find yourself standing alone. Fortunately, The Online Dating Tango is predisposed to personalization and personal taste, so now you have two choices:

1.  You can walk off and start the tango from Step 1 again. (In fact, you can stop and start the 12-Step Tango at any step, as many times as you like. It all depends upon the individual dancer. Some choose to stop for several months before beginning again. Others dance off and on over the course of years.

-or-

2.  You can tell the band to play the Solitary Samba and just stay on the damned dance floor solo!

Whatever your choice . . . I hope, like Lee Ann Womack says in her song, you'll dance.

## Chapter Twenty-five
## Week 20—Goldilocks vs the Pea Princess

I read a magazine article this weekend and learned something about myself. Apparently, I am not as unique, unusual—or unbalanced—as I thought I was. The article in question, written by Andrea Sachs and published in February 2009 by *Time* magazine, was an interview with Judith Sills discussing her book, *Getting Naked Again.* If you can't guess from its great title, this book is a self-help directed to women dating after divorce or widowhood.

According to clinical psychologist and author Sills, women reentering the dating arena after a prolonged absence tend to follow certain patterns when seeking out a new partner. These men, whom Sills labels as "transitional," fall into one of three categories. The first is a man who presents an "aspect that was an unmet need" in the prior relationship. This "opposite" relationship of the one that ended is referred to by Ms. Sills as a "palate cleanser." For example, a woman divorced from an intense Type A personality will find herself a laidback Type B boyfriend. (Makes sense.) The second type of "transitional partner" is the one Ms. Sills calls "the functional guy." The third, "the caretaker," is simply a "more intense" version of #2. Each of these two transitional boyfriend types are less about romance and more about practicality as they step up—and step in—to fulfill the so called "male responsibilities" the woman was used to having had met by her now gone ex or deceased spouse.

Wow. Talk about fitting the pattern perfectly! Looking back over the last two years of *my* dating history I saw theory come to life. My Zurich affair with a younger and very attractive exotic man had been the absolute fantasy adventure and romance—a classic example of a boring three decade plus marriage palate cleanser, if there ever was one! Following my divorce—and the end of my

Alpine magical mystery tour—I relocated and started life over, alone and single for the first time in my life. And the man I began to date then? A blue collar fix-it man who offered companionship and conversation, while providing needed transportation for errands of all sort (grocery store, doctor, Home Depot, etc.) He repaired my leaking kitchen sink, switched out a broken door knob and even put up my Christmas tree. Functional, indeed.

But here was where I deviated from Ms. Sills' suppositions. As independent and self-sufficient as I am, I had no need for a caretaker. What I did have need of, however, was more excitement than what Mr. Functional was providing. Hence I started to date the truck driver. Whom I realize now was a combination of the two: fun and function. (He took down my Christmas tree.) The problem was, he fell a bit short in every category: average looking, not bad—but not great—sex and only so-so company. By this point though, I had regained some of the confidence I had lost following the divorce and the break-up with my Swiss connection. Moreover, my car had been shipped out, I had made friends and I was handling life just fine—except for what was still missing. This was when my search went online. Enter Z who met my outstanding needs to a T. ('Til he Caspered, that is.)

So now I'm back to the starting point. Only I'm tired of weeding through the whack-a-doodles and encountering men who don't meet any of my wants, desires or needs. Yes, I know there is no such thing as the perfect man. So does Sills. Where she earns her cred (and my attention) is in the insistence that there *are* different guys perfect for different needs. A woman simply has to reevaluate and reconsider. The man who takes you to a movie may not be the one you want to take you to bed. And one who thrills between the sheets may not be so enthralling over a three course meal. In a nutshell? Stop looking for Mr. Right for Everything and start looking for Mr. Perfect to a Purpose.

My problem is I'm not finding any man capable of fulfilling anything. My fault? Probably. My sights are set too high and my wants unrealistic. Thus I've reached the stage Sills calls the "opt-out." This occurs at some point during the whole hurtful, tiresome, discouraging dating game when a woman decides she is no longer interested in dating. She is fine alone and on her own. Sills acknowledges that reentry into singledom and the search for a lover/boyfriend/companion/partner/mate are not easy feats. Persistence and self-awareness are key. If a woman truly is happy and fulfilled solo, more power to her! (It's why God invented cats, right?) Sills' only concern is if this "opt-out" decision happens because of negative feelings. In other words, the opt-outer decides she is too old, too fat, too something to keep trying.

Wonderful. From palate cleanser to functional to negative opt-out . . . I guess my case just went from merely basket to purely textbook?

But was the real problem me being "too?" Or was it that I regarded the men as "too?" Too old, too fat, too uneducated, too boring? For over two years I had been Goldilocks incarnate. Looking for the guy who "was just right," I didn't bother with any who were not—and so I'd ended up with none.

That Goldilocks reference above actually got me thinking. I'd used it before, in a journal I'd started to keep a year after I'd walked out of my dead marriage. I had joking entitled it "The Tale and Adventures of an Almost Free Woman." I went looking for it. And found it. The passage in question follows, verbatim, as I wrote it 2 ½ years ago. It merits inclusion here because it illustrates the path I have traveled. And Sills did say self-awareness was key . . .

*I am free, yet not free. What do I want? Never to be married again. I know that with absolute certainty. But I do want companionship, not permanent or exclusive, but occasional. I want to go places and do things and experience life. I tell my boys life is not a dress rehearsal. We are not going to get to do this over. I do not want to live my life with anymore regrets. So I guess my best direction at this point is to take life as it comes and to pursue options presented until circumstances and/or my inner voice dictate otherwise. I do not even know if I am capable of sexual response. My sister claims it will all come back to me. I know I am not ready to take that step regardless, I have a friend who says I will know when the right person comes along. I laugh. Considering my three "dates" I am getting closer however. Closer to knowing what I want, I guess I will find who I want when and if he appears.*

*Thus far it has been an adult version of Goldilocks' quest: too this or too that, with nothing as yet "just right." The 60+ aged businessman in Frankfurt who invited me to share a bottle of wine and then invited me to breakfast; the fellow flight attendant right around my age who took me to dinner in Tel Aviv; and the 38-year-old Turkish restaurant owner who bought me lunch and took me for a midnight swim in a Swiss lake. Each one possessed qualities that were attractive and those which were off-putting. #1, a CEO of multiple international companies, was tall, wealthy and intellectually fascinating. He was also too old. Physically he just rang no bells. #2 was ex-military with a take-charge attitude and air of strength, control and authority that was infinitely appealing to someone who has had to for so long take care of everything. Physically more attractive and in reasonably good shape for a man in his 50s, he still did not set off any bells. Not so though was the case with #3. He was my type, make no mistake. Like I said—Turkish and all that entails—dark, exotic, long black hair and an athlete's hard muscled body. But too young. Way too young. And too short. I'm not sure he is any taller than I. Yet to his credit and my chagrin, size really did prove not to matter as he succeeded where others had failed. Daring me to adventure, he challenged my boundaries and took me beyond my comfort zone. The first man I have kissed other than my husband in 36+ years. TMI! TMI! I can hear my boys exclaiming. I don't know why I am putting this in writing. Maybe for my own amusement, a journal to read when I am old and gray and want to look back.*

*My wise, wise sister/mom/friend says I am merely getting my feet wet with the Turk. (Oh, and some other parts, too.) All I know is that every time I looked in the blurry tiny airplane lav mirror the next day and saw my hair—wavy and untamed in the absence of a curling iron—I smiled. (It has been two days and I have still not washed it. And I still smile when I see it in the mirror.) Then too, as a former romance writer, I am practically honor-bound to hold fast to the visual memories, putting into words the images yet so alive in my mind:  a silver lake shimmering beneath a veiled moon . . . a far-off, seemingly floating expanse of soft gray meadow, bordered by black forest . . . and two bodies. Entwined and apart. Pale and dark—an undeniable difference in flesh tone that had gone*

*utterly unmarked in the light of day . . . Life is for*
*living. And what girl hasn't dreamt of a moonlit*
*encounter with a dark stranger in a foreign land?*

*Will I see him again? Probably. If only to take this*
*as far as it is meant to go. Surely in the*
*unforgiving light of day that which was exposed in*
*the obfuscation of night will take on its inevitable*
*importance. I am not speaking of the*
*aforementioned difference in skin so surprisingly*
*revealed in such scant light, but of the decades*
*difference in age so regretfully confessed when*
*pressed. It is funny in a sadly poignant way.*
*Compact at it was, his body was truly gorgeous. I*
*have little doubt there will never—ever—be*
*beneath my hand a more beautiful male body so*
*willing to my touch. In hindsight I do wish I had*
*explored it more.*

All righty then . . . Comments? Questions?
Reactions? Jesus! Talk about a trip down memory lane! In
a way I haven't changed one damn bit. But in another I was
actually more confident back then—and yet more afraid. I
have to laugh at one thing though . . . my wondering if I
was "capable of sexual response." (That one can definitely
be checked off the list!) Oh, and my anxiety over an age
difference? (Yep. Off the list, too.) Apparently my hair has
been a long-standing issue as well.  All joking aside, it is
beyond weird to read about where I was—knowing where I
went *and* ended up. The Turk and I became lovers a month
after I wrote that. We were together for nearly a year in a
relationship I still have trouble defining. At some point I
fell in love with him, though I realized–or admitted it—
only when it was over. It has taken a year to get over him.
Now comes the $64,000 question . . . Had I known, would I
have changed any of it? I used to say no. I went into it with

242

eyes open. I knew it was not meant to last. He awakened what I thought was dead, and the ride (as the song goes) was worth the fall. But lately I am not so sure. I think I was happier not knowing what I was missing. It's an age-old question: Is it better to have loved and lost, rather than to have never loved at all? On second thought . . . scratch that. The woman I was then, who wrote that last line about wishing in hindsight, was lamenting an opportunity lost and admitting to regret. The woman I am now has no regrets. Sadness, yes. I turned 58 in his bed. Fast forward two years and I am about to turn 60 alone. Who wouldn't be sad? But regrets? Not a damn one!

So what do I take away from this? Obviously the Turk did not grow any older or taller—and yet for a time he made me wonderfully happy. Instead of dismissing as wrong and jumping out of a "too something" option, insistent upon finding "just right," ala Goldilocks, I bedded down in a bed that I knew from day one was not right (much less "just right"). For a year I tossed and turned like that princess who felt the pea, snatching occasional moments of satisfying slumber. So I guess if we are going to use fairy tales and allegorically compare men to mattresses, the question is this: Do you want to sleep fitfully or risk not sleeping at all? Because, ladies, let's be real. In real life, "just right" might be as fairy tale as three talking, porridge-eating bears living in a freaking house!

So Monday morning I was back to trawling, aided in my efforts by two emails from two men who had seen something in my profile they apparently liked. Would that I could say the same! At first glance, neither seemed like viable options. And talk about opposites! One was too old with long gray hair, moustache and a definite hippie from the 70s look. The other was too young and bald as a cue ball. Truthfully, I have not yet firmly decided if I'm going to emulate Goldilocks or the Pea Princess during my remaining time down the rabbit-hole. (Oh, goody! *Four* children's story references now.) But I do know I need chapter pages, so I answered both.

First, the hippie, a 64-year-old Civics and Special Education teacher who thought we had "a lot of things in common." Jewish, looking for 54-74, he considered me "amazing, intelligent, attractive and very interesting." What the hell did he know? Certainly his was an opinion, not only held by a miniscule minority, but one far out-weighed by fact and numbers—as in the hundreds of men on our mutual site who had in 19+ weeks looked at my profile and passed. Still, a compliment is a compliment. I wrote back and told him we had more in common than he knew, as I had also taught both subjects once upon another lifetime ago.

Next was the cue ball, a 42-year-old seeking 28-52. Not only had he send a generic "Hi how is your Monday going?" spaghetti spam email, he had to have sent it by mistake considering his stated age preference. I said as much in my response, though I did offer to debate his choice of a favorite American classic novel I happen to have taught and abhorred.

With responses to my "suitors" dispatched, I clicked onto the link to view my daily matches. Had I had a mouthful of coffee, it would have been spewed across the computer screen. Highlighted in yellow as my special "singled out match for the day" (a feature I have *never* seen before!) was an all too familiar profile. I stared for a moment in shock before the most asinine thought occurred (since he is now listed as 43) . . . *Gee, I guess he had a birthday*. The temptation was too great to resist. I wrote, praising God's twisted sense of humor. After explaining how he had been selected as my special Monday match, I wished Z a belated birthday.

I then moved on to my other matches supplied by the site. Out of the twelve they gave me, I liked three. The first was a 44 year-old seeking 33-44, he wrote he was not interested in a "textual" relationship, was a hopeless romantic, a realist AND a dreamer looking for a woman "sweet, sassy and a little salty who is gorgeous if only to [him]." I enjoyed the sentiment of his profile. I wrote and told him so, then jokingly asked if he had an older brother. I wished him luck.

Next was a 50-year-old with great eyes and upper arms. This was an occurrence I had not previously encountered. You see . . . I had actually found Mr. Eyes and Arms on my own a week or so earlier and had written complimenting said attributes. Over the weekend he had finally responded and thanked me for the compliment. In his return email he had said I looked "charming in [my] pictures and had a great profile." He had added his name, JXXXX. Naturally I had written JX back. I thanked him for his kind words and made email small talk, asking about the weather since I was on the opposite coast on a trip and some impending hurricane was all over the news. Again, he had responded, telling me the weather was good so far. He made note that I had been blessed with wonderful children and "[had] to say" he was "proud" of me. I assumed he meant as in the job I had done raising them? It was an odd comment. He added that he was a freelance engineer. Once more I wrote, confirming that I was indeed blessed and asked what kind of engineer he was. I didn't hear back. Now, Monday morning and two days later, his profile was before me as a site-generated match? I clicked over to the message link and saw that he had not read my last message. *At least I hadn't been dumped—yet*, I thought. I wrote that I was back home, but scheduled to fly at the end of the week again. I figured I had nothing lose and would give it one last try. (He really did have great eyes and arms.)

The third and last of my interest-generating, site-generated matches was a 60-year old seeking 49-62 who had a clever and humorous profile in which he poked fun at women who posted only bathroom selfies. I wrote and invited him to look at my profile. If he saw common ground, I looked forward to hearing from him. Otherwise I wished him good fortune finding what he was looking for.

In all, I sent seven emails that morning. Within an hour three had read them, including Z—who offered no response. (Gee, I'm shocked. Not.) A couple of hours later I heard back from the hippie. Over the course of the day we exchanged several more emails via the site. I explained that I had back-to-back Frankfurt flights coming up. He suggested we might continue to text and talk when I returned to town and included his number. I said I would be in touch. By late afternoon, six of the seven men I had written had read my emails. Only one had responded, the hippie. (Pretty much par for my course.)

Early evening I received a message from JX. He explained that he had been out of town with family over the holiday weekend. He wrote a charming email, from its introductory "Hi beautiful, welcome home" to its "you are really beautiful and I wonder why you haven't been taken" conclusion. I resisted the urge to say I wondered the same. Instead I answered his question as to how long I had been online, explaining I had four months and one disastrous date under my online belt. I also commented in response to his observation that I didn't have much down time as I was always in another city. I explained that this month was an anomaly. I normally fly two or three trips max. I didn't want to get my hopes up. But I really did like his looks. And I really didn't want another disappointment or need another loser.

BTW . . . I forgot to mention previously a couple of interesting developments regarding past losers. Dark Horse looked at my profile several days after disappearing, and BB's profile now shows as unavailable. The best though, is that I heard from Mr. Baseball. Three and a half weeks after we had last spoken, my phone rang, displaying an out of state number. He explained that his cell phone battery had overheated and he had lost all of his stored information, including my number. Just minutes ago, in fact, he said, he had sent me an email through the site explaining his digital disaster. Then he said he found the number he had just called stored under my ex's first name and thought he'd take a chance since the last names matched. I could drive a truck through the holes in his story. Why wait 25 days before trying to email me? Especially as we had tentatively scheduled a date? Wouldn't logic say he'd try to get a hold of me before then? And if he had lost everything, how could my number be stored under my ex's name? He also supplied way too much detail about trying to recover lost numbers and contacts. Oh, and his computer had crashed around the same time? Sorry. I didn't believe a word of it. Not that I'm one to keep score—but I am. And according to my card, Mr. Baseball had struck out two weeks ago!

Additional profiles I encountered this week worth mentioning now (because it's too late to include them in the Brass Balls chapter where they truly belong.) . . . A 47-year-old who posted only pictures of his body parts, flexed biceps, tattooed back, naked abs, etc. He did however include one full body shot—wrapped in a towel in front of a bathroom mirror. Oh, and he also included a couple of pictures of his weight bench and weight room. But that's not *the* most bizarre part. Bodman not only stated he was African American—yet looks as white as I—seriously WASP, I swear to you—he made a point of writing that only Black women should respond. I would be shocked if any woman of any color showed this narcissist a shred of interest. In my opinion, a guy much more deserving of some woman's interest somewhere was a 63-year-old, disabled army vet who has MS.

As Week 20 drew to a close I cast a few more seeds into the online dating cyber wind. Most never land, much less sprout, root and break through the soil. But hope is mental Miracle-Grow©. (And until my 6 month membership ends and my journey concludes, I'll still need something to put on paper.) I wrote a 50-year-old seeking 36-66 who shares my love of travel. I also wrote a 66-year-old who had sent me a wink and a like. He was seeking 50-70. His profile offered the most reasonable of assertions regarding dating: "If it happens, it happens. But why not a pleasant dinner anyways?" The remaining seeds tossed to waft on the wind? A 51-year-old design architect seeking 38-50 and a 55-year-old also seeking younger, 34-50. He had posted vacation pics of a Sahara vacation—a place on my bucket list since I was eleven and read *The Sheik.*

BTW . . . by Thursday JX had still had not read my last email. In a weird way, I was pleased. I figured it was a definite positive in his favor that he didn't live on this fricking site. If he continued to follow past behavior, I wouldn't hear from him until the weekend. I'd be in Europe. Hoping this particular seed had at least found a little dirt to land in, I gave it a bit of water. I wrote and thanked him again for his email, telling him (in all honesty), it had been the nicest anyone had been to me during this whole online thing. I told him I really hoped we might continue to communicate. Then I reiterated that I would be back and forth across the pond until Monday. But, as I am able to receive texts overseas, I was including my number. Not to play favorites—though to be sure I had them—I also emailed the hippie. (Hereafter to be known as Hippie-Dippie, a moniker bestowed by one of my oldest and dearest girlfriends.) I wished him a good weekend, repeating my promise to be in touch during the upcoming week.

By the weekend's end, Hippie-Dippie had responded, making for an actual landed seed. Mr. Reasonable had also responded and suggested we get together. With two flights scheduled over the upcoming week, out-of-town company coming the following and two flights the week thereafter, I simply had no immediate time available for a meet or a "date." I wrote back and offered the first week in October as a possibility. In the meantime, JX pulled a Casper. He never wrote again. My emails to him still showed as unread, yet a search on site revealed he *had* been online within the last three days. Another seed lost to what now felt like obvious hot air . . .

I logged on one last time as the week closed. Nothing and no one of interest. Way back in the 1960s, Bob Dylan wrote a song popular in my own hippie-esque youth. Its lyrical assertion was that the answers to life's questions are "blowing in the wind." Answers *and* desires, Bob. They are all up there, riding some cosmic thermal current, beyond the reach of man—or woman.

# Chapter Twenty-six
## Week 21—A Grain of Salt

*Legend says when Roman legions defeated Carthage in 149 BC, they plowed the city over, sowing the soil with salt so that nothing could ever grow there again.*

As my 21st week of online dating commences, I am feeling completely Carthaginian. My own little plot of personal dating dirt might not be strewn with NaCl (metaphorically speaking, of course—and FYI, historians don't buy into the whole salting the earth story anyway), but it might as well be . . . 'cause as of the commencement of Week 21, nary a single cyber seed has taken. And God knows, I've planted plenty! Gardening gurus (addressing real-life gardening issues and not cutesy-clever online dating metaphors) call this condition "a complete failure of germination." According to such expert seeders, weeders, sowers and mowers, there are three probable causes for an empty bed (pun intended):

    1.) planting too deep (can't imagine THAT ever being a bad thing)

    2.) cold soil (DEFINITELY not my problem)

    3.) just poor seed.

I'll take door number 3, please. *Just poor seed.* I like that one. It takes the onus off of me—save for the fact I obviously have the uncanny ability to pick and plant bad seeds. (Oooh, extended metaphor AND double entendre!) What's a hoe to do? (Okay, that one was bad.)

But, seriously, a rational person has to begin to wonder. After all . . . the only constant in this cavalcade of weirdos, whack-jobs and bewildering vanishers *is* me. Whether I've opted for a younger and physically appealing Adonis or compromised on a tolerably older and oh-so-average Joe, the end result has been the same. I'm still sleeping single in a double bed. (Actually, it's a queen.) Clearly it's time (again) for a new strategy. Moving now off the gardening shtick—and likening my situation to a hit 1980s song by Bonnie Tyler—my current *holding out for a hero* course of action has produced none: No "superman to sweep me off my feet" (sorry, Bonnie) . . . no "white knight upon a fiery steed" . . ." Fuck! (Not!) Nowadays, I'm impressed if mild-mannered Clark Kent in a broken down Pinto returns a freaking email! Yep. Without doubt it's time for a new plan . . .

Clearly, the Mohammed Method isn't working. Moreover, I don't have the time for trawling anymore. My work schedule has changed. Instead of my usual "Reserve" line, aka sitting home on call, twiddling my keyboard tapping thumbs and flying once or twice a month, I'm now holding a "hard" line. In flight attendant-speak, this means I've been assigned a full month's worth of flights to work. (The horror! The horror!) From none or one . . . and possibly (maybe, highly unlikely, could happen but don't count on it) two . . . to *six*? (And did I mention half are *domestic*? NOW we are talking horror!) In the past 18 days, I've been home only 3. To further divert my focus and frustrate my futile efforts to find that aforementioned white knight upon his fiery steed, I've had the out-of-town company previously mentioned.

So to recap . . . Hippie-Dippie and Mr. Reasonable, 64 and 66 respectively (Christ! How far down the fantasy-lover ladder *have* I fallen?), remain viable prospects who have both expressed an interest to meet. Both are still on hold, postponed until after my back-to-backs to Frankfurt at the end of the month. (Yeah, I know. It must be nice . . . but trust me. It ain't all Rhine River Riesling rainbows and *Lederhosen*-wearing unicorns.) Mr. Baseball is goooooone from any further consideration, and JX is a ghost. Twelve days of silence say a lot. Although my last email to him still posts as "unread," a username search confirmed he had, in fact, been on online within the week. (Maybe when one reads an email through their email server, rather than through the site, the email doesn't show as "read?" I don't know. I do know if he were interested, I'd have heard from him.)

Speaking of interest . . . during the past week I have received a few new nibbles (wink, like, fav, etc.) as yet unanswered. Time to trawl literally hundreds of profiles is one thing. Simple sentence responses and/or swipe and click perusals are another. With minimal effort I responded, first to a 55-year-old who had winked at me. He described himself as loving, sweet and caring. Not bad traits to have. He was more religious than I like, but what the hell? The next was a polar opposite. An atheist, ex-marine, also in his late 50s. He had sent a photo like. As did a 60-year-old Jewish guy, who seemed nice enough, and yet is now totally unmemorable. The last guy had made me one of his favs. A 59-year-old widower, his profile said he wasn't looking for a serious relationship. As he preferred women 54-59 who were "confident with self," I figured I had a shot.

Among my daily matches (supplied by the site and therefore requiring no trawling time), I found a 47-year-old seeking 40-58. His openness to going older was appealing. Besides, he had great eyes and a sarcastically witty profile, writing that women should read his profile first, and only then could they "feel free to ignore." I also wrote a 52-year-old, seeking 52-57. In his profile he admitted to being extremely ticklish himself and yet liking tickle fights, because he was "playful by nature" and that activity revealed whether a woman was "affectionate or not, or liked to be touched." His not-so-subtle hint towards sex was straight up enough. But the whole tickle thing? I found it tilting towards weird. Still, I wrote. I asked what happened if a woman wasn't ticklish at all. The final, remotely feasible "match," was a 57-year old, who by his username appeared to be German. According to his profile he spoke the language at least. I wrote him—in German.

I also wrote and reached out to an oldie but goody. Remember Mr. Nice Guy Too Old? I figured, why not? As of late, my daily matches were consistently over 59 anyway. Clearly, the universe was trying to tell me something. Like . . . "larger than life" Young Stud *wasn't* showing up? I needed to stop clinging to my *I Need a Hero* fantasy mentality and develop a new *carpe diem*/seize what (who) came strategy. Ergo, the following plan of attack . . .

Step 1: Despite my inclinations, I needed to abandon my preference for younger. I needed to open up the figurative playbook—and myself—to the 60s as a decade of possibility. NGTO had sent some of the most sincere and well written emails I had received. And let's be frank. Trying to start something with men who couldn't spell, while barely responding in complete sentences, had gotten me nowhere. Moreover, I know from experience, overlooking an obvious intellectual/educational gap in favor of physical appeal doesn't pay off in the long run.

Casual and chatty, I told NGTO I was just checking in. I was looking forward to my membership ending in a couple weeks. It hadn't worked for me, but oh well, I philosophized. Wondering how he was faring and hoping he'd had success and found his match, I invited him to drop a quick note of friendly response.

Step 2: I went next to my history. If I was going to go older, I needed to take a second look at the two who had "liked me" last week. The first was a 68-year-old homebody who "loves nothing better than curling up on the couch with a good book or interesting show on TV." (Yes, me too. But it sounds oh so boring and pathetic when written down!) I opted out. Again.

The other I was more willing to consider. He was a 6'4" 58-year-old PhD employed in public service. Wearing a sport coat and sweater vest, with a Tom Selleck moustache and a decent head of dark, slightly graying hair, his look screamed "academic." Fittingly, his profile opened with a literary allusion and a hardly inaccurate observation: "What an interesting forum, not unlike looking into the mirror and seeing the many faces of Eve." He went on to describe himself as "enigmatic, thoughtful, well-educated, funny, sincere and often dopey romantic." His list of favorite activities was as extensive as his self-description: good conversation, reading, the arts, travel, cooking and nature. I'm guessing the field he works in doesn't pay all that well, as he made a point of stating he was not rich "in the conventional sense."

Income is a check- off item falling lower on my list. Wit and intelligence are much higher priority boxes—both of which this guy artfully ticked off with a passage stating he was fine alone, but recently had "felt the creep of loneliness." (A great line!) "Limbic resonance aside," he went on, "I am comfortable in my own skin." (Note: If I have to grab a dictionary, color me impressed.) While he doesn't care for crowds, PhD enjoys good conversation. And reading. In fact, his list of last read books was as impressive as his vocabulary. Seriously, who reads a narrative history of the Plantagenets for fun? (I do. I do.) And McCuller's *The Heart is a Lonely Hunter*? Color me smitten.

I crafted a suitably intellectual and articulate email (or so *I* thought). Within the hour, like clockwork, my message to PhD showed as read. However, no response was forthcoming. I know shocking, right? (FYI, the next day there was still no response.) I have to admit I was disappointed. Something about the profile had really appealed to me. Oh well . . .

Undaunted (okay, a little daunted), I returned my attention to Step 1 of my new "settle, surrender and seize the day" strategy, which shall now be known simply as SSSS. I needed to physically change my stated preference for younger men. Dutifully I scrolled and clicked, updating my age preference (again) from 45-60 to 50-60. A small change, yet monumental in mental acceptance—and reluctant acknowledgment. The time had come to dispatch my Swiss connection and three lovers since (38, 37, 45 & 42 if you're curious and counting) to the same place my size 2 skirts went: The land of lovely memories.

Step 3 in SSSS was to "*re*" myself. A prefix with Latin roots, *re* imparts the meaning of "do it again." And so I did, or rather *re*did my online persona, *re*working, *re*writing and *re*freshing my profile, thereby *re*inventing— or at least *re*defining—the woman called "jamada." I deleted her "sass with class" headline and replaced it with smalz—"It will happen when you least expect it." Not only was it a line I'd heard incessantly from concerned family and friends over the past year, it was one I'd repeatedly told my sons. (Nothing like banal advice coming back to haunt you!) Next up another concession . . . toning down the written paragraph so as to have jamada come across more purring pussy cat and less "I am woman hear me roar." (Only those of my age will recognize THAT reference, I'm sure.) At this odyssey's onset I'd made the conscious choice not to "dumb" it down or "soften" it up. I'd wanted a man who would see the challenge and ala superman/white knight rise to it. Clearly those men don't exist, at least not online, or that I'd found. And since—if we are going to be perfectly honest here—what I was really wanting now was *not* a sixty-something-year-old, but rather enough material over the next few weeks to close out this book, I relented. (Sorta kinda, leopards and spots, you know . . .)

So here it is. Third time's the charm and all that rot:


*Independent, intelligent, well-traveled. Strong and resilient. A bit sarcastic and a lot cynical. Stubborn too. But I love to be proven wrong. I*

*clean up pretty well and have a penchant for*
*high heels. I am reserved until I know someone.*
*Great in a crisis, yet I'm a sucker for dogs and*
*babies and sappy Budweiser Clydesdale*
*commercials. I've lived enough life to know*
*who I am, what I am and what I want. I want*
*the triumvirate—intellect, sex and love—what*
*girl doesn't? The whole online thing mystifies*
*me. Whatever happened to just meeting and*
*talking and seeing if something develops? E-*
*flirt??? Seriously, that even exists?*


I also added my ethnic make up—half Italian/half Russian. (It's an east coast thing: one's nationality. In Arizona I don't ever recall the subject coming up. People were White, Black or Hispanic. Period.) I answered the "favorite things" question which had formerly been left blank:

*Fog and church bells. Trains. Puppies and*
*babies. Commercials that make me cry. Movies*
*from the 40s and 50s. Good conversation. Red*
*wine. Black coffee. Pizza and pretty much*
*anything Italian—especially food and shoes.*

"Favorite activities" was another formerly blank section response now not:

*Flea markets and vintage shops and finding*
*that thing I didn't know I needed and now can't*
*live without. Going where I've never been.*

Would these small changes made me more marketable, more socially and romantically desirable, less stand-offish or aloof? In a word—more dateable? I had no idea. But what did I have to lose? I had to try, even though I didn't—and still don't—believe any of these hoops matter beyond the photo. Speaking of . . . I deleted the pictures that were posted sideways and upside down—the selfie and the one of me in uniform with two other flight attendants. (Their topsy-turvy, screwed up orientations had pissed me off from day one. Plus, their sarcastic captions probably weren't helping my cause.) I added one taken with my grandbaby and grand dog (more smalz) and another with my youngest son that had always been one of my favorites. (Great smile, good hair *and* I looked really thin. The photo trifecta for women everywhere.)

I concluded the week with a needed bookkeeping/maintenance issue. I logged on and arranged to cancel Site #2, thankfully set to expire soon. (**Note:** All sites work the same. **If you don't cancel, they will automatically renew your membership and charge your card.** Be proactive if you don't want to be stuck paying for another unwanted tour of Web World's Field of Dating Dreams.) As far as Site #2 . . . been there, done that, had the T-shirt. And it was going in the Goodwill box.

Despite *some* of their members' higher levels of education and elevated professions, this self-professed site for the more educated and "sophisticated" online dater had resulted neither in better choices nor a more rewarding online dating experience. If anything, it was less so. As time went on, the percentage of men without photos seemingly increased. The profiles declined in quality as well, becoming less substantive. I saw fewer and fewer fully complete profiles. My guess? I had run through the ones serious enough to pay and was now relegated to the looky-loo level, where all those personality type-measuring response questions were way too demanding of time and effort for the unpaying curiosity-seekers perusing for free.

But one never knows if one doesn't try. What doesn't work for one, might well pan out beautifully for another. Only a couple of days ago a friend told me about a couple she knows, 48 and 52. A year after meeting on a site for professional singles, they were now buying a house together. *Mosel tov!* My friend didn't remember the name of that site, but it wasn't either of mine. (Gee, go figure.)

Along your online journey, just always remember one irrefutable truth: Online dating sites are in business as a business. Consider this telling fact, appearing in an April 2015 article by *Washington Post's* Drew Harwell: "According to company filings for 2014, Match Group (which includes Tinder, Match, and OkCupid—betcha didn't know that! I sure didn't.) brought in more than $600 million in the U.S. alone." I say again, *in business as a business*. Ergo, three caveats to keep in mind . . .    1) Dating site mottos (such as "It's real life, but better" and "Do you want fast or forever") are advertising hype designed to attract *paying* members.    2) So too those smiling photos of attractive people who are supposedly already members—or even better, satisfied former members who found their Prince or Princess Charming. (Ever hear the expression "salting the mine?") 3) Beware and be smart. That enticing tag line "you have the right be demanding" does *not* mean they have the responsibility to deliver. Oh, and BTW and FYI:  According to the same Washington Post article mentioned above, "The industry is expected to grow by *another* $100 million every year through 2019." *Caveat emptor,* people. *Caveat emptor.*

In conclusion:  Ladies, it might be helpful to think of falling in love as making a stew.  Men are the meat. (No pun intended.) Once upon a time, this necessary component used to take time to tenderize and flavorize. Not anymore. Today, thanks to the internet, it's all been pre-prepared with the dial on high. Moreover, in that crockpot of quick and easy which is online dating, hard sell propaganda is an always present ingredient. Before you ladle out a serving, best to stir in a pinch of skepticism.    And always—always—taste with a grain of salt.

## Chapter Twenty-seven
## Month 5—Age is a Number

*Age is an issue of mind over matter. If you don't mind,*
*it doesn't matter . . . .* Mark Twain

Given jamada's lack of attention from men born in the 1970s or even 60s, the decision to "go old(er)" was pretty much a no-brainer. *Addio a notti Cougar. Ciao a giorni Codger.* (Translation: Goodbye cougar nights. Hello codger days.) And yes, it's Italian. Because if you're still believing in that whole "age is a just number" mindset— and good for you!—you're likely going to need a foreign language. American men may say it—however, European men . . . But enough of me and my vampish past. Let's return to jamada's revamped profile . . .

**I'll be damned!** (Probably so. That's another topic. See above.) **It worked!** My new SSSS strategy of "out with the heroes" did indeed solicit new interest. And fittingly, a new theme song: *Send in the Clowns.* Oops! On second thought . . . *don't bother. They're here* . . . They showed up IMMEDIATELY after I changed my profile. But I'm getting ahead of myself. Let's backtrack, shall we?

Whether just making changes triggered some algorithm which made my profile *appear* new—or my less intellectual, more romantic and sensitive self was more attractive, I'll never know. Maybe, too, the golden ticket to the golden oldies was changing my age preference? Older men, threatened by my wanting younger, were now less put off? (If you'll recall, according to NSA, my stated younger man preference might have been working against me.) Whatever the reason, numbers don't lie. And there were *a lot* of numbers!

Just to be sure, I went back and counted. In the previous two weeks I had been averaging 2 or 3 profile views a day, with a "like," or "he's interested in you" or a "fav" or "wink" message once a week. After submitting the redo, "jamada" received 36 views the first day! Granted, three quarters of them passed her by uninterested. But 25% didn't. In a single day, nine men clicked on a "yes, "fav" or "interested" button.

Before anyone gets too excited, they were:

- 63, seeking 41-59 (fyi, looked *much* older.)
- 72, seeking 55-68 (definitely too old.)
- 63, seeking 45-60 (overweight and creepy looking)
- 55, seeking 54-65, went the extra mile and also sent a wink. (a viable prospect)

[He stood out because he was the only man open to women substantially older. His user ID was, however, a turn-off—*Hotready4her*. Seriously? His looks weren't off-putting and his profile wasn't half bad though. He described himself as being possessive of (my word, not his) a positive attitude and old school etiquette. "Keep your glass half full and I'll refill the wine," he wrote. It was a cute line. In a black and white photo, that was a great picture, he looked to really love his grandbaby. Points in my book, to be sure.]

- 62, seeking 50-70, wrote "i love god" in his beginning paragraph (too religious)
- 37, seeking 19-70, a stocky Hispanic (19-70? No)

[He must have run his profile though an iTranslate program given his syntax and verb usage: I like to have fun and drink. I'm better to see if you can because very nice."]

- 58, seeking 50-69 with a hidden profile, residing in NC (NC? nope)
- 54, seeking 40-50, also with a hidden profile and no photo (no— learned my no photo lesson with BB)
- 63, seeking 41-59, also no photo (and no)

In addition to the nine men above who clicked their minimal interest with minimal effort, three men actually bothered to write. Below (and verbatim) are the unsolicited emails which arrived that first day, including any response from me, mental, written or otherwise:

- 69, seeking 58-72. *I would have emailed u, but y waste my time since ur looking for younger men.* Dude! Pot calling the kettle black! Plus his use of text shorthand bugged me. I wrote back just for spite: "lol so 2 r u looking 4 younger. Good luck 2 us both." (Shockingly, I never heard back.)
- 58 year-old, Jewish, who listed himself as "average." His photos indicated heavier. *I like your profile and pictures... the smoking? I'm good with it . . . no issues.* Well, thank you very much! I was annoyed—but still went back and changed my "trying to quit" to "occasional." Truthfully, I

considering just lying and clicking on the "no way" option, but figured screw it! I am not going to lie— even if 80% of the others do. (I didn't respond)

- 33 Black, seeking 18-99. *well I don't know what to say.* His profile headline said plenty: *Let's be friends and see where it leads what do you have to loose*{sic} (I passed and didn't respond)

Day 2 produced fewer hits and responses. Yet the numbers were still up in comparison to prior weeks: 29 views with 1 like, 1 fav and 1 unsolicited email. Among them:

- 66, separated, seeking 55-66. At least he was honest regarding his "a few extra pounds" weight designation. (I didn't respond. I still don't do separated.)
- 63, seeking 57-64, a 5'6" retired teacher who loves museums, looking for a woman who "doesn't mind reading subtitles." He says he is not a believer in organized religion, but is spiritual. He is trying to be a writer. (Despite his height, I found him somewhat interesting. I responded. I never heard back.)
- 58, Hispanic, seeking 40-57, whose profile read: "DON'T FORGET MY INGLES IS NOT TO {sic} GOD {sic}. He wrote, *hi how are you If it's ok w/you I would like to know you* (I didn't respond)

In total, jamada's reworked profile received 77 views the first three days. (FYI, on the fourth day, interest greatly subsided, returning to the normal couple hits a day.) To be honest, I didn't see a winner in the bunch. But at least now there *was* a bunch. Which segues to my recommendation now . . .

Online dating's success hinges on random chance inevitably occurring *if* the numbers are high enough. (Think monkey pecking away at a keyboard—eventually Cheetah will type out a coherent sentence.) Therefore any action which has the potential to increase those numbers should be entertained. If you are finding yourself in a shallow dating pool with inflowing interest slowed to a trickle, by all means! Rework your profile. The action will essentially turn the spigot on high for a couple days. One never knows . . . in the ensuing flood, a winner might just plop into your pool and bob to the surface.

For me, the success I achieved was what I had been aiming for. Sorta. While I didn't actually unearth a new man for chapter inspiration *per se*, I did stumble upon a new topic for research and exploration:   A-G-E. More specifically, **age preference** and **age gap** as they apply to the male/female relationship in general, to dating overall and to online dating in particular.

In truth, the entire subject of age differences and preferences as they relate to mating, dating or marrying is neither a new nor unrecognized issue. From the beginning of time, men have preferred younger women, while women have preferred older men. Conventional wisdom attributes these preferences to pure physiological urge and need:  the male urge to procreate and the female need to be provided for. In simplest terms, while Cavewoman Barbie was bearing and birthing Caveman Ken's procreations, she needed him to go out and hunt down a hunk of meat to throw on the fire so that they could all survive. Fast forward a few million years (give or take) and Modern Barbie is still bearing and birthing, only now she needs Modern Ken to go work for a wad of cash to throw in the bank so they can all survive. Toss in the two facts that 1) a woman's fertility *decreases* with age and 2) a man's resources *increase* with age and there you have it. (Drum roll, please) The tried, trite and true male preference for younger and the female for older.

Note: Before you get all woman's lib on me . . . yes, today's Feminist Barbie *can* indeed do it alone—she can bring home the bacon and fry it up in a pan and still pop out kiddos some anonymous sperm donor jacked off in a specimen cup for. That's not my point here.

Historical and contemporary examples of the older man/younger woman pattern abound. The past is loaded with old-ass royalty marrying essentially children. During the Middle Ages the Church had to pass an edict, proclaiming the "legal" age of consent to be 12. Lest you think ancient history, consider Hollywood. Woody Allen and Soon-yi, anyone? But the heart wants what the heart wants . . . so no judgment. (Yeah, right.) An older man and 20 year plus younger woman rarely raises an eyebrow, in real life and on film. Hollywood is notorious for casting much younger actresses as the romantic interest of a much more "mature" actor. It's even been an integral plot point. Ever see *Sabrina*? Btw, in real life Bogie was 25 years older than Becall. When they married, he was 46 and she 21. And it's not just actresses from the Golden Age of Hollywood inclined to go golden oldies older. When Michael Douglas married Catherine Zeta-jones in 2000, he was 56 and she was 31. Larry Kings' 8th wife is 26 years younger. There are, however, larger age gaps. Ask Robert Duvall. His wife is 41 years younger. While the age gap pattern overwhelmingly features older man/younger woman, it is not exclusively such. Demi Moore, Tina Turner, J-lo and Madonna are just a few who come immediately to mind.

So what *is* society's *acceptable* age gap between a couple—married or dating? I'm glad you asked.

Apparently there is a well-known rule of thumb I never heard of. It's a mathematical formula that research, conducted and published in 1992 by a couple of behaviorists named Kendrick and Keefe, shows to be pretty accurate *for men*. (Gee, color me surprised). The rule is to take your current age, divide it in half and then add 7 years. Example: a 50 year old man . . . divided by 2 is 25, add 7. *Voila!* His youngest "acceptable" woman is 32. For a 60-year-old man, she would be 37 and for an 80-year-old geezer, the woman changing his diapers would be 47. We all know of couples that personify that gap—and then some. Anna Nicole? But an 80-year-old woman with a 47-year-old man? Yeah . . . not so likely, but probably in existence somewhere. Were I to personally utilize the "half plus 7 rule," my youngest "acceptable" man would be 37. (Oops. Guilty as charged. Once. In Munich. Told ya . . . European.) Moving on . . .

In addition to historical and pop cultural anecdotal examples there is actual hardcore data. For example, the following—regarding the age difference in American heterosexual married couples—comes from the 2013 US Current Population Survey:

| Age difference | % of All Married Couples |
|---|---|
| Husband 20+ years older than wife | 1.0 |
| Husband 15–19 years older than wife | 1.6 |
| Husband 10–14 years older than wife | 4.8 |
| Husband 6–9 years older than wife | 11.6 |
| Husband 4–5 years older than wife | 13.3 |
| Husband 2–3 years older than wife | 20.4 |
| Husband and wife within 1 year | 33.2 |
| Wife 2–3 years older than husband | 3.5 |
| Wife 4–5 years older than husband | 3.3 |
| Wife 6–9 years older than husband | 2.7 |
| Wife 10–14 years older than husband | 1.0 |
| Wife 15–19 years older than husband | 0.3 |

A quick glance reveals that over a third of American married couples in 2013 are within a 1 year age difference from one another. That sounds pretty good . . . until one does some math and realizes the following:

- 52.7% of **all** married men in the United States are married to younger women, while only 14.1% of women are married to younger men.
- 24.9% of married American men have wives 9-5 years older, while 6% of women have husbands 9-5 years younger.
- 18% of all wedded American males are married to women, who are either almost—or definitely—young enough to be their daughters, while only 4.3% of women are similarly robbing the cradle.
- In fact, in every age gap grouping except 20 years and older, men's younger spouse numbers are 4 times higher than women's.
- In the 20 and plus years group, men are married only 3 times as often to younger spouses than are women.

Reinforcing the data above (while demonstrating how little the female marrying preference has changed in 20 years) is a 1994 study regarding women's marrying preferences:

- At age 20-29 women were willing to marry 10 years older
- at 30-39 they were willing to marry 8 years older

- at 40-49 the age gap decreases to a preference of 6 years older
- over 50 their ideal match is 6 years older.

All of the preceding statistics concern marriage, however. Let's turn now to the topic of age gap in **dating**, specifically dating in the 40 and above age groups, where the older man/younger woman age disparity is less influenced by evolutionary urge and need.

Once and if the desire for children is off the table, one might expect women in their 40s to become more desirable to men in their own age bracket. Similar life's experiences, values, frames of cultural reference, etc. right? Wrong. According to a 2010 British psychological study about human behavior, most men *regardless of age* prefer younger, physically attractive women, while most women *of any age* prefer successful, established men their age or older. The societal norm deck is stacked in the man's favor, because a younger woman on an older man's arm is viewed as vindication of masculinity and proof of sexual prowess. Women with a younger man yen are, however, are less lauded by society.

Attitudes may change though, as time goes on and the pairing of younger man and older woman becomes more commonplace. History has done nothing if not to show how much longer it takes for barriers to fall and for women to earn and/or enjoy the rights, privileges and freedoms men do. The right to vote for American women didn't happen until 1920. Hell! We weren't even eligible to sit on juries in Mississippi until 1968! Equal pay for equal work still doesn't exist.

Aiding our "equal right to date younger" cause are a couple facts of modern life. Life expectancy continues to rise as both genders take better care of themselves (exercise, diet, medical advancements, etc.). But look at a photograph of any couple over 50. I will bet you $100 she looks better than he does. Make-up, hair dye, cosmetic procedures . . . subterfuge that works! Moreover, "older" women today not only look younger than their grandmothers just two generations ago, they act younger. I can remember my own grandmother, who was probably around the age I am now. She was the classic Old World grandma—black-clad, heavy stockings, sturdy shoes, every day Mass going, rosary bead counting Italian widow. Seeing her as a sexual being would have been like looking up the skirt of the Virgin Mary statue! And yet, sexual we are! Women over 50 might be seen by society as invisible and undesirable—and past the age of playing bedroom checkers—but nothing could be further from the truth.

It is not hard to theorize that as today's older women embrace their still viable sexuality, they may well in ever increasing numbers go younger. Someday women may actually reverse their longstanding and traditional preference and do as men have been doing for a long time—forgoing older altogether. In fact, many older woman already do, particularly those who nursed a now deceased spouse. These former caregivers are extremely reluctant to repeat the Florence Nightingale routine and therefore are nixing an older partner from the get-go for fear of future health issues.

Seriously, ladies . . . the movement has started! A 2003 AARP survey published in *Time* magazine revealed that 34% of 40 and older women were dating younger men. A subsequent AARP poll in 2008 reconfirmed that nearly 1/3 of women between the ages of 40 and 69 were dating men at least 10 years younger. I suggest reading *Older Women, Younger Men.* One of its co-authors, Susan Winter, does an excellent job of explaining the factors between older women and younger men that create "a powerful chemistry between them."

Finally, let's examine age preference and age gap as they specifically relate to **online dating.** Surprise! Surprise! In general, most people dating online want younger. *Time* magazine's Alexandra Sifferlin writes, "Numbers culled from various dating sites have consistently shown both sexes prefer to date down the age spectrum rather than up." So, how far down, one might ask. Elite Singles, an over 50 dating site, tried to find out by analyzing the upper and lower age search limits of more than 450,000 of their members. Their findings revealed that not only did the older man desiring younger women stereotype hold true, it held true by a substantial margin. Men between the ages of 60-69 preferred on average a partner up to 11 years younger. At the opposite end of their stated preference, the maximum age they desired in a match was a single year older. In fact, according to research conducted with the members of other dating sites, 42% of men surveyed wouldn't even consider a woman older. (Yet 22% of that 42% did say they would respond if she writes first.) For women over 50, their preferred age gap preference was 6 years older and no more than 5 years younger. However, women are five times more likely to shown interest in a man five years younger as opposed to five years older.

While googling the whole age gap in online dating issue I stumbled across a male forum/chat room dedicated to online dating age issues. It was rather eye-opening, to say the least. Pretty much it was men in their 30s and 40s lying about being younger because they want women in their 20s. One 36-year-old man openly admitted he prefers to hang out with "and fuck" women in their mid to late twenties. Since he is (in his opinion) in good shape and easily passes for younger, his question was whether or not he should cop to his real age. The consensus from his forum buddies? Go for it, dude. Lie—if you can get away with it. "After all, women lie," was an oft cited response.

Push-up bras, fake nails and hair, blah, blah, being given as examples of the "two wrongs make a right" justification. One guy recommended "going as low as you can pass." His reasoning was, "Later it won't matter, if something is there." From what I could gather reading the posts, it was not an concern of any sort that men 35-40 were dating and banging girls 18-26. High fives and fist bumps for all! There was a sole exception, however, one charming asshole who questioned the need to lie at all. He personally had no problem admitting his real age because it presented no problem, since "men's value increase with age unlike women's." He cited status and material wealth as the reasons younger women didn't care. (Sad, but true.)

Considering the widespread preference for younger, I was less than shocked by several other tidbits uncovered during my quest for information about age-preference, age-gap and simply age-related online dating issues. Whether it was Facebook posts, online chat rooms, dating blogs or published articles, a recurring theme was truthfulness. Or rather the lack thereof. People complaining about people lying about their ages in their dating profiles was by far the most common protest—which made coming across the instructions on how to change one's age on a particular dating site all the more hilarious! Hint: you have to go in and change your birth**date**. (Duh!) The mere fact this question—and its answer—exist, says a lot. The issue is not gender specific. The overall consensus is that both sexes lie. Ergo, the universal recommendation is to go—exactly as the male forum advised—as low as you can pass. When you do, never fear. There are other chat rooms, posts and blogs available to discuss the fallout. So what happens if you *do* connect with someone younger and now are forced to tell the truth? Again, the forum guys nailed it. The consensus was overwhelming, too. If there's a real and mutual attraction, it won't matter *after the fact*. So why eliminate a contender at the gate? Go young or go home!

All of this newly acquired information aroused my curiosity. How did my own SSSS-inspired trip to Old(er) Man Town compare to official studies and published statistics? To take a closer peek, I slid the entire list of men who had viewed jamada 2.0 beneath the preference lens of the age-gap microscope. The men ranged themselves in age from 50 to 74. (I'm not counting the language-challenged 37-year-old with his 19-70 preference nor a 33-year-old without a photo who was interested in 18-99.) At the lower (younger) end of their preference spectrum, *all* 75 of them wanted younger than their own professed age, anywhere from 33 years to a single year younger. The average preference, however, was **13 years younger**. On the higher (older) end, more than 26% *still* preferred women younger than themselves, while 15% were actually willing to go as old as their own age. And the rest? The over 58% willing to open the door to older? Well . . . they didn't open it by much. Despite their 13 year preference for younger, their average *maximum* desired age was **5 years older**.

According to the Elite study mentioned previously, men 60-69 had an on average age gap preference of 11 years older and only a single year older. My viewers had an average age preference of 13 years older and 5 years older. Take what you will from those numbers. What I took from it was a profound sense of being screwed in every way except the one that matters.

The challenge of being a "mature" woman looking for a partner, mate, companion or date is not for the faint of heart. Trust me. "Sixty is the new sexy" is just a cute tag line. Online or off, you are not what men your own age are looking for—much less what younger men want! "Our time," my ass!

So what's an old broad online looking to do? If you can't beat 'em, join 'em? Do you lie about your age in the hope the fib levels the field? Do you stick to your principles and refuse to settle, holding fast to the belief what is meant to be, will be? Or do you cling to a different cliché. If there is a mutual attraction, age truly is just a number.

The choice to try online dating is a personal decision. Likewise the decision on how—or even if—to proceed once you've been discouraged. My best advice is this: Don't immediately jump ship and abort the whole mission. Try breathing new life into that old profile with some updated material. Another recommendation is to refocus on the end game and whatever your *most* important goal might be. Know it will probably require concessions. Looks, money, personality, sense of adventure, cultured tastes, sexual attraction, companionship . . . sure it would be great to find them all. And perhaps you will. However, you should also be prepared for a dial-back of expectations. You may have to compromise and go older, heavier, balder, shorter. But do it stages. Think jettisoned fuel tanks falling away in order to reach altitude.

By all means, shoot for the moon to start. Pack your romance rocket with all the power you can: hope, excitement, lofty expectations, idealistic fantasies and happily ever after dreams. Blast off and soar! But if/when your lunar dreams fail to materialize and you find yourself leveling off, the time to adjust your trajectory might be at hand. Maybe outer space isn't attainable. But Earth has five layers of atmosphere. Defying gravity and reaching the stratosphere or troposphere *could* turn out to be a hell of a ride.

Life rarely—if ever—delivers all desires. I always think back on a sign I once saw hanging in a printing shop:

*You can have it quick, cheap or good.*
*Pick two.*

## Chapter Twenty-eight
## Week 22—It's In His Kiss

To say I'm cynical about love in general would be an understatement. After all, happily ever after didn't happen when I was young. Now I'm older, thicker, grayer and shrewder on the outside—and annoyingly, every bit as insecure, self-doubting and stupid on the inside. Acne and braces and bad decisions don't seem so incongruous. But age spots and wrinkles and poor choices? Seriously, just WHEN do pheromones and hormones lose their power and wisdom and common sense kick in? Talk about frustrating! To be old enough to know better—and yet to NOT act smarter. *Single at Sixty and Still Stupid.* I wonder if that title would sell? But once again I'm getting ahead of myself figuratively and quite literally . . .

As my 22$^{nd}$ week down the dot com dating rabbit-hole approached its midpoint, I was still searching for a chapter topic. What to write that hadn't already been covered? The thought of another list of ages and preferences and usernames made me cringe. By now I had surely made my point—and my case. After five months traversing an online dating minefield rife with rejection, disappointment and frustration, to say I'm not discouraged about ever finding someone would be a lie. And yet when I started this experiment some 150 days ago, I think I really *did* secretly believe in love, in second chances, do-overs and new beginnings. In short, in possibilities. Time and experiences since have taught me differently.

At the conclusion of the previous chapter, I wrote about the need to examine one's primary focus for going online. Curiosity, amusement? Hope in general? (Ahhhh . . . hope . . . life's individual flotation device. No matter the challenge—just slip your arms through the straps and hug the hope cushion close to your chest . . . Sorry. Couldn't resist the flight attendant metaphor.) Or are the goals more specific? In simplest terms, ladies, you need to ask yourself what you're *really* wanting: affection, attention, courtship, romantic love or carnal satisfaction? There's no right or wrong answer. Each woman has her own desires based upon her own financial, physical, emotional, social or sexual situation. The key to finding is identifying. (Sorry. Another metaphor ahead.)

I liken my own discovery process to having poured any and all desires, wants and needs into a pot with the heat set on high. For five months I watched the resultant broth bubble. I stirred it constantly and even added new ingredients, waiting anxiously, ever hopeful in my deepest recesses. Only the process didn't produce what I had expected. Like rendering fat out of meat, thickening juices into sauce or reducing drippings to gravy, the process boiled away the liquid, leaving a slurry-like paste at the bottom of the pot: in essence and over time, extracting from a plethora of possibilities my essential and single most important want. So what *do* I want? For right now, let's table that.

In *Getting Naked Again* (Yes, I bought the book) psychologist, PhD and author Judith Sills writes a truly valuable how-to guide for women 40 and older starting over after divorce, death or being dumped. Considering the fact that prior to my online experiment, I pretty much managed—over a span of four freaking months—to qualify (in order) on *all three* grounds, I consider myself the quintessential textbook example of an over 50, nearing 60, year-old woman starting over. I may not be a PhD, but I've got life framed on my wall.

So . . . here you have it, with an assist from Dr. Sills . . . lessons lived and learned—and condensed into a handy-dandy 3 step starting over synopsis:

1. **Rejection**. Don't kid yourself. It happens. And it hurts! Whether online or

off—and even if you really don't even want the balding, potbellied loser—being stood up or ghosted by him still stings! Furthermore, it erodes your self-esteem and resurrects even long dormant insecurities. Let's face it, after 486 profile views, only 52 email contacts and a scant score of replies that resulted in 1 lousy dinner date . . . How could any human in her right mind *not* feel rejected?

2.  **Self-doubt**. Being rejected during the dating/starting over process—*especially* if you were the one dumped or divorced—inevitably leads to the belief that something is wrong with you. And then whoa, Nellie! Suddenly your "toos" (too old, too fat, too needy, too controlling, too whatever) become a torrent, raging down Rebuff Mountain to sweep you in self-pity and drown you in doubt. Before you realize it, you are convinced you are undesirable and unworthy of being loved—especially if you were left, dumped or divorced for a better model with obvious upgrades. But even if you divorced him, society has a tendency to still consider *you* the one lacking. Whether he was an alcoholic, abuser, control freak . . . it doesn't matter. YOU walked, so YOU failed to make it work. YOU failed to honor the whole "for better for worse til death do us part" promise, and so YOU broke up the family—happy or not. "No wonder no one wants you now!" screams your

inner insecure self. Dr. Sills calls this spate of emotions a "flood."

3. **Giving up**. At some point, the feelings faucet turns off. Hot emotion turns to icy indifference. Dr. Sills refers to this as the "freeze." I call it the "fuck it" phase. No one is ever going to want you—not now, not later, not ever—so what's the fucking point of trying? You might as well throw in the dating towel, take up knitting and get a cat. (I love the TV promo I recently saw for an upcoming episode of some comedy show. The mom asks her adult daughter, "So, now that I'm undesirable to men, do the cats just show up? Or do I need to go to the shelter and pick some out?" I may have misquoted it, but the essence, humor and truth are certainly there.)

According to Dr. Sills (who I am sure *does* have a PhD framed on her wall), all of the emotions and reactions above are normal. She calls the whole process "healing." And healing, she says, "is slow and it does not occur in a straight line." Healing entails answering a lot of questions, too. For example, what it is that you want now? And what is it that you'll want later? You might not know right away. And that is ok. Here is where Dr. Sills believes dating of any form helps, online or off. (Personally, I'm not too sure—but I'll defer to the expert.) Even if all you learn from the experience is what you don't want, that's progress. It gets you closer to what you do. (I'll buy that.) Dr. Sills talks at length about the need to "relax your requirements," "check your attitude" and "cut yourself and the guy across the table a break." She also advocates re-examining one's objectives, contending that are "different men for different purposes," whether they be for travel, dinner, conversation or sex. She believes lowering expectations and shifting thinking will put "more fun and less fret" into the dating experience. Her final big piece of advice: "Slow down and resist your urge to hunt for The One" and look instead "for a little while, to date the many," because "even a lousy date can pay off in several ways." She lists them on pages 139-140 of her book, if you are interested.

For me, I had been there, done that. I was moving on. I was now poised over the stove and staring down at a glob of goop in the bottom of a pot. At some point down the dating road you, too, may be looking at the substance in your own pot, seeking to identify it. For one woman, it might turn out to be travel—with the overweight guy with ample financial means for expensive dinners and luxury vacations. For another woman, it may be a social life— obtained on the arm of a distinguished pillar of country club society with a very *un*pillar-like penis, who nevertheless looks great in a tux as he escorts her to the theater and ballet. For a third, it could be romantic gestures and fawning attention—received from a balding couch potato who opens the car door and buys her flowers every Friday without fail. For my beautiful, tall, leggy, blond, goofball (her word, not mine) girlfriend with a quirky sense of humor, her slurry/sludge essential substance *was* humor. (Found, since the original writing of this chapter, in a short sports director she met on a flight who makes her laugh.) As for me . . . well, my slurry turned out to be a little three letter word, beginning with S and ending with X, delivered—quite ironically—on the evening of my 60th birthday by a broad-shouldered 51-year-old French Canadian airline mechanic, with (so going against my type!!) *short blond* hair, fine features and great forearms.

The *Cliff's Notes* version is that I met him in a bar. He walked in. We talked. We clicked a little. We kissed.

We clicked a lot. He spent the night. I saved his number. The point of going into any further detail is to illustrate this chapter's true theme: How and why online cyber dating can never really compete with old-school offline, organic boy meets girl encounters. In order to tell the whole story, the scene needs to be set and my frame of mind explained. (It may be far too much detail, but I've always loved to write "when first sparks fly" passages . . . so just consider the following as pages in a romance novel—or skip them. Your choice. But since it's my book, they stay.)

I had been dreading my 60th birthday for months and been mentally preparing for it for weeks. But like most of life's momentous moments, nothing truly prepares. At least, that's how it was for me. The actual day, September 28th, had dawned in Germany. I had worked the Frankfurt flight over and was headed home. Thankfully, not alone. A girlfriend and fellow flight attendant had made it her personal mission that I celebrate the dreaded event. To that end, she'd grabbed a free seat (perks of the biz) on my flight. She had never been to Mainz before, so I enjoyed playing tour guide, showing her the sights of our layover city: cathedral, river, medieval open-timbered houses, fountains and town squares . . . the whole postcard perfect package. We'd drunk wine sitting outside at a café nestled on a narrow cobble-stone street and had dinner in a four-hundred-year-old as authentic as they get German restaurant. And we had shopped. From the outside, it was the perfect girls' get-away. On the inside, however, I was a depressed mess, trying to pretend all was right in my world when it so wasn't. The effusive birthday wishes from my crewmembers and passengers rang hollow and meant nothing. I was misery in red heels, ready to go home and wallow.

Landing in Philly around 2 pm, I was over the day. Not only was I still on 6 hours ahead European time (and so technically an hour or so from bed), I was tired of pretending there was anything to celebrate. My girlfriend was of a different mindset, now viewing the actual day of my birth as one calling for continued and obligatory merriment. Sealing my doom was a call she received while we were on the employee bus headed to the parking lot. It was from her ex, a pilot. They had broken up, but were doing the "still friends" thing. Still in love with him, she jumped at the chance to see him—using me and my birthday as a convenient excuse to innocently meet up with him at an Irish bar in my neighborhood. "For the birthday drink you have to have on your official birthday," was how she put it. I went along with the farce, because that's what friends do.

At my place we changed. We were both in uniform and that's a big no-no in a bar. She agonized over her appearance. She truly does not understand how beautiful she is. A leggy, mid-40s blond with a killer personality, I see Grace Kelly in her. She sees a giant goofball. (We women are so fucking hard on ourselves!) I tell her otherwise constantly. She doesn't believe me. Of course, I don't believe her either. She is my biggest cheerleader, dubbing me "Executive Platinum" and too good for the losers I've encountered online. At any rate, Goofball Grace wore a cute tunic and leggings, while I threw on my go-to black skirt, a burgundy top, gray heels and my new gray scarf—a birthday gift from GG and a memento of our Mainz excursion. Hair frizzy and kinky. I didn't care. It had been up for work in a uniform-compliant top knot. And I hate it up. Down I can hide behind it. It makes me look younger. It takes the focus off my face. One sees the dark lips, wild hair, prominent nose for sure and eyebrows—then the wrinkles. (I think.)

The bar is just down the street, so we walked. A typical local tavern with high tables, blaring TVs, mediocre live music and a booming after work crowd. GG's ex-boyfriend/and still current object of interest was already there, sipping on a Coke since he was on call. Of course I'd seen pictures. But my first thought was still: yuck! He was short and bald. She could do so much better! Knowing how he had hurt her, I was fully prepared to dislike him. Nonetheless, I was friendly, albeit at a loss. What did she see in him? And yet, she glowed. She was absolutely animated and so comfortable with him. And he with her. There was clearly a past between them far from resolved.

Fast forward an hour, a surprisingly good shepherd's pie and glass of terribly generic merlot later, and the short little bald shit had grown on me. (Yes, the same SLBS I wrote about before.) He was trying very hard to treat me well. Because he knew I mattered to her, he wanted to make a good impression. And damned if he wasn't. SLBS was actually beginning to appear attractive. Tired of being the third wheel and realizing the re-sparking love birds required some space, I headed for the patio and a needed cigarette. There were 6 or 7 left in the pack I'd bought in Mainz. Determined to quit (again) when they were gone, I'd carved in mental stone the day after my birthday as my new quit day. Maybe something good could come out of turning sixty? My last cigarette on my big 6-O.

Awash in memories of where I'd been my past two birthdays, in my Zurich lover's bed for my 58th and in my new Philly apartment looking at 42 boxes to unpack for my 59th, one cigarette quickly turned into two. I considered going back in. But it was hot inside, noisy and crowded, so I remained outside and people-watched. A few men came and went. None paid me any attention. Not that I expected otherwise. I am feeling pretty invisible these days. Some kind of office party in progress created an interesting, far ends of the socio-economic spectrum, clientele: men in shirts and ties alongside real working stiffs clad in a variety of uniforms—Fed Ex, UPS, US Postal, delivery drivers and surprisingly airline and airport workers. (Apparently, only flight attendants and pilots are subject to the no-drinking in uniform rule?) Women were in a definite minority. And I was the only one in heels and hose and a skirt—pretty out of place attire for a blue collar bar. Big surprise. I'm used to it. I'm out of place most places. In fact, I have been so all of my life—a byproduct of being a military brat and moving every other year. In my youth, I rather reveled in it. In my old age, I simply accept it. I don't give much of a fuck any more. I even do it on purpose, I think. A preemptive action, if you will. I distance myself first, so when the world does it, it's a lesser blow—which, BTW, never hurts as much as the one that takes you by surprise.

At least two cigarettes later, maybe three, a guy entered the patio from the parking lot. Since I was sitting alone at a centrally located table intended for 4 or 5 and I was watching him, it didn't take much for our glances to meet.

"Mind if I sit with you?" he asked, gesturing with the cigarette in his hand.

I figured he wanted use of the ashtray. "Sure. Why not?" I either said it or thought it.

Compared to the rest of the beer-bellied, Philadelphia sports team logo-wearing salt-of-the earth types that populated the place, he wasn't half bad. Really, really short blond hair, broad shoulders and nice forearms, a black T-shirt sans logo and jeans. He had pleasant, rather fine features, teeth a little spaced and a certain swagger. It seemed everyone on the damn patio knew him by name.

He asked if I was part of the office group.

"Nope, just trying to get away from it. It's crowded inside." (In hindsight his presumption made perfect sense. Remember, I was wearing a skirt, heels and hose—hardly the normal hoodie, tennies and jeggings look of a local.)

I honestly don't remember a lot of what transpired next. I remember the middle and the end. Just not the beginning. But I can tell you this . . . what I can't remember is EXACTLY why online dating doesn't work for me. It happened instantaneously . . . fast, intense, unscripted, undefined . . . a barrage of signals and responses, nuances and triggers. While online dating proceeds in a linear step by step movement—i.e. attraction begets contact, contact begets more contact, more contact creates more interest, etc., etc. until the actual face-to-face meet . . . offline is a star-burst in reverse. So much is incoming via an only subconsciously readable process that only raw instinct can respond to it. There is no time to think, to contemplate, weigh or deliberate. Bam! Fireworks! Explosion! What we all know as THE SPARK.

For how else can I explain what occurred next . . .

He introduced himself and said he was a mechanic. When he mentioned his employer's name, I laughed and pointed to myself.

"Flight attendant, same company."

He looked deliberately and pointedly at my legs. "I should have guessed . . . stockings and high heels."

"Not necessarily," I answered. "Less actually wear them than you'd think."

We chatted about travel, free flight benefits and other superficial stuff. The necessary steps in the verbal dance men and women do when they first meet, all for the purpose of learning background, compatibility and availability.

*(Pause here for an editorial comment . . . Read the following verbal exchange and tell me how it compares to sitting in front of a computer screen, scanning an online profile for "Marital Status." Go ahead. Read it. Then then tell me you don't feel heat.)*

I pulled another cigarette from my quickly emptying pack. When he made a move to light it, I let my touch on his hand linger. Then I took his hand and turned it to see if a wedding ring was present.

"Got a wife?" I asked.

"Nope. Got two ex ones though." He tossed his lighter back onto the table.

"Where are they?"

He shrugged. "Don't know. Don't give a fuck." He looked at me. "Where's yours?"

"Dead."

And so the whole issue of availability was resolved.

*(So? Is it just me—or is that not hot?)*

Conversation continued and I learned more. He was sure of him, for sure! A bad boy, who preferred to party in Vegas or Florida. He probably drank too much, but worked just as hard. Not relationship material by a long shot, but then . . . I wasn't looking for a relationship.

"I've met you before," he said.

"No. You haven't."

"Yeah . . . I have. I'm sure of it. I've met you before."

Was he talking past lives? If it was a line, it was one I'd never heard before. He said he was a Taurus. (I wasn't surprised.) He asked what kind of music I liked.

"Pretty much anything, except rap. I like R & B and Mo-town, especially."

He talked about rock music's roots in Blues.

"Muddy Waters," I responded, "influenced the Beatles a lot."

He seemed impressed. We talked about education as well. I was impressed when, after I opined over the lack of relevance our system has for most teenagers, he complimented me on the perfect word choice: "relevance." Who knew a mechanic could be so layered?

My girlfriend came out to check on me. She smiled knowingly. She knew.

"You have to come in and have another birthday drink," GG said, before turning her focus to him. "It's her birthday today."

"Happy Birthday," he said.

"Yeah, whatever," I answered, waving as GG judiciously exited stage right. "It's not exactly one I want to celebrate."

"Why not?"

"I don't want to be as old as it makes me."

He shrugged. "Age is just a number. I'm 51."

"I'm more."

He shrugged again and smartly dropped the subject. He introduced me to the bar's owner, now schmoozing with his patrons on the patio, then the owner's wife. They were clearly fond of him. I gathered he was a regular and hitting on a random female was probably not out of his ordinary. He went back to his car for his cigarettes, then got another drink: vodka, neat. I knew something was developing—and developing fast. The question was, did I let it continue? It was nice to have male attention. It had been four months since Z. Dr. Sills was whispering in my ear: "Go for it! Sometimes Mr. Right is just Mr. Right for right now."

I asked if he'd like to come back inside and join me and my friends. I half expected him to decline. He didn't. He sat down and easily introduced himself to GG's pilot. The fact we all four worked for the same airline created a superficial rapport for the quartet. However, it was the male connection that instantly formed between the men that truly fascinated me: two alphas respecting the other's turf as each moved in on their respective targeted for the night female . . . It was like watching *Wild Kingdom* live.

Talking airline, mine leaned in to better hear GG's over the music. At the same time I slipped my hand down the table to grab my wine, inadvertently (or not) creating contact. He touched my fingertips and played with them for a moment. Casual, natural, physical.

When conversation split again between couples, I turned in my stool to face him. He did the same, opening his legs to create room for me to move in closer.

"So which birthday is it?" he asked.

I copped to it, and he shrugged, indifferent as hell to my deep, dark secret.

*At least in this vodka/merlot fueled moment, age **didn't** matter, I thought. God bless alcohol—the elixir of equality responsible for getting fat, ugly **and** old women laid for centuries!*

"Why does it matter?" he then asked.

"Because women at a certain age become invisible."

"My mother is 72. And my mom *isn't* invisible."

"Ok. Not invisible," I conceded. "But they're not desirable. Even 50 or 60 year-old men are looking at 30 and 40. Why go with a 60-year-old?"

"Intellect," he answered. "There has to be something there to talk about afterwards."

Damn! He was earning points and clearly indicating he was interested. The next move was clearly mine to make—or not.

I leaned in to talk into his ear, above the noise. "So French Canadian, huh? I've never had one of those . . . ever fuck a grandmother?"

*(Yeah. I know, classy. And subtle. But subtlety and restraint have never been strong suites of mine. I'm all in— or all out.)*

He answered something I didn't hear, then apologized. "Too much? Too soon?"

I laughed. "I opened the door."

He leaned forward and gently swept aside my hair. "You're not invisible," he said with a light kiss.

285

Then he paused. Deliberately waiting for my signal? Whether it was my half smile or soft sigh or something else on a totally different sensory plane, I gave it. And he got it.

He placed both hands on either side of my face and kissed me, this time nipping at my lower lip and slipping his tongue inside as soon as I allowed it. Oh, he was good! (Later I would learn from GG, who had gotten it firsthand from SLBS, that the full on and in kiss did not go unobserved.)

After a very enjoyable moment, reason returned. Feeling foolishly on display, I broke it off and said I needed a cigarette. Without waiting to see if he would follow, I headed back to the patio. He followed. At a corner table we took up where we'd left off. Blame it on the wine, four months of celibacy, five months of rejection or depression over turning 60 . . . whatever the catalyst, we made out like a couple of horny teenagers.

Eventually we came up for air. "So you just walked here?" he asked, referencing an earlier exchange wherein I told him I lived close by.

"Just down the street," I answered.

He looked at me. One of those looks that speaks volumes . . . "Let's take a walk."

I went inside to retrieve my purse and scarf and to tell GG I was leaving. "I'm going to need a little time before you come over."

She laughed. "Text me."

"Don't worry," SLBS chimed in, "we've been talking. She can stay at my place."

Normally I would never do that to a girlfriend, but extraordinary circumstances call for . . . moreover, I was clearly doing her a favor. She had been wanting to get back together with him for months. Besides, I didn't actually figure it would take that long. (Wam-bam, thank you ma'ams never do.)

We walked down the street toward my house. At some point he laughed and told me to slow down. I wasn't in a hurry, I've just always walked fast.

Inside my apartment he paused and looked around. "This is nice," he said, before pulling me to him. His hands went up under my top as we kissed. He fumbled with the bra's clasp, then just yanked. Hard and two-handed.

*Fuck! That was my red Victoria Secret! The most expensive bra I own!* I remember thinking. It was kind of sexy though, I had to admit. (The next day I bent the hook back and sewed in a new eye.)

Once he had the access he wanted, he was slow, deliberate, tactile, lusty and dominant. And good. In the middle of it all, the most ridiculous thought popped into my head, a recently read piece of horoscope trivia: Taurus is the most sensual of all the signs; "if anyone can make your skin feel good, it's a Taurus man" . . . No shit!

Afterward, he said he needed a cigarette. He threw on his jeans. I grabbed a robe. My lease dictates no smoking, so we stood on the front porch. The wind was blowing, and it had started to rain. Shirtless, he pulled me close and held me. He asked if he could stay.

I don't do sleepovers. It's a firm rule of mine, yet I said yes. We headed back inside. After round 2 (even better than round 1), he said he was starving. He hadn't eaten. He was going to walk to the corner convenience store for a sandwich.

"I'll back in bit. If it's still ok I stay?"

In the meantime GG had texted and asked if I would leave the door unlocked so she could come get her stuff. When he came back, we went to bed. (I never heard her come in, though she told me the next day she and SLBS had both laughed at the way clothes were thrown around the living room.)

Following round 3 (difference skill set, but just as good), he held me for a long time. Then he started to snore.

I used to hate the sound. But after so many years of sleeping alone, it was strangely comforting. I rolled over and fell asleep with the strains of that stupid song running through my head: "Happy birthday to me, happy birthday to me. . ."

For the purpose of full disclosure, I need to tell you now that what comes next was written several weeks after the fact. I have seen him since, but that fact is not germane to my cause here, which is to discuss the inexplicable attraction of sexual attraction as it pertains to online versus offline dating.

That abstract, indefinable phenomenon of instant visual attraction and emotional appeal is often called THE SPARK by some and CHEMISTRY by others. It happens—or not—within seconds of meeting someone in the flesh. The feeling varies with the individual. It can be a very real sensation of actual heat, a pleasant flickering in the belly—the proverbial butterflies—or it can be a mere realization, conscious or not. To bastardize a famous quote about pornography by US Supreme Court Justice Potter Stewart . . . I can't define it. But I know it when I feel it.

In a dating advice article posted by eharmony, Melanie Schilling, a psychologist and dating coach, claims there are actually two types of sparks: the Wow and the Ahhh. The Wow, which tends to burn hard and fast, "creates amazing casual encounters." (Ya think, Melanie?) Yet it is short-lived, blowing out rather quickly. The Ahhh, on the other hand, is a slower burning, less intense, more comfortable and sustaining spark—ergo the type you probably want "as the basis of a long term relationship." Ms. Schilling contends that even if initially absent, the Ahhh "can develop over time." Thanks, but I'll pass. Trial and error have taught me when I don't feel it initially, it's "square peg in a round hole" time. It doesn't work, and trying is a waste of effort. (Of course, I'm single at sixty, so what the fuck do I know?)

Because sexual attraction often occurs seemingly upon reception of specific triggers—we all know what floats our boat—we tend to think there is an actual template—a certain set of desired characteristics like hair color, height, intellect, personality, body type, etc. which can manufacture it. Ergo, online dating sites' lists of preferences and the boxes we mentally check off when considering someone we encounter online.

Herein lies the fundamental problem of online dating, as I see it. We humans possess five senses, in addition to our brain, with its powers of thought, analysis, deductive reasoning, etc. While the online dating method is able to beautifully tap into our brains and all their technical and analytical abilities, our senses are pretty much left out of the selection for a mate/date process—except for the sense of sight. Semi-satisfied, at best, by a one dimensional photograph. (Big whoop!) Even eventually adding in the sound of someone's voice via a real phone call does not provide the full panoply. Furthermore, only a small percentage of the human brain processes verbal communication. We are wired for more and function thusly—sending and receiving wordless cues in a conscious and unconscious encoding and decoding process that cannot be recreated in virtual reality. "In living color" is more than an expression or a 90s TV show!

Think body language: facial expressions, gestures, eye contact, posture, distance proximity . . . According to the experts (and Wikipedia), these nonverbal behaviors comprise 75-85% of all human communication. Factor in tone of voice (hearing is 11%), touch (2%), taste (1%) and smell (3%), and now you have the full picture of human interaction and communication. The look in his eye, the crook of his smile, the tilt of his head . . . sure. Those can be relayed on a computer screen. But what about the smell of his skin, the taste of his kiss, the touch of his caress . . . how do you get those from a profile or a photo? Oh, you could—in person, of course! But chances are either or both of you will eliminate the other long before that *final stage of online dating* can be reached. For here's the curse of online: The numbers, the sheer volume of choices, create a "what if there's something better out there?" mentality that is a constant plug-puller on countless flickering interests. Before true current can flow, the off switch has been flipped. It is the exact opposite in organic dating. The face-to-face meet is *offline's first step*—not it's last.

The dating sites have sold us a bill of goods, convincing us we are "communicating" online. No. We are not. At least, not very much. We are typing on a keyboard, texting and emailing. There's a reason we had to invent emojis, people! Absent tone, inflection and accompanying visual cues, the written word is an ineffectual, ambiguous, subject to false interpretation means of connecting to an emotional end. Certainly, anyone who has ever had a text message "taken the wrong way" can attest to my point here.

Give me a man in the flesh. Let me read the nonverbal signals—how long he looks at me, how close he holds me, the fact he rinsed out his coffee cup the next morning before he put it in the sink . . . I'll take that any day over staring at a text and trying to decide if his use of ellipses indicates continued interest—or not.

In a nutshell . . . a keyboard is a means of contact. It is not a means of connection.

My slurry may change. But for now, I know what I what—and what I don't. I don't want to be hurt again. I don't want to give up my independence or lose my identity. I'm not interested in ever being married again. I don't want to play house. And I don't need a travel, dinner or social companion. That's what girlfriends are for. But most importantly, I don't want to ever settle again. Particularly if I think "less than what I want" is *as good as I can get.*

Maybe it's just another form of preemptive action? Perhaps. But at this space in time, as of this chapter's close, I am more secure than when I started.         A         final thought regarding who you find online . . . as opposed to stumbling across in life . . .

Online you know a lot—and feel nothing. Offline you know nothing—and feel everything.

# Chapter Twenty-nine
## Week 23—You've Got Mail

There's a supreme irony to this week's theme. After spending much of the last chapter finding fault with online dating's *modus communicationis*, here I am—still utilizing it! But when in Rome . . .

In summary and as previously discussed (no doubt to *ad nauseam*), for anyone over 40, what passes for "dating" in online dating is not so much dating, as it is an online social activity induced by a photo. Using a mathematical term to illustrate (and I HATE math!), the whole process begins as an algebraic equation: $p + i = o$. In plain English—**p**hoto plus **i**nterest equals **o**utreach. Often the outreach is merely a safe and anonymous toe-in-the water-testing wink, fav, like, etc. Occasionally, when interest and/or attraction is stronger, these easy, no effort required button-click options are skipped over in favor of an actual email, which usually includes an actual name, rather than a user ID. Sent without true knowledge of any common interest and/or attraction, this unsolicited email is online's equivalent of a cold call in sales. (The chances for a metaphorical hang-up are huge.) With curiosity, hope and adrenalin flowing, the recipient heads straight for the sender's profile to look at *their* photo. At which point, the process precedes a step. Math-wise, the equation expands—into one of two possibilities:

1) $o + p + 0(i) = 0$   (**o**utreach + **p**hoto + zero interest = zero response back)
2) $o + p + r(i) = e$   (**o**utreach + **p**hoto + **r**eciprocal **i**nterest = **e**mail)

It is important to remember that a response to an email *may not* trigger additional emails. However, should a flow of back and forth emails commence and continue . . . well, congratulations, Houston, you have lift-off. Let the digital dating begin! A term used to describe this first exciting flurry of electronic messages is **e-flirt.** There are articles written and webinars to attend available to teach the techniques and rules. For example:   keep it light, be mysterious and keep him hanging and wanting more. In essence, e-flirt is basically playing hard to get—cyber style. Just know that this little virtual world you have entered into of typed sweet nothings, witty word play and clever innuendo IS NOT REAL.

Eventually, if the emails continue long enough and the e-flirting is doing its job, one or both of the interested parties may suggest leaving the site. Phone numbers are exchanged, and the next phase of virtual dating starts: texting. Whoo-hoo! More typing. Chances are good, however, that this is the point at which digital contact will become a cellular intercourse of *both* texted and verbal communication. But wait! Don't go telling everyone (like in the commercials) that you "have met someone" just yet. BECAUSE YOU HAVEN'T. While phones calls are much closer to the real world, they are still not there yet. Ergo, the final and most difficult step for man and that one giant leap for woman—and the Holy Grail goal of online dating: the face-to-face meet.

My lack of success in progressing from email, to text, to meet is well documented in the previous chapters. And the losing streak has continued. During Week 21, I wrote to five men. (Two of the five had reached out to me.) Within a day, four of the total five had read my emails, but none responded. Then, a few days later, I heard from the guy whose B&W photo with his grandchild I had complimented. He wrote: "Thanks." (No name, no follow up remark, no interest. No surprise.) The next day Tickle Me Elmo wrote. In answer to my question as to how his tickle-o-meter worked if a woman was not ticklish at all, he wrote: "You have an interesting point . . . hummm . . . a situation I've never encountered. It certainly bears exploration . . ." I wrote back, reading interest between the lines. Apparently I read wrong. I never heard from Elmo again. Nor did I ever hear from Mr. Subtitles—who had WTF-faved me in the first place!

Nevertheless, as of this writing, I do still have four men in a holding pattern of sorts. While I was researching and writing the previous chapter, Nice Guy Too Old wrote back. (You'll recall, my outreach to him was part of SSSS in Chapter 26.) He informed me that it hadn't worked out with the woman he'd dropped me for. Having no grandchildren herself, she didn't get "the occasional Little League game" and other such obligations. Understandable. NGTO and I exchanged a few more emails and then, according to form, cell numbers. In one waaaay longer than I wanted phone call, I learned a lot: He was Italian, a retired hospital administrator, a widower with four adult kids. Frankly, he talked too much. About himself. It was difficult to get the proverbial word in edgewise. Hoping he was just nervous or maybe simply out of practice, I was willing to give him the doubt—and a shot. (At this point, I was still determined to adhere to SSSS.) We made plans to meet for coffee at 3 o'clock the Thursday next.

Coincidentally, my now firmly scheduled date for a Happy Hour drink with Hippie-Dippie on Monday next is also at 3 o'clock. I'm apathetic and not expecting much from either "meet." I figure I have three out of four good causes for pessimism: namely, Al Gomer, Traveler and BB. In the flesh, only Z delivered on his photo. Mr. Reasonable remains in limbo, technically on hold and awaiting the go-ahead from me. Our last email exchange was mutually non-committal. He wasn't going anywhere. (His words, not mine.) When I had time, I should let him know and we could meet up for dinner. The fourth in the hold queue is a newcomer: PhD, from Chapter 26. We shall delve into his story in greater depth shortly.

The whole A-G-E thing (especially in view of my recent S-E-Xcapade) remains an issue for me. A huge issue. Dr. Sills insists that older women should give dating older a chance. Based upon her clinical experiences, as relayed in her book, I am not exceptional. I am not the only woman in her 60s who can't see herself in bed with an old man. (Okay. Fine. I'm not unique. But damn, doc! And this is just between us Judiths now . . . I don't know about the other women you've treated or interviewed, but *I* had a 2 ½ year run of young! How in hell am I supposed to be happy at the prospect of jumping in the sack now with 58, 64, 66, or 67?) But I'm trying. I'm trying to give it a chance, taking what I can from each experience and learning whatever there is to be learned.

I have learned being single at sixty sucks! Literally, hundreds of men have looked at my profile on two different sites—and passed. Only a very, very small percentage reached out—and the vast majority of them were repulsive! Pray tell . . . what am I supposed to take from that? That homely, balding, overweight, lonely, bathroom-selfie taking Social Security collectors are all I can attract? Neither am I alone in my frustration. I have a friend, a police detective. Early 40s, long black hair, divorced, a beautiful and accomplished woman. She's a different decade and different person, but like me, she is ready to enter the fuck it phase. She sums up the men who have contacted her online with a long laugh, a short expletive and the following statement: "I don't mean to sound conceited, because I'm not. (She's not.) But what makes this gross guy think he could possibly have a shot at me?" She and I have compared notes. Discussing the online loser in his many manifestations, we wonder if the answer is this: Because a woman is online, they think she is so desperate she will take anything in pants with a penis and a pulse?

But enough about the men I wouldn't consider anyway and anyhow. Let's get back to talking about email.

Specifically, my apparent inability to write one. *How hard can it be?* I thought initially. Literate, well-educated and multi-published, I could write a decent one—I thought. Apparently not. Whether initial quick volleys that suddenly fizzle or lengthy exchanges that abruptly end without explanation, my email rate of return is abysmal.

Now the questions start. Why do men write or outreach at all, if they are not interested at all? And why when they seemingly are, they suddenly aren't? Clearly I did something wrong. But what? How can I turn off a guy in a few sentences? Or was it too many sentences? Do I come across too . . . too *what*? Too wordy? Too needy and anxious? Too educated or aloof? How about too good for this whole stupid-ass money-generating, ego-destroying scam? (Whoa, girl! Rein in the rage.)

What follows is the actual email exchange with PhD. If you can see where I go wrong, you are far more astute than I. E-flirt is clearly not my e-forté. Yes. It's difficult to admit. But evidently true. I don't give good text. (BTW: If you think reading through this is boring after the last chapter . . . well, honey, you should have tried living through it!)

> Me: *Good morning. I don't know how I missed seeing your "interest." I can only claim disenchantment and disinterest with this site and the process which puts the foibles of human nature on painful cyber display. That said, I must compliment you on a great line: "The many faces of Eve." Trust me. The many faces of Adam are no better. Moreover, you have totally captivated me with several other comments. If you knew me, you would know how rare it is that I am impressed. You would also know that I don't compliment without cause and am*

*painfully—often to my detriment—honest. So before you run off to the hills intimidated and frightened by a forthright woman who truly doesn't give a shit anymore about proprieties and the male/female game which dictates caution and counterfeit, I shall continue. I know alone also. I have also been very, very good at it. Your line about recently feeling "the creep of loneliness" hit a profound note with me. Me too. Then you had me at "limbric resonance." Honey, where have you been all my life? All kidding aside–but not—I am comfortable in my own skin, I don't care for crowds, I love to read and am starved for good conversation. At this point, if the past is indeed predicate, you will no doubt do three things. First, you will quickly go and look at my profile. Then you will decide based upon my appearance to most likely ignore this email. You may justify that inaction by thinking me a kook or a flake or one of those cray-cray types who so abound online. I am not. But physical attraction is either there or not. I get it. So thank you for the absolute best profile I have read. And good luck to you. I truly hope you find a woman who satisfies what you are looking for. In the very, very off chance, you do the third and respond, please know I look forward to hearing from you. And by the way, I share your thinking on one thing else. I know how to kiss. Well.*

He (nearly a week later): *Good morning. Thank you for a thoughtful and personal message. Seems like we share several perspectives. Being one that cherishes the 'off chance,' and an attractive woman, I'll venture the third option. We could continue chatting or meet, whatever you feel most comfortable with. Either way, enjoy your day and be well. Tim* (NOT HIS REAL NAME)

Me (same day): *Good morning, Tim. What a pleasant surprise! I would indeed like to continue to communicate and also to meet. I have a ridiculously full (and very abnormally so) schedule over the next week or so. I am a flight attendant for American. I currently have out-of-town company until Thursday. So how does Friday work for you? Lol. Saturday I must fly to Dallas for training for 2 days, then I have a 3 day international flight to Frankfurt and a 3 day domestic the day after I return to Philly. Honestly, this never happens! I didn't fly a single day last month. Feast or famine, as they say. Perhaps we may continue to chat online until I have substantial time off? I fly every weekend in October, but am off the 3rd-7th and the 10th-14th. As you desire. Enjoy this overcast day. I look forward to chatting further. Judith*

He (2 days later): *Judith, good evening. I must say, what an enticing feast. I can take or leave Dallas but Frankfurt, now there's a city to explore with a significant other: the river, the zoo, the parks and cathedrals, as my mother would say about Chicago "my kind of town." I envy you. Unfortunately, Friday probably won't work. I'll know more tomorrow, but I hope early October may offer a possibility if you're still up for it. I love Europe in the fall and was hoping to get there this year, but alas, next spring hopefully. So many places to still see and so little time. Be safe, and send me a photo from your travels. It would be really nice to see you upon your return. Happy equinox. Tim*

Me (next day): *Hi, Tim. It was very nice to hear from you! I share your opinion about Dallas. Lol it is our headquarters, ergo its nickname "Mecca" for those of us from the US Airways side. You actually have me at a disadvantage regarding Frankfurt. As many times as I have flown into the city, I've never seen anything but the airport and train station. We layover in Mainz, a lovely medieval university town (Gutenburg Bible) about 40 minutes away. I look forward to meeting you next month. If you would care to share your phone number, I shall indeed send you a couple of pictures of Mainz next week. It is beautiful in the fall (and spring). Take care Judith* (READ THE SAME DAY IT WAS SENT)

Me (3 days later): *Hi Tim. Just a quick update. I didn't get back to Philly until 11 last night. (thunderstorms=delays) Legal now to keep flying for another year, I head to Frankfurt tonight, Tampa on Friday. I look forward to planning something next week. Stay well. Judith (READ SAME DAY)*

*Me* (1 week later): *Good morning, Tim. Happy Monday in a new month. . . with a profound shift in weather. What happened to autumn? ;) I am working Frankfurt tonight (again), but would like to schedule our meet now that I have some upcoming down time, Thur or Fri this week or Mon thru Thurs next? The proverbial ball is in your court. Judith (READ WITHIN A COUPLE HOURS)*

I never received a response, nor another email. I implemented my "no-response in a week" rule of elimination and relegated the PhD to the ranks of the weird and disappeared.

In contrast, Hippie-Dippie and I are still in contact, of a sorts. Our planned meet has been moved to Friday next. (In further proof I wasn't particularly interested in him, I had picked up an extra Frankfurt flight instead.) To read how that date went, as well as the one with NGTO, please see the next chapter. As far as Mr. Reasonable? He didn't make the cut over to next week. I kept putting him off because of work and disinterest until one day his profile just popped up as "unavailable." Having never exchanged more than a sentence or two regarding a possible, sometime down the road meeting, I didn't care. He obviously didn't either, as I had supplied my phone number, and he never texted or called it.

*Que sera sera . . .*

I am not alone in realizing the inherent defects in the online dating process as previously discussed in several chapters now. As far as online sites' ubiquitous email exchange program passing itself off as flirting or interacting or connecting or dating? Again, I'm not the only soprano in the choir singing "it's not real." Dr. Sills recommends no more than 3 or 4 back and forths. She calls them "volleys." After which, according to this bona fide expert, you need to leave the fantasy world ASAP and "move your interchange to the telephone, [which] connects you to the real world much faster [so] you won't have so much emotionally invested in your e-mail fantasy lover." After "a positive telephone call," she advises following it up "by a brief escapable meeting, say for coffee or drinks, in (of course) a safe public place."

Reading Dr. Sills' book, I saw myself in a hundred places on those pages. And as it turns out . . . after writing this chapter, I realized she was right about that "learning what there is to learn" guidance after all. I'm not a product of the digital age, nor am I a fan of social media. (In fact, I pretty much despise it.) Therefore I am more than willing to concede that my profound lack of success with online e-mailing, e-flirting and e-dating is my own fault and flaw and failure to adapt. As a universal and successful forum for meeting people, online dating (in all its foibles) has an indisputable track record as a viable option and valuable resource. So don't be put off by my experiences. Use it. It's a useful tool in the modern woman's dating tool belt. It just doesn't fit in mine.

See . . . my tool belt is old school and old-fashioned. It only has a little metal loop. You know . . . that open round thingy meant to hold a good hammer . . . ;)

# Chapter Thirty
## Week 24—This Dud's For You

This was a banner week in my online dating odyssey—or so it appeared at its onset. I had two actual face-to-face, real in-person, dates scheduled. First up was NGTO, who was beginning to wear on my nerves. Second, was Hippie-Dippie, who had already done so. But more on him later.

In the week since we had arranged our coffee get-together, Nice Guy had called and/or texted a half dozen times. He had flown to visit his daughter out-of-state and now felt compelled to tell me his TSA tales of woe. (I don't care. Seriously! And what's the point? Last time I looked at my badge, it said American Airlines lowly flight attendant—not Transportation Security Administrator.) Plus, he just talked too much, leaving long voice mails and effusively telling me how much he was looking forward to meeting me. (I know. After five months of ghosts, goobers, geeks and gross-outs, I should have been thrilled with the attention.) But his chatty-Charlie proclivity was annoying as fuck—though it did have an upside. A date would progress quickly. Because there was never going to be a lull. Yippee—couldn't wait. (We are NOT venturing into obvious territory. "She Got Laid, So Now Doesn't Care" Land is off limits.)

NGTO had picked the place, a Starbucks with *the* worst parking lot access. Moreover, the small lot was packed. (Talk about a genius business model . . . convincing people the world over that a 15 cent in my youth cup-o-joe needs to be flavored, foamed or frappéed so you can charge $5.) I parked in the grocery store lot across the street and walked. I was purposed ten minutes early so I could buy my own latte. If he was insufferable in the flesh, I didn't want to feel obligated to stay because he was the one to pay.

Waiting off to the side to pick up my order, I saw the door open from out of the corner of my eye. In the sudden slice of bright light a slight figure appeared and walked in.

"Judith?"

*Oh crap!* Inside I winced. Outside I wheeled and feigned dumb. I stared at the thin little old man before me and smiled my flight attendant faux "Can I help you?" smile.

"Yes?"

"I'm George." (nhrn)

*Of course you are.* I forced an animated greeting. An awkward moment then ensued, as Geezer George went in high for a hug, and I went out low for a handshake. I uttered a silent prayer of thanksgiving that I was wearing sunglasses dark enough to hide my rolling eyes. I gestured to my waiting latte and suggested I go outside and secure a table while he ordered his own.

I had barely managed to text GG an "OMG! He's ancient!" text, before George reappeared.

He had made an effort, I was willing to concede. Dressed in dress slacks and carrying a sports coat, he made a favorable impression—at least wardrobe-wise. As he sat down, I summoned every Sills-ism I could recall: *Maybe not THE ONE, but a one. Date different men to different purposes. Even a bad date can have value. Cut him some slack.*

Unfortunately, the only slack I could focus on was in his upper arms. I tried not to stare. But I couldn't look away. He was wearing a black t-shirt that revealed the crepiest-looking skin and flabbiest, saggiest upper arms I'd ever seen on a man. His shoulders were narrower than mine. And he had that weird bony bird chest old men have. In comparison to his torso, though, his face was strangely youthful—smooth even. (No wonder the profile picture had fooled me!) He'd probably not been bad looking 20 or 30

303

years ago. By a long mile he was not as repulsive as BB, but there were definitely no fireworks going to fly. No force on this earth can spark ignition in a dud.

I casually mentioned I had to pick up a girlfriend from the airport in an hour or so. (GG wasn't flying in, I was flying out—on this date—ASAP.)

We spent the next hour talking—about the past. His past. His dead wife in particular. I heard the whole story of how they met and about the business she'd started up from scratch. He was so stereotypic, I had to laugh (to myself) . . . the textbook widower who had had a good/great marriage and good/great life until she got sick and died. It had only been a year. He was still in grief counseling, using the online thing as therapy to move on.

I'm not an uncompassionate person, but we were in two different places, coming from two very different histories—and looking to go in two totally different directions. He was looking for another relationship. I was looking at the clock. (*Only 20 minutes to go . . .*)

At one point he asked if I was cold, as we were sitting in the shade.

"No, not at all," I answered.

"I can give you my jacket," he offered.

"No, thank you. That's very sweet. But really, I'm fine."

A few minutes later he asked again.

Again I declined.

"If you don't need it, I'll slip it on then," he said. "I'm getting a little chilly."

*Of course you are.* And in that moment the thoughts I had successfully been holding at bay, burst through my mind in a Technicolor collage of comparison I could not halt: Another man . . . in a black T-shirt, too . . . with hard biceps and great forearms, broad shoulders . . .

The contrast was crushing! One needed a coat to sit in the shade to sip on an over-priced cup of coffee. The other had stood bare-chested in the sleeting rain to drag on a post-sex cigarette.

I exhaled. And took another surreptitious look at the time. (*Five minute to go-time-go.*)

At last the minute hand that had seemingly stopped moving, landed onto the needed number. I made my move, gathering up my cell and empty cup. "I really should be going. My girlfriend's plane lands in 20 minutes."

He stood when I did. I had a feeling what was coming.

"Would like me to call you again?"

I paused to take a deep breath before I answered. "Honestly, George, no. I'm sorry. But I'm not the right woman for you . . . I'm really not. What you are looking for is out there. But it's not me." I put out my hand. "Thank you. It was nice to meet you. I wish you luck and I do hope you'll let me know when you find her."

He didn't appear crushed or surprised. "Can I give you a quick hug?"

"Of course."

I made a beeline for the Acme parking lot, my high heels clicking on the concrete sidewalk in time to the classic rock Queen song running in my head: *And another one down. And another one down. And another one bites the dust . . .*

And no. I would *not* have felt differently if I hadn't banged the mechanic a week earlier. Nice Guy Too Old George was just that—too old.

*Next . . .*


In the days leading up to our date Hippie-Dippie hadn't done much to inspire hope. Following my cancellation of Monday's meet, our effort to reschedule had turned into a test (of my patience) by text. After finally agreeing upon the upcoming Friday, I figured the hard part was done. I wrote that I would check back with him

Thursday to firm and confirm. *Mission accomplished*, I thought. Immediately he texted back and asked what time I was thinking. I had assumed the same time, around 3:00. But to hedge my bet I suggested 3:30 or 4:00. He said he had a workshop from 3:30 – 4:30. (Then why hadn't he said that to start!?) I asked if that wouldn't make for a long day for him. Perhaps we should just aim for the following week, I wrote, especially because I was off Tuesday thru Thursday.

His answer was, "How do you know how long it is? Lol I'm not sure yet how long it will be. Should know by Wednesday."

I explained that I had assumed he'd be teaching all day and then have the workshop after class, which was what we did when I was teaching.

"You saying I am old!" he wrote back.

"No. I was trying to be cognizant of the end of the week burnout and the 'just want to head home and veg' syndrome teachers get on Fridays." (Jesus! Did this have to be so complicated?) I added a "lol" to my text, but in truth I was peeved. I further explained that I remembered how I had felt at the end of the week when I'd been teaching. (And I'd been 34—not 64 like him!) "If you are up for a drink after your workshop, let me know."

Again he had to drag it out and nitpick. "But I'm off Monday and tomorrow. So no burnout. The Jewish holiday so only working three days this week but thanks for your concern."

I didn't like the tone the whole exchange had taken. But I checked my temper, responding: "Perfect. Pick a time Friday and text me the address."

He called instead and set the time for 6 o'clock.

I wasn't crazy about it: 6 is a far cry from our initial 3. Not only was traffic going to quadruple, I had planned to be home by 9, in my jammies and on the couch. *Blue Bloods* is on at 10. Besides, I had a flight to Munich the next day. I was also annoyed that an afternoon happy hour drink after work had turned into more of a dinner thing. I didn't want him buying me dinner, and I sure as hell didn't want to spend money on a meal I probably wasn't going to enjoy with someone I probably wasn't going to like. I was getting a bad vibe—but ignored it. I texted him to remind him to send me the address.

"I certainly will. Be great to finally meet you. Have a great day!"

I certainly didn't concur. I was going to see it through, though. The next couple days passed without incidence—or contact. I didn't think twice about it until Thursday afternoon. Having not heard from him, I was beginning to feel relieved, hoping I was off the hook. That evening I received a text. *Crap!*

"Here you go!"

But there was no address. "Try again," I wrote. "Nothing came through." This time it did. A name and a highway number. I googled directions and a description popped up. A brew house. (Oh goody. I don't drink beer, and it looked like a dive.) It was about 35 minutes away, a good hour with rush hour traffic. "Got it. Thanks see you at 6."

"cool beans."

I'm seriously surprised my eyes didn't get permanently stuck, rolling as far back as they did. There was no way this was going to go well . . . no way in hell.

I wore pretty much my usual. (The thought that this outfit could be cursed has begun to occur.) The black skirt which hit mid thick calf (according to BB), black heels and a black long-sleeved top (instead of the black and white striped knit top I'd worn to meet NGTO.) I did blow out my hair, but only because I was working the next day. I truly could not have cared less regarding the impression I was going to make. He'd already made his with me—and it wasn't good.

I had just gotten in the car a little before 5, when he texted.

"Make it 6:30," he wrote, explaining that he was running over time.

I answered, "Ok." Further annoyed (if that was even possible), I left the phone in the car and went back inside to watch the news. At 5:30 when I got back in the car, I saw he had texted again.

"just found out we are getting out at 6:30! Is 7:30 ok to meet?"

Maybe if he had apologized (profusely) or taken responsibility ala "Gee I really messed this up—I guess in hindsight we should have set a date next week," I would have typed "ok." But I doubt it—and I didn't. I was done. And over Hippie-Dippie, his brew house and his beans—cool or otherwise.

"No. I have an early flight tomorrow." (I lied. I had a 4:30 pm check-in.) "Maybe another time."

Instead of expressing regret and/or ownership of his scheduling screw-up, Dippie got his back up and his sarcasm on. Two texts arrived about ten seconds apart. "So you can meet at 6:30 but 7:30 is too late?" "Ok. Take care."

I exhibited extreme restraint and simply shut off my phone. Dressed up and no place to go, I took myself out to dinner. I had been wanting to try a nearby Italian place with great reviews. According to Yelp, it was a hidden gem known to locals for decades.

*Decades* was the word, all right—as in the age of the place's décor: mauve and slate blue florals and 1980s golden oak at their dated worst. The small one-room restaurant was packed however: multi-generational families, couples of all age ranges and several tables of old dudes in their 70s. *Sans* reservation on a Friday night, I was lucky to be seated at a tiny one-top beneath the bar with a full view of the room. I loved it! It was a floor show just to watch the two servers, a couple of Old World Italians in their 60s, work and schmooze the crowd of obvious regulars. When I asked about their red wine selection, I was informed the place was BYOB.

"*Ma*," my waiter said with a wink, "*va bene. Signora*, I bringa you *uno vino buono*."

And he did. (A very generous pour of an excellent Chianti.) I ordered the branzino and a goat cheese salad. When it came, I gaped. The damn fish, from intact head to fanned tail, extended the length of an 18 inch platter. Giuseppe or Vito or whatever my Vino angel was called, asked if I'd like him to take the skin off and the bones out.

Realizing my oops—for at no time in his description of the evening's special had my waiter included the word "fillet"—I was grateful and relieved. "*Si, prego. Grazie*," I answered, utilizing pretty much the extent of my Italian.

With two large spoons, he gracefully lopped off the head and tail, skinned it—and then proceeded to debone it. The whole backbone and everything lifted out IN ONE PIECE. I'd never seen the likes—talk about a table-side treat and a feat of practiced skill that was sheer performance art! A drizzle of olive oil and a squeeze of lemon . . . followed with a twist of black pepper . . . and I was good to go. The salad had been delicious, but the branzino? Seriously the best fish (whole or otherwise) I have eaten in my entire life! When the bill came, there was no charge for the wine. The tab was $47. I left an $18 tip. It had been worth every dime. For the experience alone.

Clicking my way across the parking lot, I silently applauded. *Kudos to the Judiths tonight.* While I'd enjoyed fish out of fiasco, proving there *is* something always to be learned and savored, Dr. Sills had earned another feather in her credibility cap. I wonder if she knew . . . it wasn't just a lousy date that could have value, but an un-one, too? (My sixty-something sisters should recognize this allusion to a famous 1970's ad campaign which sought to market 7-Up as the "un-cola.")

That night, before cuddling up on the couch with Mr. Selleck, I deleted all 29 texts from Hippie-Dippie. I also deleted him from my contacts. While I was at it, I went back and deleted NGTO, Mr. Baseball, NSA, Traveler and Stalker Doctor. In fact, I deleted every phone number of—and text from—every loser I had connected with through either site, including Z. (That one hurt.)

The next morning I got out the calendar and counted remaining days. I had a little over two weeks left before my 6 month membership expired. I honestly didn't think I could stomach going back online. Melodramatic, I know. But fear not . . . being a Libra means every extreme emotion has its counter weight in logic. My inner voice of reason wasted no time in speaking: *Oh, pleeeeeeze! Your measly handful of face-to-face meets may have been with guys more dud than stud—but they hardly qualify as the worst dates in online history!* Which got me to wondering what *actually* might . . .

I belong to a closed membership Facebook page for women only, mostly flight attendants. It's a chat support group basically for all things female. Women write asking for advice and input on every subject under the sun. And sometimes it's an outlet for simple bitching and moaning (venting being an essential component of coping for most women). I wrote asking for online dating stories anyone cared to share. Curious what I would get, I put no parameters on them. I said they could be humorous or hideous, fabulous or frightening. I explained what I was working on and promised no names would be used.

Several women responded immediately. Theirs were the good stories—the success stories. (Yes, Alice. They DO exist!) Women who had met their significant others through dating sites. One, who said she was in her 40s when she met her husband on PlentyofFish, has to be the poster girl for over 40 women everywhere. She said she "went on lots of dates" while she was online, but she wasn't really on the site "all that long" before she met her "soulmate." (Cut! Cue violins and cherubs, release the doves, roll closing credits—and get me an airsick bag.)

I know I had asked for any and all stories. But "happily ever after" wasn't really what I was aiming for. It's human nature. We're drawn stronger to the dark, the bizarre and the offbeat. Fortunately, my cyber sisters did not disappoint. Varied as they were, the stories I received all possessed an underlying thread of commonality: men met through dating sites who were in person *nothing* like their photos, profiles, emails, texts and phone calls. Apparently, if Snow White were going online to find her seven companions today, they'd be named Cheap, Grab-ass, Slovenly, Silent, Boring, Sneezing and Odd. Maybe someday I'll compile an anthology. But for now and to my purpose here, I've selected two stories from amongst those many.

Second place—and winner of the first runner-up ribbon for my favorite Worst Online Date Story—goes to Melinda (nhrn) from Milwaukee. Melinda, an attractive late 30s brunette backpacker Bohemian-type, with a nose ring and a leaning toward New Age, had been in steady correspondence with a guy from an online site for a few weeks when he suggested they meet. Both music lovers, an upcoming concert seemed the perfect choice for their first date. She relayed to me how she had felt comfortable enough to give him her apartment building address. They had been talking extensively on the phone, and she was feeling a definite connection/attraction. She was downstairs awaiting his arrival when a guy on a motorcycle pulled up. The minute his visor went up, she recognized her date, Robby (nhrn). He asked if she was up for climbing on and going to the concert by bike. He said he had figured it would be easier with traffic and had brought an extra helmet even. She told me she remembered the exact words she said to herself: *Why not? I'm a fun person up for new experiences.* She told Easy Rider Robby to just give her two minutes to run upstairs and switch her shoes. When she came back down Easy Rider Robby had rabbited. Of course she texted and called, certain there had been some dire emergency. It took until the next day for her to accept the fact that Robby was a rat.

Ouch. But at least Rabbiting Rat Robby was real . . . which segues to the blue ribbon winner of my Worst Online Date Story.

Congratulations, Marisol (nhrn) from Miami! Judging from her Facebook photo, Marisol is a gorgeous long-haired blond in her mid-40s. We spoke by phone for nearly an hour. Here is her story:

> *I knew he was a widower with a 10-year-old child. We had talked a couple times briefly when he invited me to dinner. Though I usually never did dinner as a first date, I do Starbuck during the day, I said ok to dinner. He sounded normal. Oh, boy! Was I ever wrong! We met at a restaurant. I got there before he did, so I got a table close to the window. I could see him parking the car. His hair was all messy and he was wearing a T-shirt with a fish—like a marlin—on it. You know, the $5 souvenir type? He opens the trunk and pulls out a shirt and puts it on. Watching all this, I'm already thinking I should go NOW. But I stayed. Don't get me wrong. I'm not shallow. But if you are meeting someone, the minimum you do is iron the shirt you wear and comb your hair. Just saying.*
>
> *He walked in and walked to the table. We said hello. The table was for four. I was seated on one side of the table with an empty seat on my*

side. He was seated across from me. I just want you to picture the whole situation for what's coming next.

He started mumbling things that I had to ask myself if it was English. English is my second language, so maybe I was forgetting the language, I thought. I just had to look at him and smile. I had no idea what was happening. Then he stopped talking, and it was silent. I had no idea what to say. A few minutes passed. I decided to ask about his dead wife. He'd mentioned earlier that he was ok talking about it.

They'd known each since high school, he said.

I asked how long ago she passed away.
"March."
"Last year?"
"No, this year."

It was the beginning of April—meaning she died just a few weeks—or even days—before! My eyes popped really big, I guess. Then the BOMB!

"Oh, don't feel bad," he said. "It's ok. As a matter of fact, she's sitting next to you and she is telling me you would be an excellent mother to our child."

Well . . . it's not too many times in my life when I had no idea what to do or how to do it. I put a smile on my face, put my napkin on the table and asked him to excuse me to use the restroom. I took my purse and flew out of the restaurant.

For weeks he called me. Messages that were so intimidating I had to change my number. He was so mad at me. He called me all kinds of names. I don't know what anybody would have done, but I had no other solution. Running was the only way out!

313

*True story. I hope it was helpful to you. I had a bunch of retarded idiots coming my way in the few month I was online dating. I had to get off because it was insane, I blamed myself for attracting loco people. If you need more stories, let me know. I have more. Not as good as that one. That's my #1."*

Mine, too, Marisol. Thank you for sharing it, for reinforcing my faith in fact—ever stranger than fiction—and for making me feel really good about *my* online losers. I'll take "cool beans" and bony birdman chests over your "I see dead people" ghost whisperer any day!

# Chapter Thirty-one
## Week 25—Real Men Tell Tales

I've gone on now for hundreds of pages about my pet peeves and deal-breakers, my losers and ghosts—in short, my online odyssey. I've also told plenty of tales of other women's online dating woes. But turnaround is fair play. It's time to let the men take their turn.

Unlike women, men are usually more circumspect and less inclined to open up and share. Still, I have easily read 1000 online dating profiles of men between 40 and 60-something. Their paragraphs are laden with subtle and not so subtle disclaimers and warnings regarding both their pet-peeves and their deal-breakers. And surprisingly—or not—many are the same as women's. Moreover, some men *are* willing to share, if you know the right stimulus. "Misery loves company" works well for women, but men are competitive by nature. All I had to do was open the door with a whack-job story of my own—or better yet of another male—and most were more than willing to "one up" it. Based upon the information I gathered and the men I spoke to who did fess up, I am damn confident declaring that Disillusioned Street runs both ways through Dot Com Dating Town.

First up, pet peeves . . . Photos are the number one fodder for male complaint. No photo (as with women) is men's major irritation. Old photos run a close second—actually anything that smacks of deliberate misrepresentation is a goat-getter. Given our skill with make-up and the proliferation of filters and other such selfie aids, I'm not surprised. Hell! I sometimes shock myself in the freaking morning mirror—and *I know* what I look like without make-up. But apparently female subterfuge goes further than wrinkle-minimizing foundation, artful contouring and well-lined lips. One guy told me how a woman he had met on a dating site had to confess upon their first meeting that the photo she was using for her profile pic was, in fact, that of her daughter! But at least there was a DNA connection. Not so the woman who admitted using a friend's photo (more on that date later). I also heard complaints about women whose profiles featured only a single photo or who posted exclusively selfies. "Could you show me you actually do something and go somewhere besides your bathroom to pose in the mirror?" is how one guy put it to me.

Shockingly, cleavage, lingerie shots and lots of bare skin were also turnoffs for a lot of men. (Trust me. I was shocked too. But I heard it from multiple men and read it in numerous profiles.) Pictures featuring dressed up pets was a huge no-no. Group photos with a gaggle of girlfriends were also not so much appreciated. Nor were photos containing phone numbers and email addresses. I asked if they thought profiles with such photos might not be dating profiles at all, but rather an innovative form of advertising for a tech-savvy pimp—or a "thinking out of the box" call girl. The men I questioned weren't sure. Most said they had wondered the same thing. All said they had passed on such profiles. (ah-huh)

After photo-related issues, women lying about their weight or age was the second greatest complaint. One guy told me that he had honestly listed his age as 59 and given his preferred range as 50-65. He was getting contacts from women who claimed to fit into his preference—yet from their photos clearly didn't. He said he often wondered "if a walker wasn't somewhere just out of the frame."

Serial daters were the third most mentioned complaint. (As you will recall, this bane of the middle-aged online dating male's existence was first revealed during my speed dating foray.) I'm guessing the irritation has to do with their presumption that a woman busy lunching and dining with multiple men isn't going to be serving up dessert. Apparently the phenomenon of women actually *living off* of dinner dates acquired through dating sites is quite prevalent. So much so, a term for it has been coined—and all men know it: "rolled by Match." A pilot acquaintance told me the following story of his introduction to the "rolled" experience.

Michael (nhrn) is mid-50s and trust me, nothing to look at. Short and balding, he nevertheless possesses the elevated sense of self-worth and ego all pilots are issued upon completion of flight school. That said, Michael has never been married. I doubt he ever will be. Flight attendants call the syndrome "Peter Pan Pilot," but that is beside the point. What is the point is that Michael joined an online dating site, through which he was able to connect with a multitude of women in their 40s, his preferred age range. (Like the 15,000+ female flight attendants he flies with aren't a large enough dating pool! But of course, we flight attendant KNOW PILOTS and the way they function AND think. Take for example, their two-state rule—if you're two states away, it's not cheating.)

So things progress as expected in the online dating realm, and Michael asks one of his cyber sweeties (tall, blond, very attractive, early 40s, I'm guessing) out for a first date. (I should also repeat the fact that pilots are, as a rule, CHEAP.) Michael selects a reasonably nice (priced) place for drinks. In telling me his story, he reiterated the fact *several times* that they had discussed and agreed to meet "for drinks." And yet, the minute the woman sits down, she reaches for the menu. Not wanting to appear cheap, Michael asks if she might like to maybe split an appetizer or two? "Oh, no!" she answers. "I'm starving. I'm going to need my own." The woman goes on to order an appetizer *and* one of the pricier dinner entrees, half of which she has wrapped up into a doggie bag to go. Of course when the tab comes, Michael pays it—about 3x what he had planned on spending for a first time meet with a woman he would likely never see again. (He didn't.)

317

When Michael got home later that evening, his crash pad buddies asked how his date had gone. When he told them, they roared. "Dude! You just got rolled by Match!" This was the first time Michael had heard the expression. But it wasn't the last time he'd experience it. According to Michael, it happened to him two more times that same month. He'd arrange a date for drinks, and each time the woman sat down, she'd reach for the menu and proceed to order *a lot*. As of this writing, and to the detriment of starving tall blonds in their 40s in the greater Philadelphia area, Michael is sorta back with his long suffering ex and kinda off the dating market. (Sorry, ladies.)

Additional male complaints and pet peeves in no particular order of frequency or level of annoyance follow:

- profiles with email addresses added in as the profile name or requests such as "write me@.gmail.com" ("I'm paying for this membership. I think it's only fair they do too," explained the guy who was particularly annoyed with it.)
- hook-up emails (As much as this one surprised me, it's an apparently frequent occurrence for men, as I heard about it from multiple men. "It's rare to have a response to an email. The majority of mail messages I get is 'do you want get together and have sex?'" explained one guy I spoke to.)
- very attractive women in their desired age range looking for older men (Irony at its best! I could only laugh that men in their 40s and 50s were frustrated by 30-something-year-old women looking for 60-year-old men.)

- women normally a 5 or 6 on the 1-10 Looks Scale acting like they were a 7 or 8 (I have already mentioned this male irritant in a previous chapter. Engendered by the assumption there are a greater number of men than women online, this supposed "buyer's market" for females creates "an elevated and false sense of their own value" in women, according to men. [Guilty, as charged—just ask BB.] I have, however, read the exact opposite—that there are actually *more* women over 50 online dating than men.)

- reasonably attractive women in their desired age range looking for younger men (One guy, 42 and seeking 35-45 with "no drama," actually wrote in his profile that he found "a 44 year-old woman, seeking 18-32 with no drama, to be a very funny, but confusing profile." Really? I'm not confused at all. Can you spell? Try this: s-e-x. I'll bet he has no similar problem with a 44-year-old man seeking 18-32 women with no drama. Again, I laughed.)

Along the subject of online dating profiles, preferences, and such . . . none of the men I spoke to (and none of the profiles I read) indicated any issues with the contents of women's written profile paragraphs. I'm guessing they don't really read them—or don't care.

Speaking of profile paragraphs, however, a lot can be gleaned from men's regarding their frustrations with online dating. The number of men who make a point of addressing the subject of "baggage," as well as dishonesty, infidelity, integrity, loyalty and drama is astounding. Specific requests such as "if you are still dealing with your ex, please don't bother to respond," tell me it's a frequent occurrence. Women planning the wedding after two dates are more likely to be encountered by younger men. Men in their 50s and beyond get clingy women without lives—if one is to believe this not uncommon thread: "I lead a full life and am looking for a woman with a life of her own. Looking for a healthy relationship, not one based on need or conditions." I was particularly taken with a 47-year-old, seeking 33-45, who stresses he is not a drunk, doesn't do drugs, owns a house, pays child support, has a job and is not still hung up on his ex. One needs merely to connect the dots to see the underlying picture: Either he expects a merit badge for doing what used to be considered normal moral behavior—or he is tired of running into women who don't appreciate such qualities? BTW, he was a decent-looking guy!

(I must pause now and go on record. Much of what follows in the next two paragraphs is inference and supposition on my part.)

Men are specific, direct and perhaps more honest and straightforward in their profiles than women, I believe. Consider the following excerpts:

- " . . . just an average guy looking for someone to spend some time with. Not looking for to{sic} serious a relationship."
- "Must like kissing and kiss well."
- "I need to lose some weight but I'm an awesome guy."
- "If I'm interested I will send an email. If a fav, like or wink is received, you should know I hit something in error."

- "I prefer a night in with that someone special. If you are a woman who requires wining and dining, please move on."

I was, in fact, surprised at the huge number of men on dating sites willing to admit they like to stay at home. Yes, that "cuddle on the couch" crap gets old, but points for honesty—if that's what it is. In their dating profiles, women try to portray themselves as fun go-doers. Men, on the other hand, appear to stress their stay-at-homeness. I wonder . . . is this because it's what each gender *thinks* the other one wants? He believes women prefer Homebody Bob over Cat-about Tom, and she's convinced men want Good Time Gal Sal over Hausfrau Fran? Maybe so . . . but really? At the end of the day, when it's all said and done, think about it. Couch Potato Pete and Active Alice? How likely is such a match to last? "Opposites attract," is crap. But as I said, this is just my personal opinion and impressions. Let's turn now to an "expert" or two . . .

In 2014 *Huffington Post* actually published an article by Ann Brenoff that discloses just how lousy "Baby Boomers" (a term conventionally understood to encompass and define those of us born between 1946 - 1964) are at online dating. As I am on the subject of men and online dating, I'll start with the mistakes men make. According to dating coach and author Ken Salin, who was quoted in this article, the biggest error Boomer men getting back into dating make is "chasing younger women." They think younger women are easier because they are "not jaded," while Boomer women are "bitter and angry." (BTW, Ken says this isn't true. Personally, I'm not so sure.)

Another mistake the male online dater makes is thinking with the wrong head. (Gee . . . *that* never happens off line!) Men need "to put their libidos on hold," according Ms. Brenoff, who has written extensively on Baby Boomer issues. Ken agrees, explaining that men "are sometimes so eager to be sexually active again," they go for the "sexually-fueled rocket ride," ignoring all the danger signs. Then they wonder why they crash and burn.

A third cause for Boomer men (and women) "floundering when it comes to finding online romance" is that they (and women, too) keep "celebrating Groundhog Day." Stop dating the same person with different names, advise the experts. The "hung up on one type" dating pattern has two inherent flaws: #1) it eliminates a good percentage of available prospects who don't fit the "type" and #2) repeating a pattern repeats mistakes. (Been there, done that!)

As a related side note . . . I find it amusing the number of men who protested "high maintenance" prima donna behavior in their profiles (or to me in person). Here's a newsflash, gentlemen . . . if you don't want high maintenance, high drama prima donnas, DON'T DATE THEM!

The article also touched on a prevalent problem for men of any age online dating: the soulmate fantasy/kid in a candy store with a pocket full of change/grass is greener syndrome. I have previously stated men believe in the perfect soulmate concept more than women do—ergo, they are in constant search for her. Couple that search for impossible perfection with a near limitless bounty of choices online, together with the human tendency to wonder if something better isn't still out there, on top of the fact monogamy isn't in their hard-wiring to start—and ta-da! Small surprise they are always looking to upgrade! Thinking the next could be better, they fade quickly and ghost easily, guiltlessly moving on to the new flavor of the day. But I digress . . .

During the last 25 weeks I have heard a fair number of online dating "gone bad" stories from men. Many were either simple no-show stories or stories less of "bad" dates than they were of "failure to spark" encounters. The remaining fell easily into one of four categories, featuring women who were:

- ❖ Rude—such as the woman who proceeded to swipe and rate matches while on an actual date. Or the one who was on her phone the entire time, texting her girl friend to keep her apprised in real time. (The saddest thing is . . . he would have asked her out again! We are addicted to sharing our lives on social media to the detriment of *living* our lives!) The most numerous of offenders in this category were women with the expectation of being taken out and having money spent on them. In other words, men feeling like they were being taken for a ride–and not the kind they were wanting. The women excusing themselves to use the restroom—never to return—also fall under this grouping. (Personally, however, I think they should have gone with the next option . . .

- ❖ Lying—the woman who received the "emergency" phone call from a friend or work, forcing her to leave within moments of laying eyes on her date. (Guilty, as charged!) I'll go out on a limb here and guess that women use this ruse more than men. I think it's in our make up to want to spare someone's feelings, so we lie. Another member of this group is the woman who was always too busy to commit to a "real" date. Ploy or truth? Your guess is as good as mine. Naturally, all of the women who falsified their photos and/or profiles belong here.

- ❖ Boring—this group is for the women who hardly spoke, who looked freaking miserable and who acted as if they preferred to be anywhere else. (We are much more apt to sit through a bad date than to no-show it. It's in our DNA to fake it.) Also the woman who monopolized the conversation, the one who hadn't seen a movie or a TV show in 10 years and the one who showed a hundred cell phone pictures of her Yosemite vacation.

❖ Bizarre—the woman intentionally already seated in the restaurant when he arrived, so as to conceal her wheelchair. It wasn't until she pushed back to use the restroom that he realized her condition. (I went back and forth over which category to put her in. Is just omitting the fact you are paralyzed really a lie? In the end, I decided anything out of the dater's expected ordinary qualified as bizarre.) BTW, this same guy also had a date with a girl with a tracheotomy stoma. Of which he also had no prior knowledge. He met both through one of the largest and most popular dating sites around. (As I've said multiple times—you can't make this shit up!) The woman who had to pee every 10-15 minutes and the one who wore a large button with her late brother's photo on it round out this group. (FYI, he died three years ago, wasn't military, and they had been estranged for years. No judgment, just saying.)

As I did with the stories I heard from women, I have selected two winners—a male second place and a male first place. Runner up goes to Al Gomer. (Yes, my Al Gomer from Chapter Ten.) Al had arranged to go on a riding date with a woman he'd been texting through an online dating site. Both were cycle enthusiasts. Logically, their first face to face occurred in the parking lot of some park with extensive bike trails where they had agreed to meet and ride. After polite pleasantries, they mounted up. In his words, "She took off and left me in her dust." As if it weren't bad enough that his male ego was bruised because she'd "out-ridden" him, he was "brought even lower" when he reached their prearranged stop for water and a snack break location. Biking Betty was nowhere in sight. He tried calling her thinking she might have had an accident. He waited. And he waited. After an hour Al headed back to the parking lot. He was surprised to see her car still there. He had figured she had bailed. Worried now that something might have really happened to her, he contemplated calling the police. A few moments later Biking Betty Bail-out rode up. "Clearly annoyed I was still there," he added. With minimal conversation and no explanation or excuse, Betty loaded up her bike and drove off. Ouch.

The men's first place winning story is a doozy, worth of enshrinement in Online Dating's Worst Date Hall of Fame. Ladies, I give you "In a Clutch," featuring protagonist Donald. Donald (nhrn) is a well-educated, successful professional in his early 40s who decided reluctantly, upon urging of friends, to try online dating. Which is where he met Rhonda, a literature professor at a prestigious university. A few years older (48 as opposed his 42) Rhonda was a tall (5' 10'' according to her profile) fairly attractive brunette with short hair and light-colored eyes behind her glasses. After multiple texts and phone calls, whereby mutual interest and attraction appeared evident, they arranged to meet for drinks and dinner. Rhonda didn't drive, but Donald's car had been acting up. Plus, it was an hour and a half drive for him. Still, he didn't mind. He liked the way things had been progressing.

The restaurant she recommended was packed with a Friday night crowd. Very glad he had made reservations, he checked in with the hostess and then walked into the bar area to look for the woman he had been texting and talking to. At 6'4" Donald has a pretty good height advantage—which he proceeded to utilize as he scanned the throng for a tall short-haired brunette who might or might not be wearing glasses. As his eyes swept the throng, he felt a tug on the back of his coat. When he turned, he heard a woman say, "Hi."

"Ah, hi," he answered automatically. His eyes elevated and still searching, he turned away. Again he felt a tug and again he turned.

The same woman was there, looking up at him and smiling. "Donald?"

He looked at her, confused. "I'm sorry. Do I know you?"

"I'm Rhonda."

Donald told me his "jaw unhinged and hit the floor" He felt the air leave his lungs in an audible gasp. The woman he was looking down at, 5 foot tall at best, weighed a good 300 pounds. She did not resemble—in any way—any of the pictures he had seen online.

"I guess you're surprised," she said.

"A little," was all he could manage.

"I hope you don't mind," she said.

At this point Donald said his shock was beginning to wear off. He said he started looking for the cameras. He was sure his friends—the same ones who had urged him to try online dating—were punking him and recording the whole thing. "This is a joke, right?" he said, his head twisting side to side, looking for a familiar face laughing its head off.

"I figured I wouldn't have a shot if I showed my real self."

Donald was still looking for his friends, still believing he'd been set up, but the truth was beginning to dawn. "You're not kidding, are you?" he asked.

Rhonda shook her head. "I hope you're okay with it."

Donald was speechless. "I was at a loss how to handle the situation," he told me. "I didn't want to be rude or come across as some superficial, shallow jerk. On top of that, I'd just driven an hour and a half. I figured I might as well see the date through. Especially since the hostess started calling my name, you know . . . 'Donald, party of 2.'"

Donald and Rhonda had "a pleasant enough" dinner, during the course of which she said that while her photo had been a lie (The woman in the pictures was a friend, who didn't even know her image was been hijacked for use on a dating site!), the rest of her profile was fact. She did—or at least said she did—have the profession she'd claimed, etc.. After dinner Rhonda invited Donald back to her place. She had taken a cab to get there, and he felt obliged to drive her home. (As he had felt obliged to pay for drinks and dinner. I guess my son is right . . . the guys just always pay.) However, he felt absolutely no chemistry with her and wanted no part of a nightcap for two. As previously mentioned, he'd been having trouble with his car—it was stalling at stop signs and lights unless he popped the clutch, or something.

Well, whatever that "something" was, he didn't do it. On the drive back to her house, he deliberately let the car faux stall. Telling her he had a long drive ahead and it was best if he just headed back after dropping her off since the car was acting up, he let Round Rhonda out at the curb. Without passing go or collecting any metaphorical 200 dating dollars, Donald drove directly home. True story.

But truth is in the eye of the beholder. As is the veracity of any dating story. I have no doubt were BB to tell the story of our meeting, the stories would not mesh. But the intent of this chapter was not to paint true stories truthfully, but rather to illustrate examples of a universal frustration. The advertising hype surrounding online dating sites create a picture of online dating that for many is not occurring. Nor is technology always the answer to human problems. As of this writing, my 33-year-old son (he of the wheelchair and stoma dates) is seeing a lovely woman in her mid-thirties. They met the old-fashioned way: at work—when he least expected it—and wasn't looking. Go figure . . .

# Chapter Thirty-two
## Week 26—Money, Money

Oh happy day! It's finally here—my last week. I have lost all interest in this process. Emails, likes, winks and favs have trickled down to a handful. I'm getting more contact from the damn site trying to get me to renew my about-to-expire subscription than anything else. The one today particularly amused me: *Sometimes it takes extra time . . . get 50% off on your next renewal*

"Extra time?" Oh no! Oh hell to the no! It could be effin' FREE, and my answer would still be no fucking way! Color this single-at-sixty DONE! However . . . I still have a chapter to write. So here went my final week of online dating . . .

Bored and looking for an online dating-related topic to research or write about, I somehow stumbled across an internet article by Gigi Engle (ironically posted through my second site's website). Its subject matter was horoscope signs, dating, and do and don't astrological matches.

I am a Libra. In Gigi's words: "the most self-aware sign in the Zodiac." According to Gigi, "the Libra woman knows what she wants and won't stop until she gets it . . . She is logical and balanced. (Duh! Scales . . .) She will never settle for anything other than the best. She is driven, grounded and great with communication." Still, according to Gigi, I am also hard-headed and alpha, goal-oriented, down-to-earth, fiercely loyal and needing of challenge. (Damn!!! Nailed it, girl!) As far as a match, Gigi contends I shouldn't date Capricorns, who are "too free-spirited and directionless" for me. While the chemistry is often there, she says, "the passion tends to burn out quickly." (Interesting . . . my ex-husband was a Capricorn . . . I was married to him happily [at times] and faithfully [until the last year when I left] for nearly 36 years.) "Unabashedly honest," I also "don't mix well with—and have no tolerance for—Pisces men, who are highly sensitive and meek." A Sagittarius man is an "unlikely match" for a Libra woman, as he is "an adventurous free-spirit" and she "a grounded alpha," and yet . . . since both have "incredible minds, it just works" and is a "happy match." Gigi's final recommendation for Libra-me is a Leo. According to her, he is a handful and has an ego, is independent, yet loyal. Also demanding, intense and dominating, Leo the lion is, however, "a strong partner and a great match for the equally strong Libra." Alrighty then, Gig . . . here kitty, kitty . . . (Just kidding.)

Meanwhile, back on the online dating front, my email inbox boasts three new contacts:

- 60, seeking 55-70, writes: "*A wonderful profile and pictures. Im {sic} John (nhrn) and hope we get to find out more about each other.*" Looking closer to 70, than 60, John sports a ball cap, glasses and no chin. No thank you.

- 67, seeking 55-68, has a receding forehead and glasses, reminding me of Mr. McGoo. I'll pass.

- 45, seeking 42-56, who has no photo, writes twice, both messages are responses to profile pictures. To the smiling me on the cruise one he writes: *"You are a cutie bugg!"* (Ewww!) To the one of me and my military son at his wedding, he writes: *"I thank him for his service!"* I

330

respect his respect for our military, but no photo . . . no interest.

The remaining emails cramming my box are from my site itself. All are trying to entice me to re-up. The thought of spending more money on this endeavor never occurs. What does occur, however, is the topic of money. From the beginning I was bombarded with offers, how-to webinars, additional features, extra services—all to increase my chances of dating success. And all for an additional nominal fee. In hindsight, I probably should have addressed the subject of these "offers" earlier. But better late than never . . .

As I have repeatedly said, online dating sites are big business. According to a *Marketwatch* article by Quentin Fottrell, (originally written in 2008 and updated in 2015), the entire dating industry is worth $2.4 billion, with $1.1 B earned from online dating sites, $576 M from mobile apps and the rest from matchmakers and singles' events. Interestingly (I thought), the revenue from dating sites is "split between advertising and subscription services."

As Quentin explains, originally, back in their decade or so ago infancy days, dating sites were free to join or they charged small fees. But as their popularity rose, so did their prices. Mark Brooks, a dating industry analyst quoted in Quentin's article, explains that the simple business reason for charging low to no fees in the beginning was "to stock the sea of love with fish." (Consider it stocked, Mark. I think the issue now is *quality* not quantity. But that's just me venting an opinion . . .)

Nowadays they charge. They charge for basic memberships, for upgraded "premium" memberships and for additional services and features. Indeed, given what dating sites will charge extra for—and what online daters will pay for—these people are marketing geniuses! Sites vary, of course. Many "free" sites allow the online dater to browse, wink and even to respond to emails for free. *But—* and here is where those billions come from—if Winking Willy or Browsing Brittany wants to initiate an email . . . well, the free ride ends. It's time to get out the credit card.

Here is just a partial list of services and features different dating sites offer/sell to their paying members. Some are included in a basic membership, but most require an upgraded subscription or an additional fee:

- ✓ Ad-free browsing
- ✓ Preferential placement in search results
- ✓ Storage for up 5,000 messages
- ✓ Anonymous browsing
- ✓ Control over who sees your profile
- ✓ A guarantee they will get your email
- ✓ Allowances for more matches*
- ✓ Read alerts when your e-mail is read
- ✓ Upping your daily matches*
- ✓ Activities (speed dating, outings, mixers, events)
- ✓ Skip to the top of search results
- ✓ Get 3x more views and emails*
- ✓ Try top spot and get twice the attention
- ✓ For $3.33 a month you can talk on your own phone but keep your number confidential
- ✓ Send a virtual gift
- ✓ Webinars with dating tip topic titles such as
    How to e-flirt
    Be a better dater
    Profile pictures you need now

(* Remember, it's a numbers game!)

Once again, to be fair (and truthful), I must stress the point: *not all of the above are pay for perks.* For example, some websites provide free mixer weekends or other such "no charge" windows, during which you can chat and play games and even email without cost or obligation. I'm guessing if you actually want to continue to communicate with whomever you connected with after the window closes, you'll have to join however. After all, this is the bread and butter, carrot and stick, meat and potatoes concept behind the business of online dating: Create interest and convince the prospective customer their perfect someone is out there just waiting to connect with them—if they sign up.

Ergo, the anonymous (no username attached) emails and enticements arriving in my inbox the week *after* my subscription expired. Here is a short sampling:

- *He's interested in you! You both have a graduate degree and dig dining out. View his profile now.* (Of course, to do so requires I hit the "subscribe" button.)

- *He's interested! Subscribe and start chatting.*

- *He just emailed you! You caught his eye and now he's interested in you. Could he be the one?* (This one actually featured a photo—mid 50s, I'd guess, dark hair, round face, eh)

- *You caught his attention! He also has kids who live away from home. You both dig dining out. You share a birth month.* (Another photo, mid 60s, balding. If I did catch his attention, consider it thrown back.)

- *See who's on. It's free to look!*

- *Limited time offer to renew at a discounted rate!* (If I click on the displayed blue renew button, the link takes me to a screen which explains my 25% discounted rate is $137.94 for 6 months, instead of $183.22. My credit card info is conveniently already populated in the necessary boxes.)

In conclusion and for a final time . . . online dating sites are big business. *Caveat emptor*, people. As for me, I'm done. Mark Brooks, the industry expert, says dating site users "typically stick to a site for 3 months before moving on." Then, according to him, "roughly 1/5 on the big sites return within 18 months." I don't think so, Mark. Not this girl. In hindsight (always 20/20) perhaps I *should* have made better use of the extra features available. But I didn't. Now that ship on your "sea of love" has sailed. And as the saying goes . . . no sense crying over spilled milk . . .

Or I *could* pour it in a saucer and head for the nearest bar patio . . . What do you think, Gig? Here kitty, kitty . . .

## Chapter Thirty-three
## Month Six—Rabbit-hole Recap

The true purpose of life's endeavors is growth (and learning). Evaluation is more than a useful tool to that end, it is vital. That "what did I do?" look backward, in order to see –and appreciate—where you have arrived, is beyond necessary. Then, once that progress is measured—and appreciated—the next steps toward where you still need to go can commence. So . . . here is my after-action report, if you will . . . the recap of my trip down the rabbit-hole that is online dating.

First and foremost . . . I'm glad I did it. The cast of characters I have encountered along this journey gave constant proof to the adage that fact is stranger than fiction, a needed touchstone. Never could have I have conjured them up! Such knowledge keeps a writer humble—and inspired.

Second, please know I tried very hard to be honest and open. Perhaps at times I was too much so. If I offended anyone, I do apologize—for that was never, ever my intent. If I shocked . . . well, for that I do not apologize. I am sixty, but I am not dead. The feelings and emotions I experienced are part of life. And life is for living.

Third . . . to my immense surprise this journey down the rabbit-hole, turned out to be *not* about dating and/or finding love. Sure . . . in the beginning I thought there might be some self-awareness and discovery. But I had no idea *how much*! This is an utterly new phase of life. I know now, as I did not before, that I'll need time to adjust, to regroup and to refocus.

That being said, now that the six months are over I have several thoughts to share. In a way, I'm right back where I started. I'm still single. My circumstances have not changed. *I* have *not* changed. But I *am* different. And stronger. I learned more than a few things about myself.

Most importantly, to thine own self be true. I didn't think I could settle. Now I *know* I can't. It's not about the going and doing, but rather the person to go and do with. If that spark is not there, *it* is not there. Every woman must decide for herself what she wants and what matters. What is essential, inconsequential or negotiable. I learned it's not looks *per se*, but chemistry. That indescribable thing that sparks between two people, sometimes flying in the face of logic or reason.

At this point I need to pause in order to say a few words about online dating. Ladies, it's not going away. Drew Harwell, a *Washington Post* reporter, described its all-pervading import perfectly in a 2015 article. Calling online dating "the bedrock of the American love life," he went to support his claim with the following Nielson data: *One in 10 adults now average more than an hour a day on a dating site or app.* Prognosticators see no decrease on the horizon. In fact, the online dating industry is expected to grow. According to analysts and Drew's article, another $100 M every year is expected to fall into that $2.2 B earnings bucket through 2019. Conventional wisdom might therefore threaten a "snooze and lose" reality for anyone still hesitating. Climb aboard—or miss the relationship train to Love Town, is pretty much the subliminal message of every online dating site TV ad running.

Personally, the R-train can hit the tracks without me. In case there are any doubts, let me be clear: It ain't ever, ever, ever going to happen again. I bought the ticket, hated the journey and couldn't wait for the trip to end. But that's me. If another woman decides to take the chance, I wish her nothing but success. And a useful analogy . . .

Online dating is not unlike shoe shopping. One woman can hit DSW, try on and discard everything, leaving the store empty-handed. Another may buy what she thinks she loves—and it sits in the box, never to be worn. Yet another will buy it because it's cheap or different and, damn! if it doesn't become her favorite pair. One never knows. Or it might take a while to decide. I knew in 5 months and 4 "dates" online looking wasn't for me. A 47-year-old fellow flight attendant gave it a much longer and valiant effort: 7 years and 100 dates! Her end result? The same as mine: NEVER AGAIN. Actually, her *exact* words were: "I'm done, done, done. Done!" Many months after this conversation, when I told her she would be in the book, she told me to make sure I got every one of her "dones" in. Done, D ;)

There are very few positives about being 60. But there are some. The greatest one is the ability not only to more freely speak my mind—but to actually KNOW it. I've played nice my whole life, went along to get along and didn't rock the boat. The Libra in me, I guess. At sixty it's time to say: Screw it! (Pun intended.) Life's calamities and blows have hardened my will—and softened my restraint.

Men . . . I know what I like—and want. The sex with the mechanic was (in his word, not mine) "amazing." Yes, it was. Even the sleepover wasn't bad. I have to admit (to myself most of all) it was nice to be held and to have a warm body to back up against. I didn't know how much I craved both. Living alone and being independent has a lot of perks. But there are two sides to every sword. It's a funny thing about life and its experiences, how certain vignettes of memory become indelible . . . throwing on a robe to stand on the porch in the wind and drizzle for a cigarette/his arm around me while the occasional car sloshed by/my robe opening to flash any driver who cared to look—while I didn't care a fuck. Exciting, sexy, daring, naughty. But oh so necessary—for me. THAT'S what I want. The adventure. And honestly, for now, the sex. And what's wrong with that? Life isn't a dress rehearsal with the opportunity to do it over—or better.

As far as online dating goes . . . see above. It's not for me. I do better in person. Period.

As far as finding THE ONE . . . *que sera*. What will be, will be. I'm not naïve. I know it may not happen. In fact, the odds are stacking against me. In an October 2016 *New York Times* article by Paula Span, entitled "The Gray Gender Gap: Older Women Are Likelier To Go It Alone," some pretty scary statistics are presented, courtesy of a report called "Older Americans 2016," put out by some federal agency. Whether it's because women outlive men in greater numbers or not, the numbers don't lie. In the age group 65-74, 75% of the men were married, as opposed to 58% of women in the same group. At age 75-85, 75% of the men were still married, while the percentage for women dropped to 42%. Over 85, 60% of men were married. For women over 85 years of age, the percentage who were married dropped to 17%. If those aren't depressing enough statistics for single women in their 60s, consider this one: In the over 65-year-old dating pool, there are 2.55 women for every man. (BTW, it climbs to 3.27 women for every man in the over 85 pool.) Personally, I don't much care if my statistically allotted man is 100% mine or 39.2156862745% mine. If there is no spark, I'll be passing on him either way.

Before I close, I promised dating advice for women over 60. According to lots of experts, we Boomer women need to learn to make the first move. We need to smile, make eye contact and flirt. Some experts say we need to go where we enjoy—museums, book stores, plays. Yet others recommend going where the men go—sporting events, car races, gun shows. (Sh*t, take up golf!) Still other suggest re-visting the past—high school reunions, alum groups, and the like. (I *can* tell you, the number of women I've worked with who have reconnected with former flames or high boyfriends is astonishing!) In short . . . whether you meet anyone or not . . . go, do and enjoy. Stop trying to be anyone but yourself. Keep it in perspective. Parents with Alzheimer's, siblings with cancer, adult children with money, marital or addiction issues, grandchildren in the hospital—*those* are real problems.

Therefore . . . get over it. Whatever it is. Live. Laugh—or cry. Learn. And love. It will take time. It will probably hurt. But at the end of the day, you must be at peace with the prospect of being forever alone. Only then can you be picky enough—and strong enough—to not just end up with someone in order to avoid that said "being forever alone" thing. Think the Serenity Prayer—learn to live with and accept what is beyond your control. But have the courage and willpower to change what you can—your weight, wardrobe, appearance. Have the wisdom to know the difference. Accept the consequences of your choices: past, present and future. Join a gym. (That one is universally recommended.) The better you feel about yourself, the better and more confident you will come across to others.

This six month journey was character-building, life-affirming and self-teaching. Honestly wanting to find someone to love, I embarked upon it in hope—and on a bet, thinking of it as an experiment I might turn into a book. If I found someone to love, well then, obviously I had won. Even if I didn't, I'd still win (the bet and the book). And I did—on all counts. I won the bet. I wrote the book. And I found someone to love. Not necessarily the person I wanted to love, mind you. But the person I *needed* to love.

As it turns out, I really don't know her at all—and yet I do. She's not the insecure teenager she was—and yet she is. She's not the organized and independent, has-it-together wife and mother she was—and yet she is. She is me—and yet not me. Not yet. But now that I have found her, it's time to learn to love her. I figure it's only fair if I spend as much time learning as I spend looking.

Yep. Like Whitney Houston so immortally sang . . . the greatest love is learning how to love yourself. So I guess I'll start. In the meantime should I stumble—and I am sure I shall—there will always be bar patios and Leos. And Tauruses, too. (Oh, my!)

Well, dear Reader . . . if you have stuck it out and read to here, thank you! I hope you learned a little. But mostly, I hope you laughed a lot. Now it's time to end the odyssey and put this book to bed. If you are in the same boat, adrift as me upon the Looking for Love Sea, I wish you luck. And ask the same. In the interim, I'll be taking it one day at a time. Tonight I have a "date" . . . with the mechanic ;) As for tomorrow . . . hell, it's all day *Blue Bloods* Thursday! Raggedy-ass sweat pants just came out of the dryer—and I'm pretty sure I've got the number for Femi's Pizza on speed dial . . .

# Epilogue

Sometimes the end is not the end. Since concluding this book 3 ½ months ago, life has naturally continued—with a few new developments that really do now merit mention.

**First**, for the first time in a year, I'm holding a solid international line next month. Yes! Yes! Yes! Despite the will of the all-powerful Lord of Seniority and the machinations of his incompetent sidekick PBS (Preferential Bidding System), I will be flying three normal 3-day Frankfurt trips and one rare 4-day Munich. (NOTE: 4-day transatlantic pairings are VERY hard to get because you're there for two *whole* days. Many flight attendants therefore bring along spouses, significant others, family and non-airline friends for what is, in essence, a company-paid 2-day European vacation.)

**Second**, I have quit smoking. In fact, as of this writing (exactly six months from my big 6-O promise to self) I have been a nonsmoker for 38 days.

**Third**, in the same timeframe, I have lost 10 pounds. I'd like to be able to say the weight loss was a result of dedication, perseverance and exercise. (I'd like to, but can't.) The simple truth is I am happy. Plus Wellbutrin helps.

Btw, here's another simple truth. This one is a funny, not ha-ha, but rather ironic—because God has a sense of humor—truth about life. It can change on a Roosevelt dime—or an Irish bar's patio. (Pause now for an important revelation: I have a thing for hidden meanings in calendar dates.)

Six months ago *to this very day* I unhappily turned 60. If anyone had tried to cheer me up with some trite "Be patient. See where you are in six months. Life can surprise you." B.S., my rolling eyes would *still* be stuck in the back of my head! Yeah, well . . . fast forward said six months, and *damn*! FDR and Liberty are spinning. Me too.

Please know I am making NO assumptions. Cynical Cindy has NOT left the building. Nor do I, for one effing minute, think the Happy Ending Fairy has finally found my freaking address. But fact *is* fact. And at this very moment, at the U.S. Department of State's local office in Philadelphia, there is a blond short-haired, broad-shouldered mechanic getting his passport . . .

# References

2016 Online Dating Survey (17 Jul 2016) *Pew Research.* Retrieved from www.pewresearch.org/quiz/online-dating/

Adams, M. (14 Mar 2013) 15 Unconventional Matchmaking Sites That Prove There's A Dating Site For Everyone. *Arts.Mic.* Retrieved from http://mic.com/articles/29706/15-unconventional-matchmaking-sites-that-prove-theres-a-dating-site-for-everyone#. SzGgZdOrP

Brenoff, A. (11.21.2014) 6 Reasons Boomers Are Just Not Good At Online Dating. *Huffington Post.* Retrieved from www.huffingtonpost.com/online-dating_n_6153440.html

Brooks, M. (2016) Top 10 Best Rated Online Dating websites & Services. *Consumer Affairs Online.* Retrieved from http://www.consumeraffairs.com/dating_Services

Faris, S. (13 May 2016) The worst things a man can say in his online dating profile. *New York Post.* Retrieved from nypost.com/2016/05/13/the-worst-things-a man-can-say-in-his-online-dating-profile/

Farkash, H. Do you need 'the spark' for a relationship to work? *eH Advice.* Retrieved from www.eharmony.com.au/dating-advice/relationships/spark#.wDm4F_krLIU

Ferdman, R. (23 Mar 2016) How well online dating works according to someone who has been studying it for years. *Washington Post Wonkblog.* Retrieved from http://www.washingtonpost.com

Fottrell, Q. (Aug 15 2015) 10 things dating sites won't tell you. *Marketwatch.* Retrieved from www.marketwatch.com/story/10-things-dating-sites-won't-tell-you-2013-0208

Foxworth, D. (14 Feb 2013) Looking for love? Beware of Online Dating Scams. *FBI San Diego*. Retrieved from https://archives.fbi.gov/archives/sandiego/press-releases/2014/looking-for-love-beware-of-onlnedating-scams

Franke, P. (8 Oct 2013) 20 Ridiculously Specific Online Dating Sites That Actually Exist. *BuzzFeed*. Retrieved from https://www.buzzfeed.com/paul24/20-ridiculously-specific-online-dating-sites-that-b5ra

Harwell, D. (06 Apr 2015) Online dating's age wars: Inside Tinder and eHarmony's fight for our love lives. *The Washington Post*. Retrieved from https://www.washingtonpost.com/news/business/wp/2015/04/06/online-datings-age-wars-inside-tinder-and-eharmonys-fight-for-our-love-lives/?utm_term=.30888e341648

Karlinsky, N. (Aired 21 Jun 2012) Does eHarmony really work? *ABC Nightline* Report. Retrieved from youtube.com/watch?v=vYcOzFhq6_A

Kristof, K. (20 Oct 2014) 6 red flags for online dating scams. *MoneyWatch*. Retrieved from www.cbsnews.com/news/6-red-flags-of-a-romance-scam/

Laham, M. (08 Jan 2016) The Risky Side of Online Dating. *Huffington Post*. Retrieved from www.huffingtonpost.com/news/online-dating-scam/

McCarthy, E. (9 Jan 2016) What is catfishing? A brief (and sordid) history. *The Washington Post*. Retrieved from *www.washingtonpost.com/news/arts-and-entertainment/wp/2016/01/09/what-is-catfishing-a-brief-and-sordid-history/*

Our Top 5 Dating Picks for 2016. *Consumer Rankings.* Retrieved from https://www.consumer-rankings.com/dating

Price, C. (11/06/15) 10 Best Adultery Dating Sites. *DatingAdvice.com* Retrieved from www. DatingAdvice.com/for-men/10-best-adultery-dating-sites

Rogers, A. (15 Mar 2012) Models, Cheaters and Geeks: How 15 Niche Dating Websites Are Helping All Sorts Of People Find Love. *Business Insider Online.* Retrieved from http://www.businessinsider.com

Sachs, A. (04 Feb 2009) Getting Naked Again—Dating After Divorce or Widowhood. *Time.* Retrieved from http://content.time.com/time/health/article/0,8599,1876909,00.html

Sales, N. (Sept 2015) Tinder and the Dawn of the "Dating Apocalypse." *Vanity Fair.* Retrieved from www.vanityfair.com/culture/2015/08/tinder-hook-up-culture-end-of-dating

Sills, J. (2009) *Getting Naked Again.* Springboard Press

Shadel, D. and Dudly, D. (June-July 2015) 'Are You Real?'—Inside an Online Dating Scam. *AARP.* Retrieved from www.aarp.org/money/scams-fraud/info-20115/online-dating-scam.html

Smith, A. and Anderson, M. (20 Apr 2015), updated 29 Feb 2016) 5 facts about online dating. *Pew Research Center Online Post.* Retrieved from www.pewrsearch.org/fact-thank/2016/02/29/5-facts-about-online-dating/#.fHzFMDsB

Span, P. (13 May 2016) "The Gray Gender Gap: Older Women Are Likelier To Go It Alone." *The New York Times.* Retrieved from www.nytimes.com/2016/10/11/health/marital-status-elderly-health.html

Tracy, J. (13 may 2016) Inside the Online Dating Industry. *Online Dating Magazine.* Retrieved from http://www.onlinedatingmagazine.com

Whitty, M. (2007) *Truth Lies and Trust on the Internet.* Psychology Press

74821591R00205

Made in the USA
Middletown, DE
31 May 2018